Political Change and Underdevelopment

Political Change and Underdevelopment

A Critical Introduction to Third World Politics

Vicky Randall
and
Robin Theobald

Duke University Press
Durham, North Carolina 1985

First published 1985

Published in the UK by
MACMILLAN EDUCATION LTD
Houndmills, Basingstoke, Hampshire RG21 2XS
and London

Published in the USA by Duke University Press
Durham, North Carolina

Printed in Great Britain

Library of Congress Cataloging in Publication Data
Randall, Vicky.
Political change and underdevelopment.
Bibliography: p.
Includes index.
1. Developing countries — Politics and government.
2. Dependency.   I. Theobald, Robin.   II. Title.
JF60.R35   1985   320.9172′4   85–10176
ISBN 0–8223–0564–X
ISBN 0–8223–0662–X (pbk.)

Contents

Preface

In the aftermath of the Second World War, a succession of former European colonies in Africa, Asia, the West Indies and the Middle East finally acquired political independence. Western political scientists found themselves increasingly challenged to develop frameworks for understanding and predicting the politics of the new nation-states of what became known as the 'Third World'. The atmosphere of 'Cold War' with the two superpowers, the United States and the USSR, competing for international influence lent added urgency to this task. Against this background American political scientists, drawing heavily on existing social and economic theory, propounded a concept of 'political development' or 'political modernisation'. In this perspective newly emergent Third World polities would experience the same untroubled sequence of economic growth, social stability and democratisation as their Western predecessors.

The actual pattern of events rapidly confounded the optimistic prognosis of the modernisers. Recurrent military coups, communal strife, political repression and rampant corruption highlighted the evident shortcomings of this perspective, giving rise to a series of critical reactions. 'Modernisation revisionists' emphasised the need for a more subtle analysis of the way in which social traditions persisted and modified 'modernity'. Other writers put social stability before democracy: what Third World countries needed was strong government even if this meant military rule. Such critical reactions all stemmed from an essentially pro-capitalist position. From another direction altogether dependency theorists argued that Third World countries could never achieve meaningful political autonomy so long as they were economically dependent on the world capitalist system. Neo-Marxists, without entirely rejecting the dependency critique, focused on the way that dominant social class alignments, reflecting both external and indigenous economic forces, formed around the institutions of the post-colonial state.

While the debate around these questions has become increasingly sophisticated, their importance has not diminished. 'Third World' countries now make up over two-thirds of the more than 150 nation-states on our globe. The expansion of development studies in universities, polytechnics and specialised institutes of the United Kingdom is a recognition of the central relevance of the Third World to present and future world economic and political prospects.

The pertinent literature has inevitably mushroomed. There are now any number of case-studies of politics in specific Third World countries or regions, as well as expositions and applications of particular favoured approaches. Yet when, a few years ago, we came to teach a third-year undergraduate course on the politics of underdevelopment, we were surprised to find no single text, not even a collection of essays, covering the different approaches and the relationship between them. This book has arisen largely out of that need to construct a systematic introduction to a crucially important but often difficult and seemingly arcane debate. We have tried to write the book we would like to have found.

Our first objective, then, is to provide the reader with a clear account of the various approaches that have been used in analysing Third World politics, showing how the differences between them reflect changing contexts, assumptions and values. But, second, our treatment aims to be critical: we aim to show what is useful and what should be discarded. Third, we have tried to convey, as far as possible, something of what Third World politics are actually like. We have used illustrations from several countries both to make our argument clearer and to form the basis for some kind of independent yardstick. In a field so vast, and still so full of shadows, as this one, it would be hubris indeed to advocate just one perspective or one line of enquiry. But through our evaluation of existing approaches and their relevance to political reality, we hope that we have been able to make some positive suggestions as to the direction of future study.

The debts in writing a book such as this are bound to be considerable. Our first thanks are to our families and friends who have offered us continued support and understanding. In addition we would like to thank Lionel Cliffe for his constructive and encouraging comments on the first outline of this book, as well as George Philip, Jennifer Todd, Ali Mazrui and Robin Luckham for help and advice at various stages. Lastly we would especially thank Steven Kennedy for his good sense and patience.

Vicky Randall
Robin Theobald

Introduction

At the end of the Second World War the study of politics in what is now termed the Third World could hardly be said to exist. The societies of Asia, Africa and Latin America had attracted the interest of social scientists but these social scientists were overwhelmingly working in the field of social anthropology and their primary concern was to catalogue the culture and institutions of primitive and, to a lesser extent, peasant societies. They tended to view the societies they were studying as more or less discrete entities, as social systems which for analytical purposes could be separated from the broader social context in which they were located. In large part this perspective was a consequence of the policies of the colonial authorities, especially the British, who through their system of indirect rule sought to preserve, in so far as was compatible with their needs, pre-colonial structures or what they took to be pre-colonial structures. In fact it has been argued that the discipline of social anthropology and its associated craft of fieldwork was given a significant boost by colonialism as the colonial powers needed to know about the societies over which they had assumed political control. This is certainly the view of Peter Worsley who goes so far as to label social anthropology an 'epiphenomenon of colonialism' and therefore doomed to extinction in the new circumstances of liberated Africa and Asia (1967). Without getting involved in the argument over the role of social anthropology under colonialism it is beyond dispute that for the overwhelming majority of the subjugated masses of Africa and Asia 'politics', in the sense of some form of participation in a national or even a local political arena, did not exist.

The world situation in the post-war years exhibited, for our purposes, two crucial features: first by the mid-1950s a number of former colonial territories had acquired independence and most were well on their way towards this goal. The second major feature was the crystallisation of great power rivalry in the Cold

War between the West and the Soviet bloc. The onset of the Cold War saw the emergence in the US of the Truman Doctrine, the prime aim of which was to establish a bulwark against Soviet expansionism by building up strong military, political and economic links with strategically placed countries such as the 'northern tier' states of Turkey, Iran and Pakistan. In the longer term the West, the US especially, were anxious to establish or maintain economic and political influence in as many newly-independent nations as possible as well as in, particularly after the Cuban Revolution, the formally long-independent but still underdeveloped countries of Latin America. And just as French and British colonialism had given significant impetus to social anthropology, the post-colonial scramble for influence in the Third World produced in its wake an upsurge of interest amongst (mainly North American) political scientists, backed not infrequently by substantial financial resources, in the character and morphology of 'developing polities'.

Confronted with the diversity of Third World states, these political scientists were faced with the problem of locating their research findings within an appropriate conceptual framework. Since it was felt that the societies of the developing world were in the throes of the great transformation to industrialism which had taken place in Europe a century before, it was probably inevitable that the discipline whose genesis lay in attempts to conceptualise that first transformation – sociology – should come to provide much of the conceptual toolkit for the analysis of change in the developing world. It was probably also inevitable that the pronounced evolutionary strain inherent in classical sociology be transmitted via its contemporary exemplars to the study of the Third World. The industrialised societies of the West were accordingly seen to embody 'modernity' and the rapidly changing societies of Africa, Asia and Latin America were believed to be en route to this condition. The stresses and strains of the transition were likely to be dramatic but the sacrifices entailed would be amply repaid when the goal of modernity was attained. And this goal would be attained: as Huntington has pointed out, the modernisation theories of the 1950s and early 1960s were characterised by the evolutionary optimism that had pervaded the writings of the Victorian evolutionists such as Comte, Spencer and Tylor whose ideas and metaphors in one way or another had been transmitted to them via the sociological tradition (Huntington, 1971).

Although there was a wide range of approaches to the study of modernisation, some notion of movement from tradition to modernity underpinned virtually all the theories of this period. And there can be little doubt that modernity as conceived specifically in relation to the political sphere was closely identified with the liberal-democratic forms of government and pluralist politics believed to prevail in the US and other developed western societies. Political modernisation very largely signified movement towards this condition of liberal-democracy and pluralism. The basic problem therefore was for political scientists to devise criteria that would enable them to pinpoint the stage of development or modernisation at which respective polities were located.

It is our contention that the subsequent study of political change and development in the Third World can best be understood in terms of a series of reactions to the modernisation theories of the 1950s and 1960s, and one of the principal aims of this book is to discuss these reactions and the thinking that lay behind them. However, our purpose is not solely to chart the course of a somewhat lengthy conceptual debate but both to bring out the essential characteristics of politics in under-developed societies and to raise, and we hope indicate answers to, fundamental questions about the process of political change in the Third World. Questions such as, what are the definitive features of underdeveloped polities? Are there criteria enabling us to distinguish between different types of underdeveloped polity? Is there a specifically political component to develop-ment? Is it still meaningful to talk about political development? An examination of modernisation theories and the reactions they triggered should help us to tackle these and other questions, for in many ways the debate has been cumulative and in the light of its perspective we should know better how to frame our inquiry and where to look for answers.

How the Book is Organised

Our first chapter traces the emergence of the early modernisa-tion approaches. It begins with a consideration of theories of social change, and in particular the concepts of 'tradition' and 'modernity' as used both in classical and in contemporary sociology. We also look at Rostow's influential model of succeeding stages of *economic* growth (1962). This leads us on to some of the major attempts by political scientists to locate tradition, modernity and the process of development from one to the other within a specifically political context. We examine the concepts of 'political modernisation' and 'political development' and ask how, according to the writers employing these terms, a modern political system evolves and what its principal characteristics may be. Conversely what is a 'traditional' political system and what brings about its transformation?

The notion of political development, or modernisation, as originally elaborated, is now virtually defunct, though some of its underlying assumptions persist in more recent approaches. In Chapter 2 we turn to one of the first waves of critical onslaughts against modernisation theories as such, and their extension to the political sphere. This attack centred mainly on the notions of tradition and modernity as polar types and of the idea of a simplistic zero-sum relationship between them. According to these critiques, far from being superseded by modern forms, traditional forms not only survive but may be given a new lease of life in the modern context, that is to say in the process of interaction with modern parties, bureaucracies, legislatures and the like. One important consequence, we argue, of this line of criticism was a growing interest on the part of political scientists in the *content* of tradition, that is in those forms and institutions which had previously been very largely the concern of social anthropologists. And so we find political scientists from the late 1960s broadening their academic sights to take in such phenomena as caste, ethnicity and above all clientelism.

Huntington (1971) called this approach 'modernisation revisionism' and it coincided chronologically, and also to some extent in the work of particular authors, with a second kind of critique of modernisation theories, especially directed against their evolutionary optimism. Chapter 3 describes how by the second half of the 1960s it had become apparent to most scholars that the process of political change in the underdeveloped world, so far from constituting a smooth, orderly transition to modernity, was more frequently characterised by internecine conflict, instability and decay. The observation that Third World societies were riven by deep internal conflicts, in which the modern incarnations of tradition played a central part, underlay attempts to formulate models of a distinctive type of 'plural' or 'praetorian' society. Many political scientists came at this time to believe that political stability and strong governments were what really mattered and looked for the factors that seemed to explain such cohesion as existed in societies otherwise marked by overall dissensus. In institutional terms, they looked first to political parties, and especially single ruling parties, but then increasingly to the military. The military, who had originally been cast as the enemies of political development, were now depicted as agents of stability and even modernisation. At the same time political scientists invoked some modern variant of Max Weber's notion of patrimonial rule to explain the way in which the ruling party or military in practice used the state bureaucracy as a source of privilege and patronage. The arguments of the 'strong government' school of thinking lead us necessarily to a fuller examination of exactly what role the armed forces do play in underdeveloped countries. Can one usefully generalise, and if so, how far does the military live up to these optimistic expectations?

One of the most fundamental shortcomings of early modernisation theory was its failure to grasp the implications of the Third World's economic dependence on the West. The issue was again largely ignored in the two critiques we have just been discussing. Chapter 4 is concerned with the impact of the emergence of dependency theory on the study of Third World politics. While it certainly awakened most, though not all, political scientists to the importance of the economic context, we suggest that, beginning with the repercussions of A. G. Frank's critique (1971) of the sociology of development, the focus of dependency theory on the international capitalist, or even world, economic system acted in the short term to reduce politics within states virtually to the status of an epiphenomenon. In the longer term, however, the realisation of some of the shortcomings of dependency theories, particularly their tendency to gloss over substantial variations as between dependent countries, led to a refocusing of attention on the interrelationships between specific socio-economic systems and the world economic system as mediated to a given society. Writers such as Cardoso (1973) have recognised the possibility in some Third World countries of some kind of capitalist, albeit dependent, development, and have gone on to analyse the relationship between such development and class alignments around the state. And at the same time, just as in Chapter 2 we attempt to show that the critical reaction to a simplistic zero-sum view of tradition and modernity resulted in an upsurge of interest in political anthropology, so in this chapter we maintain that efforts to fill the gaps in dependency theory yet again shifted the spotlight on to social anthropology, although now usually a distinctly Marxist social anthropology. This brings us to a consideration of the relevance of the modes of production debate to the study of politics in the Third World.

Chapter 5, rather than introducing a further critique of modernisation theory, examines developments within a neo-Marxist perspective that are primarily a response to dependency theory. While accepting much of the economic analysis of the dependency theorists, these writers seek to replace a tendency to social and political reductionism by a meticulous scrutiny of the composition and alignments of emerging social classes in Third World societies. Taken in conjunction with the new interest in the modern capitalist state, this emphasis has led to an increased focus on the nature of the post-colonial state and the extent of its 'relative autonomy' from socially dominant classes. At the back of these questions has persisted the vital Marxist concern with social revolution and the attempt to identify the stages of revolutionary development and the main social forces working for and against it in a given society. In concluding this chapter, we note that a growing preoccupation with the state is similarly evident within current non-Marxist approaches to Third World politics.

Our final chapter aims to bring together the central themes and address the central questions raised in the course of the book. It considers the succeeding approaches we have traced, asking how far each has helped us to understand our subject. In particular it focuses on the most recent and influential developments in analysis, those of the neo-Marxists in one camp, and in the opposite 'liberal' camp, a concentration on policy, emphasising economic rationality and choice. In assessing both of these approaches, we point out the strain of authoritarianism which they can exhibit and which has been a constant feature of this whole area of study since the 'strong government' critique of the mid-1960s. This leads us into our closing discussion of how political change in the Third World is to be evaluated, if at all. Early concepts of political development laid great stress on the value of democracy and participation; the authoritarian argument is that democracy is neither possible nor desirable in such countries. Can political science shed any practical or empirical light on this dilemma?

It will be apparent that the study of politics in the Third World has been closely bound up with changing approaches to the way the Third World is seen as a whole. Political development theory grew out of theories of social change and to a lesser extent of economic development. The critique offered by the modernisation revisionists was in the first instance directed at modernisation theory generally, and only then applied specifically to politics. This book is concerned with the *politics* of underdevelopment. But first this cannot readily be disentangled from economic constraints and social structures and second, in so far as we *do* focus on politics, we prefer to understand that term quite broadly.

An influential tradition in the definition of political science has wanted to concentrate on national governments and central political institutions, and perceives politics as public, deliberate activity. This has perhaps posed less of a problem in the study of western 'democracies' because such institutions undoubtedly do play a central political role and because we are in any case familiar with the wider context of power relationships within which they operate. But this approach is too restrictive in the Third World context. Central political institutions which superficially resemble, indeed are often based on, western models, in practice tend to play a different, often less important, part. Too much emphasis on them results in a sterile formalism. Likewise, the definition of politics as public and self-conscious applies to a narrow range of activities in most societies, but in some parts of the Third World (with the exception of a political elite) may barely apply at all. While in writing this book we have to some extent been governed in the meaning we give to politics by the approaches under consideration, we have in the

backs of our minds a notion of politics as being about the way
that scarce resources (understanding resources in their widest
sense) are distributed within a human community. The study of
Third World politics needs to take cognisance both of the
traditionally central issues of the structure and role of public
authority and of the other mechanisms which are at least as
influential in allocating resources between human groups and
uses. This might seem to bring us close to the perspective of
'political economy'. Self-styled political economists, however,
have in the past tended to emphasise economic relations and
policy to the neglect of political ideology, organisation and in
particular the specific resources and interests of the state. More
recently both Marxist political economy and the 'public choice'
writers have balanced the two elements more evenly and to that
extent we applaud their attempt to, in Philip's words, 'put the
political back into political economy' (1980).

While we favour a broad understanding of what is meant by
politics, particularly in the context of the Third World, we by no
means intend thereby to downgrade the importance of politics.
On the contrary one of the problems in our opinion with many
of the approaches considered here is that they have precisely
accorded too slight or *passive* a role to the 'political'. A feature of
early modernisation theory was the tendency to see politics as
the typically passive product of wider forces of economic and
social development. Attitudes have been changing. And one of
the virtues of the 'strong government' thesis was that it led the
way for such a reappraisal of the role of political institutions
amongst 'liberal' political scientists, though as Heeger (1974)
points out, Huntington (one of the leaders of this school) still
assumed that political institutions would be coping, or failing to
cope, with the effects of economic change and social mobilisation that occurred independently of them. On the 'radical' side,
it is the neo-Marxists with their emphasis on the state and class
struggle *within* nations who have re-asserted a political level of
determination. This rediscovery of politics is overdue and
welcome and we hope that our book will act as a further
contribution to it.

A final word is needed about our selection of illustrative
material. The overall structure of the book is determined by the
to's and fro's of the continuing search for the most illuminating

approach to a politics of underdevelopment. But as already emphasised we do not want it to be only about theory. In the process of discussing the theoretical and conceptual issues we hope also to convey something of the feel and character of politics in the Third World. This raises the problem of which countries we select to illustrate our arguments. Initially we planned to take a group of countries which represented each of the World Bank's categories of 'low income', 'middle income', 'capital surplus oil exporters' and 'centrally planned economies'. However, this proved impracticable. Similar problems arose when we attempted to confine our illustrative material largely to one polity in each of the three main continents, Brazil, India and Nigeria. Eventually we recognised we would need to draw on case studies of a number of countries, selected according to their relevance to the topic in question and the available literature. In so doing we have managed to include a good many countries – among them India, Indonesia, Pakistan, Brazil, Argentina, Chile, Nigeria, Kenya and Tanzania – without we hope inclining too heavily toward one region or another. This nonetheless raises the issue of representativeness. In the first place our coverage is obviously not comprehensive. In the second, what is a *typical* Third World state?

As Worsley (1979) has shown, the notion of a Third World originally arose, in the early post-war period, as an attempt to class together those nations which fell neither into the western capitalist camp of the First World nor the then Soviet-dominated state socialist Second World. It implied political nonalignment, the potential for a countervailing 'third force' and perhaps also an alternative route for development. As it has become increasingly difficult to maintain this distinction, in the face of Third World disunity, an alternative and more convincing approach has been to emphasise the common status of underdeveloped nations as 'post-colonial', and more recently as 'dependent'. The Third World is simply the underdeveloped and dependent world, not only nations but regions *within* the so-called developed world. At the same time, since the 1960s international agencies such as the World Bank have placed increasing reliance on more purely economic or quantitative indicators of underdevelopment. They have used criteria such as population size and density, ratio of manufacturing to total output, literacy rates, average life expectancy and infant mortality rates, but above all GNP per head. Countries whose per capita GNP falls below a certain level are classed as belonging to the Third World. Apart from well-known problems about calculating GNP, per capita income tells us nothing about the actual distribution of income and allows for instance South Africa to be counted as a developed country, despite the extreme inequalities within, as revealed in an average life expectancy at birth of only 52 in 1976 (for some discussion of these issues, see Wolf–Phillips, 1979).

These problems of defining the Third World, of saying what Third-Worldness consists of, are compounded by the fact of tremendous diversity in most other respects amongst its potential member states. Perhaps this was less obvious in the 1950s than by the 1970s. But now the issues facing governments of the 'new industrialising countries', like Brazil or Singapore, or an oil-rich state like Kuwait, seem of an entirely different order than in economies dependent on the export of one or two food or fibre crops, such as Barbados. The World Bank, since its 1978 Report, has indeed found it necessary to separate off 38 'low income' countries, with Bhutan, Kampuchea and the Lao People's Democratic Republic at the bottom of the league, into a 'Fourth World' category and has also taken Kuwait, Saudi Arabia and Libya out of the Third World 'middle income' category into a new class of major capital surplus, oil-exporting countries. And as we shall see, dependency theorists themselves have found the two-fold division into core and satellite areas less and less satisfactory, introducing new intermediate categories such as 'semi-periphery' and 'sub-metropolitan'.

This diversity is incontrovertible and must never be lost sight of. One of the aims of this book must be to indicate the limits to legitimate generalisation. Different levels of economic development, indigenous social structures, earlier colonial experiences and more purely political traditions will all condition the political reality and possibilities of a given state. We still contend, however, that these countries have sufficient in common and distinguishing them from the rest of the world to make it not only justifiable but necessary to discuss them together. What they share is the predicament of economic dependency and backwardness. Typically their economies are closely linked with and have been largely structured by the needs of the economies of industrialised capitalist – or exceptionally communist – societies. On a whole range of indicators – perhaps the most telling are average life expectancy and infant mortality – they are socially and economically disadvantaged. From these difficulties, together in most cases with the legacy of colonial rule, stem certain political characteristics which we argue are pervasive despite the variety of regime types. In their different ways, these countries exhibit a recurrent pattern of instability, authoritarianism and military intervention.

It is this syndrome of Third World politics (how far removed from the confident expectations of the early modernisation theorists will become apparent in the next chapter) that this book takes as its subject-matter. Through its critical examination of different theoretical approaches we hope to convey the reality of political change in underdeveloped countries and the complex of forces that determine it.

1

Towards a Politics of Modernisation and Development

We must begin by going back to those earliest attempts to understand the politics of the newly emerging Third World countries which form the point of theoretical departure for this book. We need to examine the concepts of political modernisation and political development, and the approaches associated with them, which dominated these attempts. But first in order to understand why such a perspective found favour at all, it must be placed in context. The startling changes in the world that political science sought to describe coincided with changing methodological assumptions within the discipline. Above all must be stressed the extent to which these concepts and approaches did not simply evolve within the parameters of political science but were part of the attempt to make sense of the changing world scene throughout western social science, and particularly amongst sociologists and economists. Political science took up the challenge relatively late and drew much of its intellectual arsenal, including the central concept of modernisation, from its sister disciplines.

The Need for Theory

By 1950, as we have seen, the face of world politics had changed dramatically and further momentous changes could clearly be expected. There was on the one hand the growing rivalry between the US and the Soviet Union, and on the other the proliferation of newly independent Third World nations. American social scientists in particular were encouraged, often through direct government funding, to broaden their focus to include the developing world which was increasingly the target of US influence and policy. There was perhaps initially less pressure on political science than on sociologists and economists because of the early prevailing assumption, as we shall see, of a relatively unproblematic chain of causation from cultural modernisation to economic development to democracy. Still, political scientists soon were also being called upon to provide a way of looking at the politics of different societies which was first genuinely comparative and second able to identify and explain the specific process of political change.

It is hardly unfair to say that at this time the discipline was singularly ill-equipped for such an enterprise. For some time previously, and with undoubted honourable exceptions, the broad area of political studies had tended to separate out into the two strands of political theory and the study of political institutions respectively and there was little constructive dialogue between them. In the field of comparative politics (or comparative government as it was then more accurately termed), the result was an approach which was largely descriptive, concentrating on the legal and historical aspects of government institutions, 'static' in the sense of ignoring dynamic factors that accounted for change and not really comparative at all since it consisted mainly of parallel surveys of governmental arrangements in different countries (Macridis, 1955). Such an approach could nonetheless be illuminating so long as the discipline maintained its parochial preoccupation with western 'democracies'. Once comparative government turned its attention to developing countries, its narrow institutionalism was a serious limitation. Leys, for instance, in his criticism of this literature cites the examination by British political scientists of the viability of the constitutional machinery bequeathed by the departing colonial administration, and their application of Nuffield-style modes of analysis to elections held in those countries. Such questions were arguably marginal to the real political issues at stake in developing countries, and scarcely calculated to discover the mainsprings of political change (Leys, 1969).

The 'traditional' approach to comparative government was, however, coming under attack from another source. Political science was beginning to experience the 'behaviouralist revolution' which had earlier affected other social sciences. Behaviouralism has since been justly criticised for its unrealistic pretensions to 'scientific' status and the aridity of much of the work it generated, but its impact on political studies at this point was surely more beneficial than harmful. Behaviouralism connoted at least a commitment to a more systematic approach to the study of social phenomena. Its exponents looked for regularities in social behaviour that could be empirically demonstrated and serve as the basis for probabilistic generalisations. They insisted that such empirical research should be preceded by the formulation of explicit hypotheses and then be used to test and refine them. They also argued for greater interdisciplinarity, the breaking-down of conventional barriers between the social sciences. Doubtless much of what was produced under the brief of behaviouralism adhered more to the letter than to the spirit. Still, as Leys points out, its real contribution was to bring political theory into the study of empirical politics and specifically to enable political scientists to ask questions that probed beyond the forms of Third World governments.

It was in this context of pressures to become more genuinely comparative, more oriented to political change and more scientifically rigorous, that comparative political scientists felt themselves urgently in need of a suitable set of central concepts and some kind of theoretical framework. But given the state of the discipline and its preference for descriptive and narrow institutionalism, it could not generate its own framework. Instead political scientists tended to turn to the theoretical approaches already being developed and applied to Third World societies in other social science areas. Most of all they drew on current sociological theory but they were also influenced by models of economic development. It is from these sources that political science derived not only many of its organising ideas but a central preoccupation with 'modernisation', both its implications for politics and as an aspect of politics itself. It is essential therefore to begin by looking at these theories of social and economic modernisation and the assumptions they made which would then permeate political development theory.

Modernisation Theory

Two main streams of sociology feeding into modernisation theory can be distinguished. One stems from Max Weber's thesis on the relationship between protestantism and the development of capitalism and concentrates on cultural and, at the level of the individual, psychological prerequisites of modernisation. Since this line of thinking has affinities with the approach to economic development we want to discuss, we shall take it second. The other stream of influence, however, runs from the thought of Herbert Spencer through that of Emile Durkheim to contemporary sociologists such as Neil J. Smelzer and Talcott Parsons. This is an approach which focuses upon social differentiation as the central datum in social change, and which in its more recent manifestations adopts a systems perspective. In contrast with the first psycho-cultural approach it focuses much more explicitly on *structural* features of society.

In examining the background to these more structural approaches, it is not necessary to delve deeply into the ideas of Spencer and Durkheim. Suffice it to say that they and other 'founding fathers' bequeathed to modern sociology two central and related themes. The first is that development or, as it used to be known, social evolution, manifests itself as a process of social differentation as a result of which societies become structurally more complex. The second theme takes the form of a preoccupation with the resulting problem of social integration: how, as differentiation proceeds, are the increasingly diverse structural elements to be welded together?

Social differentiation, as defined by Smelzer, is the evolution from a multi-functional role structure to several more specialised role structures. For example, during a society's transition from domestic to factory production the division of labour increases and economic activities previously based on the family move to the firm. As a formal education system emerges, training functions previously performed by the family and the church are now catered for by a more specialised unit, the school. Turning to the political sphere, in a typical pre-modern society political roles are closely bound up with, if not inseparable from, kinship roles. Kinship provides the main integrative principle in such a society. However, as society becomes increasingly complex more specialised structures emerge: bureaucracies, eventually parties, assemblies and the like (see Smelzer, 1962).

Modern systems analysis may be seen as one of the many attempts in sociology to reconcile, usually at a very high level of abstraction, society's structural diversity with the integrity of the whole. This approach conceives of society as a system made up of a number of parts or subsystems. The integrity of the whole is provided for by the functional interdependence of these subsystems. The nature of this interdependence is best illustrated from the work of Talcott Parsons, perhaps one of the most influential systems theorists (see for instance Parsons, 1960).

We should note, first of all, that Parsons is firmly in the evolutionary tradition that equates increasing structural complexity with greater efficiency: that is to say, the greater the degree of social differentiation, the more specialised can the differentiated units become and the better able they are to perform their allotted functions. For Parsons all social systems must deal with four basic functional problems or imperatives: *adaptation*, which refers to the capacity of a system to control its environment for the purpose of achieving certain goals; *goal attainment*, referring to the need to relate the system's resources to the achievement of its goals; *integration*, which deals with the problem of maintaining cohesion between the units of the system; and *pattern maintenance or latency*, which refers to the imperative of maintaining a stable value system and dealing with problems of motivation.

As we shall see, the notion of 'system', the idea of exchanges between different parts of a system and with the environment, has had considerable influence in the study of political change and development. Political scientists, following Parsons, have been particularly concerned with the functions of integration and 'pattern maintenance'. One further component of Parsons' analysis, which has held a peculiar fascination in its own right for students of Third World politics, is his concept of 'pattern variables'.

A crucial part is played in Parsons' scheme by the concept of role, for it is through social roles that the structural characteristics of the system are translated into individual behaviour.

Parsons argues that social roles in all societies are patterned in such a way as to present five basic dichotomies along which individual action may proceed. In other words behaviour in any concrete situation will be oriented in one of two directions in terms of the five continua.

The first choice is between whether behaviour in a given situation and in relation to a given individual or group is to be affective or affectively neutral. Does the action situation contain an emotional element as is the case between husbands and wives, parents and children, clansmen 'or close friends? Or is such an emotional content entirely absent as in the relationship between the bank clerk and his customer, the commuter and the ticket inspector? The second dichotomy opposes self-oriented behaviour to collectively-oriented behaviour. The modern entrepreneur who is driven primarily by the desire for self-aggrandisement is an example of the former whilst the traditional trader whose economic activities are very much geared to maintaining a following of kinsmen and clients illustrates the latter. Third, a social role may prescribe that related behaviour follows universalistic or particularistic criteria. Public servants in modern bureaucracies are expected to follow universalistic criteria, dealing with all cases with the same degree of impartiality. Public servants in developing states, however, are frequently under pressure to follow particularistic criteria and favour kinsmen, personal dependants and the like. Fourth comes the dichotomy between whether we evaluate another's role performance in terms of ascriptive or achievement criteria: that is, whether we judge someone else's performance in a particular context in terms of what he does and what he has actually achieved, or in terms of who he is: the son of a well-known politician, for example. Finally the relationship between two actors may be functionally specific or it may be functionally diffuse; the exchanges, demands and obligations between them may be limited to that particular context or they may ramify into other areas of social behaviour. Relations between a modern corporation and its employees tend to be functionally specific whilst those between a medieval craftsman and his apprentices were not limited merely to the exchange of labour for wages. Parsons and subsequent writers have noted a pronounced tendency for roles in modern societies to be increasingly patterned in the direction of affective neutrality, self-orientation, universalism, achievement and functional specificity.

The other strand of sociological thinking to feed into modernisation theory is psycho-cultural. Weber (1930) of course argued that for capitalism proper to have developed in western Europe, appropriate economic conditions (whilst necessary) were not of themselves sufficient. In addition a capitalist spirit, a set of orientations and values, was required. Following Weber's lead, a number of more recent writers have emphasised the importance of values and attitudes in the achievement of industrialisation and development in the Third World. As a consequence there has emerged from the work of writers like Daniel Lerner, David McClelland, Everett Hagen and Alex Inkeles a conception of 'modern man'. Modern man is adaptable, independent, efficient, oriented to long-term planing, sees the world as amenable to change and, above all, is confident of the ability to bring change about. For this latter reason modern man is actively interested and eager to participate in politics. The counterpart, traditional man, by contrast, is anxious, suspicious, lacking in ambition, oriented towards immediate needs, fatalistic, conservative and clings to well-established procedures even when they are no longer appropriate.

One of the more controversial of these theories has been put forward by the American psychologist, David McClelland (1961), who has posited the existence of a need for achievement (Nach), which is an integral part of human personality. This need for achievement is differentially distributed not only between individuals but between cultures. McClelland claims that a number of historical studies show how an upsurge of achievement themes in children's stories, folk tales, popular literature and other cultural manifestations has been associated, after a time lag, with an upsurge in economic activity. Economic growth, McClelland therefore maintains, is closely correlated with the distribution of the achievement factor. The implications for developing countries are readily apparent: through both formal and informal processes achievement themes must be inculcated into the younger members of these societies.

McClelland's argument represents something of an extreme

in that he views development and underdevelopment almost entirely in the light of the distribution of certain personality factors. Whilst other writers in this school may place more emphasis on economic and other institutional factors, as did Weber, their approach nonetheless has a distinct psycho-cultural bias: development is seen primarily to be a function of appropriate values, attitudes and personality traits.

If these sociologically construed notions of modernisation were absorbed largely uncritically into comparative political analysis, political scientists were also impressed by current theories of economic development. Huntington indeed suggests that in producing theories of political development, they were particularly anxious to emulate models of successive stages of economic growth, with all their apparent precision and rigour (Huntington, 1971). We shall take by way of illustration here probably the most influential model, propounded by Walt Rostow (1962). In its emphasis on the psycho-cultural prerequisites of development, we can see a strong affinity with our second strand of sociological thinking (Rostow is also incidentally important as a central target for Gunder Frank's critique of modernisation theory, from a dependency perspective, to be discussed in Chapter 4).

In *The Stages of Economic Growth: A Non-Communist Manifesto*, Rostow proposes a theory of economic growth (an alternative to that of Marx), based upon five stages. In the first 'traditional' stage, it is very difficult to expand production beyond a limited ceiling, primarily because society is based upon pre-Newtonian science and technology and correspondingly pre-Newtonian attitudes towards the world, that is the world is still not regarded as being subject to knowable laws and therefore capable of manipulation. Such societies are agrarian and with social structures which are hierarchical, allowing little scope for social mobility, and in which family and clan connections play a central organising role. The dominant attitude is one of 'long-run fatalism', the belief that the range of possibilities open to one's grandchildren will be just about what they were for one's grandparents.

What initiates the transition to the second stage of 'preconditions for take-off'? These preconditions originally emerged in western Europe when the insights of modern science began to be translated into both agricultural and industrial production. Outside Europe the preconditions for take-off arise not endogenously but as a result of intrusion by more advanced societies. With such intrusion, the idea spreads that economic progress is not only possible but desirable, whether for higher profits, national dignity or some other purpose. New types of enterprising men come forward willing to mobilise savings and take risks in the pursuit of profit. Investment increases, notably in transport, communications and raw materials. But these developments proceed gradually until the threshold of the third stage, 'take-off', is reached. At this point, new industries expand rapidly yielding profits, a large proportion of which are invested in new plant. Because of their expanding demand for factory workers and the goods and services to support them these new industries stimulate the growth of others. Rostow fixes the take-off in Britain some time in the two decades after 1783; France and the US in the decades preceeding 1860; Germany in the third quarter of the nineteenth century; Japan in the last quarter of the nineteenth century; and Russia and Canada during the 25 years prior to 1914. During the 1950s India and China in their quite different ways launched their respective take-offs.

After take-off there follows a long interval of sustained growth as the expanding economy extends modern technology throughout the range of its activity. Between 10 and 20 per cent of national income is steadily reinvested so that output continues to outstrip increases in population. Some 60 years after the onset of take-off this fourth stage, the 'drive to maturity', is completed. The mature economy broadens its base to include technologically more refined and complex processes and is thus able to move beyond the industries that fuelled its take-off. With the arrival of the fifth stage, the 'age of mass consumption', leading sectors of the economy shift into the manufacture of consumer durables and the provision of services. This stage can only be reached when real income per head has risen to a point at which the consumption needs of a large section of the population have moved beyond basic food, shelter and clothing. At the time of writing (in the 1950s) it could only be found in the US, western European societies and Japan.

The crucial point in Rostow's analysis is that, although for the non-industrialised world the initial stimulus to modernisation arrives from outside through the example set by the industrialised countries, the basic problem of taking off is totally internal to the economies concerned. Essentially it is to produce enough individuals with entrepreneurial abilities.

It can be seen that all these theories or approaches to modernisation and economic development made a number of assumptions. While bold notions of the 'march of progress' had long been discredited, these approaches still contained a marked strain of evolutionary optimism. They were explicitly teleological: contemporary societies represented the end-state towards which the non-industrial world was evolving. And while there was little consensus as to what precisely constituted 'modernisation' – could it be equated for instance with industrialisation or rationalisation, or was it a bundle of related processes? – it was still assumed to be desirable (see Tipps, 1973). The experience of the western industrialised world was drawn on heavily for models and concepts to be applied to the new Third World nations, with little regard for whether their dichotomous 'before' and 'after' terms fitted a different situation. And in particular in the US there was a widespread willingness to anticipate a relatively smooth and linear process of cultural change, economic growth and stable democracy amongst not only foreign policy advisers but a significant section of the social science establishment. Packenham has attributed this to 'American exceptionalism', that is to the misplaced extrapolation from America's exceptionally fortunate experience to the view that development was easy, that all good things – such as economic growth and democracy – went together and that extremism and revolution were unnecessary (Packenham, 1973).

A Framework for Analysing Third World Politics: Almond's Structural Functionalism

Having established the context in which political scientists began to pay more sustained attention to the new Third World nations, and the kinds of modernisation theory upon which they drew, we are better placed to trace the emergence of an approach to the politics of these countries within which assumptions about a distinctive process of *political* development or modernisation were initially implicit but increasingly took on a more explicit theoretical character. The criticisms of Macridis and others of the non-comparative nature of comparative politics stimulated the setting up in 1954 by the American Social Science Research Council (SSRC) of a Committee on Comparative Politics, under the chairmanship of Gabriel Almond. This Committee saw its role both as fostering debate aimed at producing the most appropriate theoretical framework for political comparison and sponsoring case studies of politics in different countries. It was responsible, directly and indirectly, for a significant and influential share of the literature that now began to proliferate in the field of Third World politics.

While no single framework for analysis dominated the literature, since as we have seen to arrive at such a framework was one of the Committee's central objects, the approach initially proposed and subsequently refined by Almond himself was both representative and widely subscribed to. It is therefore worth pausing to examine. Almond drew on two main sources: one was Parsonian social theory, the other the political systems analysis of David Easton (1965).

One of the first political scientists to be converted wholesale to behaviouralism, Easton had already in 1953 set himself the task, which now seems wildly overambitious but was symptomatic of the intellectual optimism of the times, of providing a theoretical framework that so transcended specific political forms that it could be applied to political behaviour anywhere and would eventually form the basis for a general theory of politics. Like Parsons, Easton borrowed from the natural sciences the model of a *system* of behaviour, but whereas Parsons' notion of a system approximated a biological organism, Easton's analogy was with the inorganic, self-regulating system of electrical engineering. He saw the political system as embedded in a wider environment and constantly open to its pressures. The key question to be asked was how the political system survived at all. His answer was that to survive any system had to respond appropriately to impinging changes in its environment. In the case of the political system, this depended upon the success with which it performed its central function which Easton defined as the 'authoritative allocation of values for society'.

Consequently Easton's categories for analysing a political system were mainly concerned with its interaction with its environment. 'Inputs' from the environment, made up of both demands and supports, fed into the system. The system, through its 'authorities', in turn produced 'outputs' (policies and so on) which acted back upon the environment. These outputs formed part of a wider 'feedback loop', which, like a thermostat, allowed the system to monitor and adjust its performance.

As should be evident, there were any number of problems with this framework, not least its application to the empirical world. The most relevant to the present discussion is the vagueness and overgenerality of its categories. How, for instance, was the 'boundary' of a political system to be recognised? The approach had nonetheless the attraction for Almond of appearing to get right away from an emphasis on particular government institutions and focusing instead on processes within a broadly defined political arena.

Almond's initial idea was to elaborate what Easton had called the 'conversion functions', the way in which the political system converts inputs into outputs, and then, like Parsons, to investigate the relationship between these functions and particular structures. On the 'input' side, the first process he identified was 'political socialisation', through which individuals within a political system acquire attitudes towards it, via such agencies as families, schools and political parties. The second function, 'political recruitment', is self-explanatory. For his third and fourth functions, Almond expanded Easton's notion of demands into the 'articulation' and 'aggregation' of interests. Articulation is the process of making demands upon decisionmakers, aggregation the way in which these demands are combined into general policy alternatives, for instance by political parties or government bureaucracies.

On the 'output' side, Almond distinguished 'rule-making', 'rule-implementation' and 'rule-adjudication'. He acknowledged that these were closely derived from the legislative, executive and judicial functions embodied in the US' constitutional doctrine of the separation of powers. Rule-making centres on the making of policies or laws, rule-implementation on their application, associated in modern societies with government bureaucracy, and rule-adjudication on the process of authoritatively deciding whether a rule has been correctly applied in a given case. Over and above the input and output functions, Almond added that of 'political communication', the transmission, particularly in modern societies through the media, of political information within the system.

The approach applied: ' The Politics of the Developing Areas'

These elements of a comparative framework were set out in the introductory chapter of the book Almond edited with James Coleman, published in 1960, *The Politics of the Developing Areas.* For this book five experts had been asked to contribute an essay on the politics of the developing area in which they specialised, making use of Almond's structural-functional framework. A brief consideration of these essays will therefore help to illustrate the implications and limitations of such an approach.

The basic point about these essays is that while several of them, most outstandingly Coleman's analysis of the politics of sub-Saharan Africa, provided an excellent introduction to what was then understood about their subject, their merit owed nothing to the analytical framework they were applying. If anything it was a hindrance. Each essay followed a similar design, with sections on the background (physical setting, traditional culture, western impact), on processes of change, such as urbanisation and the spread of westernised education, with implications for politics, and on political groupings, before the final section in which political functions were directly examined. The better essays used this format to provide a great deal of pertinent information in the first three sections, which also helped to make the last section more intelligible.

The authors were asked to conceive of politics in the various nation-states as forming political systems, but several pointed out that it was questionable how far one *could* assume a single, unified political process or system. As Coleman noted, 'a system implies a set of ordered relationships having stable boundaries and a certain persistence over time' (p. 323). In practice, however, Dankwart Rustow wrote that the political process in Near Eastern countries was as yet far from perfectly integrated. Cultural and economic changes are rapidly involving ever larger segments of the population in the national political process which has so far been dominated almost entirely by the urban elites. Yet a myriad of distinct political processes in villages and tribes survive. In addition, national politics are disrupted by the uncertainty of boundaries and of national sentiment (p. 428).

Similarly Lucian Pye suggested that in South-East Asia, it was 'useful to think of the countries as possessing not a single and integrating political process but many only loosely related political processes' (p. 117).

But the more serious distortion occurred through the application of Almond's functional categories. For despite their supposed generality, these categories strongly reflected Almond's understanding of the American political system and so almost inevitably produced a misleading emphasis on certain aspects of the political process, not always of great significance in the countries under consideration, while obscuring what was most important and distinctive. They tended, moreover, to be largely *descriptive* categories which did not encourage attempts to pin down causes of political change. We can take, for instance, the primacy given to the function of interest articulation. In the first place, as one or two authors pointed out, there was not necessarily a lot of it going on. Rustow found that 'The Near Eastern process of political articulation often appears to be floating in mid-air. It commonly lacks the solid fundament of any genuine interest representation. In turn it rarely provides the basis for any impressive superstructure of national policy' (p. 433). Almond wanted to call the structures involved in interest articulation 'interest groups', but 'interest group' would be an excellent example of a concept which, as Sartori has expressed it, does not 'travel well'. It carries associations with a certain kind of political environment in which interest group formation is considered normal and legitimate, and such groups are open in their organisations and campaigns (Sartori, 1970). Almond also suggested there would be four types of interest group: 'institutional', that is based on pre-existing organisations; 'associational' or specialised structures of interest articulation, which were the most 'modern' and approved of; 'non-associational' which were intermittent and often informal, for instance kinship and lineage groups; and 'anomic', as in riots and demonstrations. This was hardly an adequate way to discuss the manner in which different sectors impinged on politics. To analyse the role of 'ethnicity' in terms of non-associational interest groups was bizarre, but most unsatisfactory was the reference to government bureaucracy, and above all the military, even where these dominated national politics, as institutional interest groups. In his remarkably bland essay on the politics of Latin America, George Blanksten made no mention of the military until around two-thirds of the way through when, in discussing institutional interest groups, he observed that 'militarism has long been recognised as a fundamental characteristic of Latin American politics' (p. 503) but then declined to elaborate. There was also a tendency in Almond's approach to assume that interests were articulated in order to influence the making of policy, whereas Myron Weiner, reviewing South Asian politics, noted that often it was the *implementation* of policy that interests sought to affect. An emphasis on interest articulation, most fundamentally, tended to ignore those interests which failed to be articulated and thus to raise questions about the distribution of political power.

As we have seen, Almond took, without apologies, his division of output functions into rule-making, rule-implementation and rule-ajudication from the American Constitution's doctrine of the separation of powers. But this very derivation imposed unwarranted assumptions upon the political systems these functional categories were used to analyse. Did rule-making, with its connotations of policy-making and legislation, really occupy the same place as in the American political system? Pye found that the transitional societies of South-East Asia had not yet fully incorporated the view 'that the appropriate goal of politics is the production of public policy in the form of laws'. Instead they exhibited continuing manifestations of the traditional belief 'that power and prestige are values to be fully enjoyed for their own sake and not rationalized into mere means to achieve policy goals' (p. 142). Coleman, too, emphasised the extent to which in African countries, 'the concept of legislation or rule-making as a positive instrument for satisfying claimant interests within the society and for bringing about social and economic change' was a western innovation (p. 355).

Many more examples of the distorting effect of these categories could be cited. The real problem though was not the connotations they brought with them – with care these could be overcome – but the manner in which they obscured the more fundamental political processes and relationships at work. Just one example of this is the difficulties it presented in any attempt to provide an adequate analysis of the role and character of the state (Almond himself repudiated the concept of the state as excessively legalistic). The emphasis on input functions, with outputs seen largely as resulting from rather than determining inputs was one aspect of this. How could one examine the case, increasingly common in the Third World context, of a government which itself assumed an initiating role? Weiner, discussing interest aggregation in India, had to point out that in fact government leaders, drawn from the westernised intelligentsia, dominated policy-making. 'These leaders view themselves and their government, rather than business and other non-governmental associations, as the major catalyst of social and economic change. They often tend to view organized interests as an impediment to rational planning, as interests to be avoided rather than accommodated' (p. 212). How, too, could one discuss the related and increasingly relevant question of authoritarianism in government? Rustow, in reporting on interest articulation, and on political recruitment and communication, in Near Eastern societies, found himself obliged to distinguish between dictatorships and more democratic systems. And under the heading of rule-application he squeezed in a necessary comment on 'the important and varied role which coercion plays in the Near Eastern governmental process' (p. 449). The structural-functional framework made it difficult to talk about the role of the state and coercion, let alone explain them.

Political Development Theory

In these essays there is little explicit reference to a process of political development, though they generally assumed that the countries under discussion were in a process of transition, politically as well as socially and economically. Most authors emphasised the importance of political integration and stability, and expressed hopes for democracy. Coleman himself, in a concluding chapter, found general statistical support, 'with certain striking deviations', for the view that social and economic development were associated with increasing democratic tendencies in the countries covered by the book (p. 538).

In the introduction, however, Almond had suggested that it might be possible to define political modernity according to the degree of differentiation and functional specialisation of political structures and the prevalence of modern 'styles' (Parsons' pattern variables) within the political culture. Thus in a modern western system each of the functions would have a specialised structure which regulated the performance of that function by other structures, and traditional styles of diffuseness, particularity, ascriptiveness and affectivity would have been extensively penetrated by rational styles of specificity, universality, achievement and affective neutrality. This was to remain the core of his theory of political development, set out in a revised and expanded form, in the book written with Bingham Powell, *Comparative Politics: A Developmental Approach* (1966).

In this later work, Almond and Powell introduced a new concept that they claimed would make it possible to show how political development was reflected in what the political system actually *did*, how it performed in its environment. They pointed to five main 'capabilities' of the political system. The 'extractive' capability described the system's ability to draw material and human resources from its environment. The 'regulative' capability referred to its control over the behaviour of individuals and groups. A system's 'distributive' capability determined its ability to allocate goods, services, honours, status and other kinds of opportunity in society. The fourth capability was 'symbolic', meaning the system's effectiveness in martialling such outputs as the display of flags, military ceremony and national anthems. Last was the 'responsive' capability, describing the relationship within the political system between inputs and outputs as a whole.

Almond and Powell expected the political system's capabilities to increase with growing differentiation of political functions and structures, together with the secularisation or modernisation of political styles. This in turn would allow it to deal more effectively with the four main problems (other writers have referred to them as 'crises') of political development. With the beginnings of modernisation, the political elite faces the problem of 'state-building', the need to create new structures that will penetrate and integrate society, and in particular an efficient bureaucracy. At the same time it faces a related but distinct problem of 'nation-building' or cultural integration, the 'process whereby people transfer loyalty from smaller tribes, villages or petty principalities to the larger central political system' (p. 36). In western liberal democracies, the crises of state and nation-building have usually been largely resolved before the other two crises loom up. These are the problems of participation, coping with increasing pressures for participation in political life, and of distribution, meeting growing demands for redistribution or welfare. Typically societies of the Third World have to deal with all four types of crises at once.

Almond was prompted to expand on his theory of political development in part by criticisms of its earlier, tentative formulation. But he was also influenced by the growing interest in political development as a concept which itself, we have suggested, may have been stimulated by the urge to produce for politics something approaching the rigour of Rostow's model. Most specifically, Riggs in a recent (1981) review of 'the rise and fall of political development' notes that in April 1960 the Ford Foundation awarded a 3-year grant to the Comparative Politics Committee to support a programme of interdisciplinary seminars and training around the theme of political development. Arising out of this programme, seven volumes of studies in political development had been published by 1971, all but one of which included the term 'political development' in the title. Riggs suggests that prior to 1960 'political development' did not have a specific meaning, that rather the Committee agreed to use the term in its application for funding.

> In the context of the day, when international technical co-operation was widely hailed as a means to bring the advantages of modern industrial society to the relatively deprived countries of the Third World, the action-oriented word 'development' clearly opened more doors than did its near synonym, 'modernization', which carried more academic and behavioural connotations. No doubt members

of the Committee, as social scientists, were more interested in the behaviourally oriented comparative analysis of political behaviour than they were in the implicit rhetoric of a more programmatic word. But they were also realists. When it became a question of securing generous financial support for the preparation and publication of an important series of books, they were prepared to adapt (p. 307).

It was with the award of the 1960 grant that the search to pin down a content for 'political development' began in earnest. And, as Riggs observes, 'The use of "political development" is strongly, if not exclusively, associated with the extraordinarily influential activities of the SSRC Committee on Comparative Politics' (p. 299), to the extent that it is very difficult to find anyone else using the term whose intellectual parentage cannot be traced to its work.

Perhaps one should raise here the question of the distinction between political development and political modernisation. The latter term was coming into use before 1960, and continued to be preferred by such writers as Apter (1965) and Rustow (1967). Certain authors believed the distinction to be an important one. Huntington, in particular, argued that political modernisation should be understood as 'the political aspects and political effects of social, economic and cultural modernisation'. This might lead to political development, or the pressures it generated might be too great for the political system and give rise to political decay (1965). In a later survey of the literature (1972), Dodd suggested that political modernisation was more open-ended as a concept, where political development implied progress towards more or less definable ends. Some such differentiation of meaning does seem intrinsically attractive: since, however, in practice the terms were often used interchangeably, to insist on the distinction would be excessively pedantic.

Almond's theory of political development, influential as it was, did not monopolise the field, especially if one includes those that were less elaborately articulated. Many writers who offered alternative versions, espoused some form of structure–functional systems framework (for instance Apter, and Riggs, 1964). As Huntington (1971) points out, two other main methods of approach were applied to issues of political development. There was first what he calls the 'social process' approach, which took particular social processes, such as urbanisation and the spread of literacy, and sought to correlate indices of these with aspects of political change (for instance Deutsch, 1961; Cutright, 1963). Second was the 'comparative history' approach, favoured indeed by several members of the Comparative Politics Committee, and which studied the actual historical development of different societies to arrive at alternative patterns of political development (for instance Black, 1966). It could be argued, however, that exponents of the social process or comparative history approaches were less able, and generally less inclined, to offer a single, general theory of political development.

Given this burgeoning literature, to what extent did a common understanding of the process of political development emerge? Looking back in 1970, Almond was sanguine, arguing that all those political scientists associated with the Committee on Comparative Politics, however diverse their interpretations, had 'been writing about movement in a particular direction' (p. 288); that there *was* a consensus. And there is little doubt that the different accounts of political development did share certain basic assumptions: that political development was desirable and to be encouraged; that it was going on, though according to some, very slowly; that this was from an original predominantly 'traditional' political system to a developed or modern one; and that the developed system would resemble in key respects existing political systems of the western world, often if not always equated with liberal democracy.

Nevertheless, while there was thus widespread agreement on these points, they were simply the assumptions that writers had set out with, borrowed from fellow disciplines and scarcely confirmed or refined by subsequent reflection or research. When it came to pinpointing exactly which process or processes constituted political development there was much less clarity or agreement. Lucian Pye, who took over from Almond as Chairman of the Comparative Politics Committee in 1963, attempted to introduce some order into the debate. In his essay on the concept of political development (1966) he listed no less than ten different interpretations, though these were less mutually exclusive than a matter of varying emphasis. They included for instance the political prerequisites for economic development, the politics typical of industrial societies and the politics of the nation-state. Despite their apparent heterogeneity, Pye argued that one could extract from them three central and recurrent themes. First was a concern, however rhetorical, with equality, as evidenced in efforts to involve the 'masses' in politics, the spread of legislation universal as opposed to particularistic in its scope and the increasing importance of merit rather than ascription as the criterion for political recruitment. Second was the growing capacity of the political system, whether in terms of its scope, efficiency or rationality. The third theme was the increasing differentiation of political roles and structures. Pye conceded that these three elements were themselves not always necessarily congruent or compatible: for instance, measures to promote equality could undermine government capacity, but he suggested that one could usefully distinguish between different paths of political development according to the different sequences in which societies tackled these three issues.

The Decline of Political Development Theory

By the end of the decade, the concept of political development and approaches based upon it were beginning to fall from favour. Its usage since has steadily declined until now one would be most surprised to find an explicit and uncritical application of political development theory to the politics of a Third World society. This is not to say that all the themes and assumptions associated with it have entirely disappeared from the literature. On the contrary, Higgott (1983) for one argues that elements of these are all too evident in recent 'liberal' or non-Marxist attempts to develop a new 'political economy' of development. Uphoff and Illchman (1972) have defined political economy in this context as an 'integrated social science of public choice' and its exponents have tended to concentrate on the political strategies which incumbent Third World political leaders should follow in order to promote specific developmental objectives. Despite the seeming pragmatism of such an approach, Higgott maintains there is often considerable continuity with the earliest paradigm. One of the more convincing examples Higgott offers is Rothchild and Curry's *Scarcity, Choice and Public Policy in Middle Africa* (1978) which draws extensively on previous political development theory, while apparently rejecting it, for its designation of the 'system goals' political decisionmakers should adopt, the 'crises' they must contend with and the strategies they should accordingly pursue. We return to this question in our final chapter.

Nonetheless political development theory, old-style, is largely disowned and the reasons are not hard to find. Riggs observes that, 'A decline of the popularity among scholars of the word "political development" can be traced to the time when the Ford Foundation's support for research on it ceased' (p. 313). The final grant expired in 1971 and from 1974 at least there was a dramatic fall in the number of new publications indexed under this heading. But this was as much a symptom as a cause of more fundamental weaknesses.

There were first of all problems with the concept of political development in its own terms. If Pye could find comfort in the belief that from ten different meanings three common themes could be distilled, Huntington was less impressed, maintaining in a much quoted phrase that if there were ten meanings then this was ten too many. Nor, he held, could political development operate satisfactorily as an 'umbrella' term, covering a number of associated processes, as 'modernisation' might claim to. The various processes grouped together for instance by Almond, or by Pye himself, to constitute political development were not necessarily related to each other at all. Huntington argued forcefully that the concept should be abandoned and 'political change' should become the proper object of academic inquiry (1971). Riggs, too, has been critical of the readiness of political scientists, including himself, to believe that a content for the expression 'political development' could be discovered. The mistake was in assuming that political development was a concept that could be defined as opposed to a useful political slogan (1981).

However, these intrinsic shortcomings were less serious than that the whole political development approach of this period was entirely unrealistic: ethnocentric, naively optimistic and failing to recognise the political implications of economic dependence upon the West. These failures require no further elaboration here. They are central themes of the chapters to follow.

2
Modernisation Revisionism

The first wave of criticism to be considered here broke in the late 1960s and focused on the oversimplified conceptualisation in political development theory of 'tradition', 'modernity' and their interrelationship. It was part of the broader reaction against underlying assumptions of modernisation theory as a whole: that there are recognisably traditional institutions, that these constitute a barrier to modernisation and that to the extent that modernisation takes place traditional institutions must decline. The criticisms were influenced by the findings of social anthropologists who, themselves challenged by developments in political science and by the changing context of the new nation-states they had to work in, were beginning to link their analysis of micro-communities with broader social and political institutions (see Vincent, 1969). Huntington called this new critical approach 'modernisation revisionism' (1971) and its exponents included amongst many others Joseph Gusfield, Reinhard Bendix, Lloyd and Suzanne Rudolph and S. N. Eisenstadt.

These writers argued first that definitions of the two concepts, tradition and modernity, were always inadequate. The concept of modernity has never been elaborated in such a way as to facilitate meaningful comparisons between societies, especially between developed and underdeveloped societies. In fact in its cruder formulations modernity is designated virtually in terms of some idealised western man:

> Modern man's character as it emerges from our study may be summed up under four headings. He is an informed participant citizen; he has a marked sense of personal efficiency; he is highly independent and autonomous in his relations to

traditional sources of influence . . . and he is ready for new experiences and ideas, that is he is relatively open-minded and cognitively stable (Inkeles and Smith, 1974, p. 290).

As for tradition, this is usually conceived as everything that is not modern, thus making it, as Huntington points out, something of a residual concept. Or, in Portes' words, 'modernity creates tradition' (Portes, 1976, p. 73). Since tradition does not represent an analytically coherent alternative to modernity, the alleged dichotomy between tradition and modernity is not a real one. Moreover the very notion of tradition is far too broad: 'Kung bushmen, the Abbasid Caliphate, the Kingdom of Ashanti and Mogul India are all traditional societies but appear to have little in common except that they are not modern. The differences within the traditional orbit are certainly as substantial as those between traditional and modern phenomena. Indeed the degree of variation *within* any one traditional society is much greater than the dichotomous approach would suggest. It has even been argued that traditional societies will be less homogeneous, because less highly integrated, than modern societies, that is they will encompass a range of traditions (see Tipps, 1973). Tradition is not a monolithic unity that is uniformly apprehended by all the members of a given society.

A particular target for criticism has been a tendency in many of the theories of modernisation to take a zero-sum view of the relationship between tradition and modernity. That is they assume, either explicitly or implicitly, that to the extent that a society becomes modern it ceases by the same degree to be traditional. Modernisation, according to this view, entails the shedding of 'tradition'. By way of criticism, a wide range of studies has attempted to show that not only may traditional institutions adapt to and co-exist with modern institutions, specifically the nation-state and its trappings but, in addition, the process of modernisation may actually revitalise dormant traditional institutions and practices. That is, as Bendix (1967) has said, modernisation, through for instance modern medicine or increased literacy, may not lead to 'modernity'. On the other hand traditional relationships may actually facilitate aspects of modernisation.

Many modernisation revisionists (for instance Gusfield, 1967;

Singer, 1971) drew their illustrations from India whose society appeared to exhibit some of the most conservative and rigid forms of tradition. Since we shall shortly be considering the political role of India's caste system, we shall take here as an example of the modernisation revisionist approach to social change Gusfield's seminal article in which he relied primarily on Indian examples to show seven prevalent fallacies.

The first fallacy was that traditional societies have been static. On the contrary, he maintains, they are the products of successive change. India's family life, religious beliefs and practices and social structure were deeply modified by foreign conquest, including most recently the Moguls and the British, and by new social and cultural movements. The second, that traditional culture is a consistent body of norms and values, has been refuted by anthropologists. They have demonstrated, for instance, the co-existence of a 'great tradition' of urban, literate Indian culture and a 'little tradition' of village communities. Even within the great tradition, contrasting values legitimate a wide range of behaviours. India provides counter-evidence also for the assumption that a traditional society must have a homogeneous social structure. Outside the dominant caste system, Indian society has incorporated 'pariah' groups like the Parsees and Jains whose life style diverges sharply from the Hindu norm and who have played an important role as economic innovators. But within the caste system itself, the Untouchables have performed taboo but economically necessary tasks while such sub-castes as the Marwari and Chettiar have taken on major entrepreneurial roles.

The interpenetration of India's 'great' and 'little' cultural traditions disproves the fallacy that old traditions are dissolved by innovation. The fifth and sixth fallacies overlap: it has been assumed that tradition and modernity are forever in conflict and that they are mutually exclusive. Yet in India the large extended families of the Tatas, Birlas and Dalmas have formed the basis of major and highly successful industrial organisations. There is finally no reason to suppose that the modernising process weakens tradition. As we shall see, many of India's lower sub-castes have sought to register their increased economic status, a result of changes associated with modernisation, through 'sanskritisation' or appeals to traditional Hindu ritual.

It was this realisation that prevalent concepts of tradition and modernity and their interrelationship were inadequate which formed the basis for our first major line of attack on the theories of political development considered in the previous chapter. In particular increasing attention was paid to a number of 'traditional' social relationships – tribalism or ethnicity, patron-client networks, caste – which appeared to play a continuing if changing role in the process of political modernisation. It is important to realise though that, as the epithet 'modernisation revisionism' suggests, such writers did not abandon the developmental perspective altogether. They sought to introduce greater realism into the approach but many, such as the Rudolphs whom we are about to consider, retained a kind of developmental optimism in the longer run.

Caste and Political Modernisation

A good starting point is the political role of India's caste system, representing to many an extreme of inflexible tradition. It is the major focus of the Rudolphs' classic statement of the modernisation revisionist position in political science, *The Modernity of Tradition: Political Development in India* (1967). The title incidentally shows the authors' intention to rescue rather than jettison the notion of political development.

When the British encountered India's caste system in the eighteenth century it was already at least 2000 years old. To summarise a highly complex reality, Hindu society was divided into a great number of 'castes' each of which was ascriptive, endogamous and distinguished from the others by various ritualistic practices. Each was also associated with a particular occupation or set of occupations, so that while rigidly maintaining their separate identities, the castes through this elaborate division of labour were socially and economically interdependent. They were moreover hierarchically ranked with notions of purity or pollution deeply embedded in gradations of social status. Individual mobility between castes was extremely rare and social mobility of a caste as a whole possible only over several generations.

According to the ancient Vedic texts of Hinduism, as

interpreted by the Brahmins or priest caste, the coherence of the caste system stemmed from the ordering of society into four great 'varnas' (literally 'colours') or broad caste divisions. Highest in rank were the three twice-born castes, so called because their male members underwent a second ceremonial birth when they donned the sacred thread. In descending ritual order they included the Brahmins, the Kshatriyas – rulers and warriors – and the Vaisyas or merchant caste. Below them were the Sudras (labourers and artisans), by far the most populous group. Outside the varnas altogether were the 'outcastes' or 'Untouchables'. Any contact with them was considered polluting for the caste Hindu and they were allotted such 'unclean' tasks as removing excrement and handling dead animals. The doctrines of 'karma' and 'dharma' encouraged acceptance of this social order and one's place within it.

It is now widely recognised that the British adopted too uncritically the Brahmin account of social reality. Indeed they may paradoxically have reinforced it, by incorporating and codifying the caste system for legal and administrative purposes. Hindu worship was never centralised, with governing institutions and a unified priesthood, as in most other great religions. Its social doctrines varied greatly through time and from region to region. Indeed a villager, in many parts of India, might be largely unaware of their place in a transcending order of varnas, experiencing caste instead as the local system of sub-castes or 'jati'. There are now estimated to be over 2000 such jati in India, a typical village including anything between six and twenty. There is tremendous variation in the caste composition of local communities between regions and even within them. Brahmins have by no means always been the dominant caste in practice, or even always highest in ritual status.

There were and are nonetheless certain universal features of the caste system. As Srinivas writes,

> Caste is undoubtedly an all-India phenomenon in the sense that there are everywhere hereditary, endogamous groups which form a hierarchy and that each of these groups has a traditional association with one or two occupations. Everywhere there are Brahmins, Untouchables, and peasant, artisan, trading and service castes. Relations between castes

are invariably expressed in terms of pollution and purity (1966, p. 3).

There has also been a close relationship between landownership and caste position: typically in rural India, landowners are from the higher castes while most Untouchables have either no land or holdings too small to be viable.

As noted earlier, the 'traditional' caste system the British came upon was in no way static. Throughout its history, war and conquest, the influx of new ethnic groups and economic change had provided opportunity for individual jatis to raise their status while others declined. Sometimes but not always this was through 'sanskritisation', defined by Srinivas as 'the process by which a "low" Hindu caste, or tribal or other group, changes its customs, ritual and ideology and way of life in the direction of a high and frequently "twice-born" caste' (p. 6). British colonial policies and processes of social and economic modernisation associated with them brought further major changes. Marx was not alone in believing that these, and particularly the introduction of modern industry, would 'dissolve the hereditary divisions of labour upon which rest the Indian castes, those decisive impediments to Indian progress' (cited by the Rudolphs, p. 22). One consequence was indeed the beginnings of 'westernisation', the adoption of western models of education, values and life-style, a process not confined to members of high-ranking castes and which might have been expected to erode caste divisions. Singer has argued, however, that even the most apparently westernised Indians were often able to compartmentalise western values, while continuing to identify with such traditional institutions as caste (Singer, 1971), and at the same time the process of sanskritisation was given new impetus. Changing fortunes of particular sub-castes, whether due to new employment or trading opportunities, expanding communications bringing previously isolated villages into closer contact with sanskritic traditions or British attempts to reconcile the multitude of jati with the Brahminical order of varnas, all fuelled concern with ritual status.

In this context, a significant development was the emergence of 'caste associations'. A caste association is an organisation of members of the same or very similar jati from several adjacent villages. While particularistic in its loyalty, it resembles an interest group in having a formal membership narrower than the potential ascriptive membership, in explicitly pursuing the interests of its members and having a regularised structure with its own finances, publications and officers. Moreover while leadership of sub-castes has traditionally been hereditary or the prerogative of 'elders', caste associations typically select officers who are relatively well educated and able to deal with government bureaucracy.

Take for example the Shanans whose original occupation as toddy tappers designated them Untouchables. As individual members of this sub-caste prospered, benefitting from new trading opportunities under the British, they campaigned to raise their social status, claiming that in fact they were descended from the Kshatriya. They eventually succeeded in changing their name to Nadars and in setting up a Nadar caste association whose pressure activities were so effective that by 1921 the Nadars were no longer listed in the Census as toddy tappers or regarded as Untouchables (Rudolph and Rudolph, 1967).

Political and economic developments following the granting of independence to India in 1947 have further modified the caste system and its political role but by no means eliminated them. The Indian Constitution adopted in 1950 established a secular state and its section on Fundamental Rights prohibited all discrimination on the basis of caste. At the same time the Constitutions provided for positive discrimination on behalf of the Scheduled Castes (roughly corresponding to the Untouchables), in for instance the allocation of assembly seats. Of equal if not greater importance for the caste system, the Constitution established a form of parliamentary democracy which, despite authoritarian elements which were highlighted during the period of Emergency Rule from 1975 to 1977, has involved a lively competition between the national political parties. The devolution of certain important decision making and administrative powers, through India's federal system, to the states, and the creation of elected councils – the panchayats – in local government have further extended the arena of electoral competition.

How have these 'modern' political structures interacted with the caste system? Initially many western observers expected

such democratic institutions, together with improved communications and increasing literacy, to transform political behaviour. Instead of following traditional authority, as in the
caste system, individuals would make their own 'rational'
judgement of party programmes and candidates. Graham has
called this the 'enlightenment' view (1975) and it rapidly
became clear that it was not happening. Certainly the level of
political participation was relatively high from the outset. In the
first General Elections after Independence just over 50 per cent
of the 176 million eligible to vote took part and turnout has
increased fairly steadily since. It was 56 per cent of an eligible
354 million by 1980. But caste identification was an important
element in such participation and gained a new dimension in
the process.

The Rudolphs were not the first to realise this but as we have
seen they took caste as an example of the mutual modification of
political tradition and modernity. For analytic purposes they
distinguished three stages of political mobilisation while pointing out that in practice these need not follow each other in strict
sequence. The first stage is 'vertical mobilisation' when one
caste (jati) dominates a village or wider area in terms of social
status and economic power and so is able to mobilise effective
electoral and other forms of support for its preferred party and
candidates. Here the traditional caste hierarchy is directly
translated into political practice.

There are a number of ways in which the political control of
the dominant caste can be undermined. Conflicts may develop
within the dominant caste and while the initial result may be a
series of vertical faction-based linkages with client castes,
competing with each other, such conflicts may also provide
(particularly when the dominant caste is numerically small)
opportunity for castes a little lower in status and economic
power but stronger in numbers to mobilise on their own account
or in alliance with one of the factions. The influence of the
dominant caste may be further eroded by growing political
awareness and by the loss of some of its traditional sources of
patronage as the village is increasingly penetrated by state
agencies and the market, so that new middlemen or 'brokers'
with contacts beyond the village assume greater importance.
Expanding communications also foster the growth of caste
associations, formed as we have seen to advance the interests of

particular jati. Caste associations have often been prominent in the panchayati raj. Where they extend across a number of districts, occasionally a whole State, they have been able to trade the votes of their caste members in exchange for material benefits. This is then the second stage, that of 'horizontal mobilisation'. While still based on caste, it is no longer hierarchical relationships but competition between castes that is the prime motor.

There is ample evidence both from the Rudolphs and from other sources that while vertical mobilisation still prevails in many areas (see for instance Blair's discussion of two villages in Bihar, 1972), horizontal mobilisation is an India-wide phenomenon. Either way caste has not lost its salience for Indian politics. However secular and egalitarian their national pronouncements, political parties, even Communist parties, have carefully weighed the caste factor in their electoral strategy and sponsored candidates whose caste is acceptable to the local electorate. In so far as horizontal mobilisation has emerged, however, the Rudolphs see the role of caste in Indian politics as on balance beneficial. Whereas, they argue, traditional social cleavages based on region, religion or ethnicity can create centrifugal pressures as they are politicised, mobilisation around caste has helped to integrate Indians into the political system.

The Rudolphs' argument goes further, for they anticipate a third stage of 'differential mobilisation', when having played its necessary part in politicising the Indian public, caste will recede in importance. The very experience, they suggest, of belonging to a caste 'whose boundaries, norms and culture are changing' (p. 88) must undermine belief in hereditary status. Through caste-based politics, the voter will come to a more independent appraisal of the merits and shortcomings of particular parties, their candidates and programmes. They find signs of this happening already. Some caste associations have for instance split into two or more separate organisations as members perceive their differing economic interests and values. In the case of the Nadars, the main caste association, the Nadar Mahajana Sangam, for long active in support of the Congress Party, has more recently refrained from direct involvement in party politics. Instead different sections of the Nadar community, whether on the basis of perceived economic interests or in response to local circumstances, pursue different political strategies. Sometimes castes or caste associations of contrasting social status have come together to form caste federations for the advancement of all their members' interests, for instance the Kshatriya Sebha of Gujarat including Bariyas (marginal peasants and landless labourers), Bhils (depressed tribals) and the twice-born Rajputs. These are all examples of differential mobilisation. Studies of recent general and State elections give qualified support to the view that the individual voter is becoming more discriminating.

The Rudolphs' examination of caste then provides our first example of the modernisation revisionist thesis as applied to politics. Caste is used to demonstrate the dialectical nature of the relationship between political tradition and modernity: caste has been politicised and in the process both caste and politics have changed. But the Rudolphs are also arguing that while the immediate effect of the politicisation of caste may have been to reinforce traditional values and authority, in the longer run it has in fact contributed to political development, or the form of political development appropriate to India, by providing motive and meaning for participation in 'modern' political processes. They go so far as to say that, 'In its transformed state, caste has helped India's peasant society make a success of representative democracy and fostered the growth of equality' (p. 11).

While this is not the place to indulge an extended criticism of the Rudolphs' argument (though for a Marxist account of caste as false consciousness see Meillassoux, 1973, and for the denial that India's caste system can any longer be considered traditional see Fox, 1970), it must be asked whether the Rudolphs do not overstate the extent of change in a democratic, egalitarian direction. The process of horizontal mobilisation they describe remains largely confined to middle status or economically dominant castes. There are admittedly numerous examples of individual backward caste or Untouchable groups which have successfully mobilised. But India is a vast country and these examples need not reflect a general trend. The famous Dr Ambedkar, himself an Untouchable and a founding father of India's Constitution, helped form a Scheduled Caste Federation in 1942 which 15 years later became the basis for the Republic

Party, supposedly representing the interests of the Untouchables though it drew mainly on the Mahars of the state of
Maharashtra. It won only four seats in the 1957 national
elections and thereafter sank into obscurity. Even by the end of
the 1970s it was doubtful how far Untouchables were learning to
organise together politically and to ally with other backward
castes, and of course when they did there were often bloody
reprisals (see Joshi, 1982).

Paul Anber and the Nigerian Civil War

Of the many further examples of writings which have highlighted the complexity of the relationship between tradition and
modernity, we choose next to consider in some detail Paul
Anber's analysis of the background to the Nigerian Civil War of
1967–70 not only because it illustrates our present theme, but
also because an outline of these events will serve to illustrate
other arguments to be dealt with later on in this book.

The immediate cause of the Civil War was the secession in
May 1967 from the Federation of Nigeria's Eastern Region and
the creation of a sovereign and independent state of Biafra.
However, the roots of the conflict lie deep in Nigeria's colonial
past and specifically in the hostility between the conservative
Muslim Hausa-Fulani people of the North and the allegedly
progressive Christian Ibos of the East. The trigger for the
upsurge of the appalling communal violence which precipitated
the secession of Biafra was the military coup of January 1966
which overthrew the civilian regime of Sir Abubakar Tafawa
Balewa. The new military government under Major-General J.
T. U. Aguiyi-Ironsi, an Ibo, justified its intervention by the
need for sweeping reforms in the country, especially the
eradication of corruption and tribalism. In an attempt to
achieve this transformation the military announced the aboli-
tion of the country's regional structure and the unification of the
civil service.

Whether the intentions of the officers behind the coup were
genuine or not, their actions were regarded by Northerners as
part of an Ibo-dominated conspiracy. Most of those killed in the
January coup, both civilians and military, were Northerners.

They included the Federation's premier, Sir Abubakar, as well as Sir Ahmadu Bello, an august Muslim notable as well as leader of the Northern People's Congress. In addition, the centralising policies of the Ironsi regime were seen as a direct assault on Northern autonomy. Northern leaders therefore used the unification decree of May 1966 as a pretext to incite their people to acts of violence against Ibos resident in the North. During the last days of May, Ibos were attacked and their property destroyed on a large scale resulting in the death or injury of over 3000 Ibos. After a brief period of calm, Northern soldiers struck in July against Ibo supremacy in the army killing 27 Ibo officers, including Ironsi, together with a number of other Ibo ranks. Between September and November, violence against Ibo civilians living in the North erupted with renewed ferocity leaving 50 000 Ibos killed and injured and provoking the flight of at least one million Ibos back to their homeland in the East.

Given communal violence on this scale, the social basis of the Federation began to disintegrate. In Ibo land a rising tide of xenophobia led to the expulsion of non-Easterners from the region. The military governor in the East, Lieutenant-Colonel Ojukwu, refused to accept the authority of the new head of state in Lagos, Lieutenant-Colonel Gowon. Various economic measures were taken in the East which had a devastating effect on the Federal economy. For example, one-third of the entire rolling stock of Nigerian Railways was impounded in the East. The refinery at Port Harcourt refused to supply oil products, initially to the North but eventually to the rest of the Federation. The inevitable outcome of spiralling hostility and vindictiveness was the secession of the East in 1967.

For Anber the birth of Biafra and the upsurge of Ibo chauvinism that lay behind it present something of a problem. This is because, of Nigeria's ethnic groups, one would have least expected the Ibos to be the country's first 'tribal insurgents'. In contrast to the northern Hausa-Fulani and the Yoruba of Western Nigeria, the Ibos since colonial contact have been more mobile and more receptive to change. Traditional Ibo culture, according to Anber, was both egalitarian and placed great emphasis on personal achievement. The drive for achievement manifested itself in a rapid adaptation to colonial culture, not however in a spirit of passive imitation but driven by a desire to embrace modernity in order to master it. Thus whilst pursuing western education and western individualistic values, the Ibos were militantly anti-colonial and, in fact, at one stage saw themselves as forming the vanguard of Nigeria's struggle against imperialism. The nationalist orientation is evidenced by the strong support given by the Ibos to the National Council for Nigerian Citizens (NCNC), the first political party to emphasise national goals and deliberately to advocate policies which aimed to transcend regional and tribal loyalties.

The Hausa-Fulani, by contrast, have always been conservative, strongly resistant to cultural penetration from outside and deeply attached to the traditional religio-political system of emirates which predated and was preserved by colonialism. Militantly conscious of itself as a separate entity, the North was a much more obvious candidate for ethnically-powered secession. Even the ostensibly more modern Western Region, Anber suggests, due primarily to internal tensions, seemed at the time to be much more prone to separatist agitation than the East. Thus, Anber concludes, we have a paradox: how do we explain the fact that Nigeria's most modern and progressive people became the country's first tribalists, abandoning a universalist nationalism for a particularist, ethnically-based perspective?

The most obvious answer to this question is that Ibo secessionism was the inevitable product of communal violence which culminated in the horrifying massacres of the autumn of 1966. Whilst there is no denying that these events constituted the immediate cause of the East's secession, an adequate understanding of the conflict requires deeper historical analysis.

First of all it is crucial that we appreciate that as recently as 50 years before the events of 1966 the Ibos did not regard themselves as one people. Ibo social structure consisted of more than two hundred groups each of which operated as a separate society. Within each of these groups decisions were taken collectively by elders and other influential men. There was no centralised political authority and no state structure capable of imposing unity. In this respect the society contrasted quite markedly with the centralised political structure of the Hausa-Fulani emirates, and the Yoruba constitutional monarchies of the West. Ibo society was to some degree united by culture, but not by power and authority.

The twentieth century has seen the migration of large numbers of Ibos, driven by population pressure on the land, to other regions in Nigeria. Some indication of the scale of this migration may be gathered from the impressive increase of Ibos resident in the North from less than 3000 in 1921 to over 130 000 by 1952. Initially migrant Ibos became traders, shopkeepers, artisans and domestic employees. However, because of their receptivity to western education the Ibos soon became the major source of Nigeria's administrators, managers, technicians and civil servants, occupying senior positions far outside their numbers. Ibo predominance in white-collar and professional occupations soon provoked hostility among the other main ethnic groups; the Yoruba and Hausa-Fulani. Particular resentment was expressed at Ibo dominance in the Federal public service. In 1966 a Northern publication claimed that Nigeria's public services were 45 per cent Ibo and that this figure would reach 60 per cent by 1968. The North on the other hand was credited wih only 10 per cent of public posts. Similar Ibo predominance was claimed to exist in the Nigerian Railway Corporation, Nigerian Ports Authority, the foreign service and in the country's two universities at Lagos and Ibadan. The publication which cited these figures, emanating as it did from Zaria in the North, was obviously tendentious. However, exaggerations aside, there can be no doubt that Ibos were disproportionately represented at the professional, managerial and public service levels. Furthermore the publication is sociologically significant as it reflected what non-Ibos were being encouraged to believe.

Given an atmosphere of ethnic conspiracy, it is not surprising that by the late 1950s Nigerian politics had firmly crystallised around ethnic, regional rivalries, with the three main parties – the Northern People's Congress, the Action Group and the National Council of Nigerian Citizens (NCNC) – representing the country's three major groups. Having begun its life advocating nationalist policies, the NCNC had by this time been pushed by the momentum of non-Ibo opposition into becoming an Ibo party. Hostility between North and East intensified with the result of the first post-Independence census in 1963 which declared the North to have an absolute majority of Nigeria's population. Polarisation between the two regions was encouraged by disunity among the Yoruba in the West which led the North to focus on the East as its major opponent. A decisive stage in the emerging struggle was reached with the Federal elections in 1964. The contestants were, on the one hand the Nigerian National Alliance (NNA), grouping the Northern People's Congress with a recently emerged Yoruba faction, the Nigerian National Democratic Party and, on the other hand, the United Progressive Grand Alliance (UPGA) which brought together the NCNC and the Action Group. In the face of violence, intimidation and widespread irregularities, the UPGA boycotted the election leaving the way clear for an NNA, that is anti-Ibo victory. The President, prominent Ibo and founder of the NCNC, Nnamdi Azikiwe, refused to appoint a prime minister on the grounds that the elections had not been free and fair. However, after three tense days, Azikiwe was forced to back down and appoint a Northerner, Sir Abubakar Tafawa Balewa. To some Ibo leaders it seemed that the East had been outmanoeuvred and excluded from power by unconstitutional means. There was talk of secession and of a proposed coup planned by disgruntled Ibo officers. The coup did not come until January 1966, the immediate stimulus being intra-tribal violence arising out of elections in the Western Region. Whether the Ibo officers who engineered the coup were indeed the dedicated anti-tribalists they claimed to be we shall never know. The point is that the pattern of politics and social conflict in the country made it inevitable that the coup be interpreted within an ethnic framework.

Concerning our present discussion of tradition and modernity, Anber's basic argument is that, contrary to the theories of writers like Parsons and Shils, educational and economic development in emerging nations do not inevitably erode tribal loyalties. The Ibo example illustrates the reverse phenomenon, with modernisation – in the sense of frequent social, economic and political contact within the context of a nation state – stimulating a tribal identification which previously had barely existed. In fact the Ibos, argues Anber, moved from a nationalist to a tribalist orientation. The root cause was the unequal pace of modernisation in Nigeria, that is the economic and educational development of one ethnic group without the corresponding development of other groups.

Again a thorough-going critique of Anber would be out of place. Nonetheless it may be productive to make one or two observations. First Anber's argument depends heavily on equating tribalism with tradition and nationalism with modernity. Yet the difference between tribalism and nationalism is never elaborated. Might not Iboism be regarded as a form of nationalism? Is not the position of the Ibos in Nigeria analogous, as Guenther Roth (1968) has suggested, to that of national minorities within the Austro–Hungarian Empire? It seems that whilst criticising the simplistic use of the tradition-modernity dichotomy, Anber substitutes his own tribal-national dichotomy without attempting to give the terms any precise meaning.

Second, Anber insufficiently acknowledges the contribution of British administrative policies in fostering regional identifications and rivalries (the parallel with British reinforcement of caste distinctions in India is striking). Coleman suggests that even the colonial administrators suffered from this regional mentality: 'A frequently heard quip was that if all the Africans were to leave Nigeria, the North and South administrations would go to war' (1958, p. 47). The favoured policy of indirect rule, through the so-called native authorities, gave new scope for 'traditional' parochialism as did the strongly federal character of successive constitutions adopted from 1946. But

> In this respect, by far the most important single feature of British policy was the effort to preserve the Muslim North in its pristine Islamic purity, by excluding Christian missionaries and limiting western education, by denying northern leaders representation in the central Nigerian Legislative Council during the period 1923–47, and by minimizing the contact between the northern peoples and the more sophisticated and nationally-minded southerners temporarily resident in the north (Coleman, 1958, p. 322).

Finally in 1951 the British confirmed southern fears of northern domination by guaranteeing the Northern Region 50 per cent representation in the central House of Representatives.

Going back to our original question about the relationship between tradition and modernity, this incidentally raises the problem, mentioned by Tipps (1973) of how the colonial experience is to be categorised. Colonial administrations would justify their policies as 'modernising' but they could be seen as creating a kind of new, hybrid 'tradition'.

More important from the point of view of this book is Anber's neglect of the economic dimension. This may be illustrated in two ways: first Anber does not discuss the strong relationship between the regionalisation of Nigeria and the exigencies of the colonial economy. A brief acquaintance with the historical emergence of the state of Nigeria readily indicates that the nature of colonial penetration in that part of West Africa was such as to create a series of economic enclaves linked not to each other but to Europe through the export of primary commodities such as tin, palm products, cocoa, peanuts and rubber. In this way a low level of economic integration worked to compartmentalise the ethnic groups who came to compose the independent state of Nigeria. Accordingly the unequal modernisation which Anber sees as the cause of subsequent communal conflict was rather a symptom of the structure of the colonial economy.

A second sense in which the economic dimension is neglected by Anber can be seen in his tendency to view the Biafran debacle almost entirely through an ethnic lens. This leads to a silence on the question of social class, especially the role of the Hausa-Fulani aristocracy and the emerging bourgeoisie of the East and West in manipulating ethnic sentiments for their own ends. To this point we shall be returning. Let us note for the time being that in peripheralising the economic, Anber's mode of analysis is very much within the ambience of the modernisation theories which he is criticising. Hence the appropriateness of Huntington's expression, 'modernisation revisionism'. Nonetheless Anber's discussion does illustrate the difficulties of identifying tradition and isolating it from modernity.

The Politics of Clientelism

Whatever the defects of modernisation revisionism, the approach did focus the attention of political scientists on traditional social and political institutions. The realisation that traditional forms were not simply superseded by modern forms led to an upsurge of interest among political scientists in the content of these forms and the nature of their interaction with 'modern' political institutions at the centre. Accordingly the second half of the 1960s saw the emergence of a new dialogue between political science and political anthropology. Nowhere is this more apparent than in the interest shown by political scientists in the phenomenon of patron-client relations. From the late 1960s there appeared in major political science journals a number of articles devoted to the conceptual elaboration of the patron-client relationship as well as to the examination of clientelism in specific empirical contexts. We propose to discuss patron-clientelism at some length not only because it illustrates the central theme of this chapter but also because in the analysis of political change in the underdeveloped world the notion of clientelism continues to occupy a central position.

The institution of clientage is probably one of the most basic forms of social relationship outside kinship. In fact it is a relationship which appears when kinship alone is unable to guarantee the necessities of existence: subsistence and physical security. Clientelism in tribal societies is well known to social anthropologists. Among the Mandari of the Southern Sudan, for example, clientship developed when individuals or families, whether through misfortune or misdeed, had become separated from their larger kinship group. In order to survive in a hostile environment such individuals or families were constrained to attach themselves to a Mandari lineage from whom they received protection and access to pasture and land. By way of return the Mandari lineage acquired manpower which could be used for defence, to work on Mandari land, to perform domestic and other menial tasks. Client status is inherited and there are important jural and customary differences between client groups and 'true' Mandari. Similarly the Bedouin of Cyrenaica (Libya), according to Emrys Peters, are divided between noble or 'free' tribes and 'tied' or client tribes. Descent is what distinguishes between the two groups; free tribes are those that can successfully claim descent from the mythical founding ancestress of all Cyrenaican tribes. In pre-colonial times, client tribes had access to pasture and water only through free tribes who alone were permitted to own these vital resources. In return for this access client tribes provided manpower, all-important in a society where there were no institutions of law and order (Peters, 1968).

From these brief examples we can derive the fundamental characteristic of the patron-client relationship: its unequal or asymmetrical nature. This is a relationship which involves an exchange between a superior patron or patron group and an inferior client or client group. The inferiority may be expressed in legal terms: clients in ancient Rome could not legally own property and were subject to other formal restrictions. However, in the case of the clientelism that has recently attracted the attention of political scientists the inequality has generally been more informal. In fact when political scientists have discussed patron-client relations it has usually been in one of two senses. As Alex Weingrod has pointed out, political scientists have for some considerable time been interested in the process whereby party politicians distribute public jobs and other resources in exchange for various kinds of political support, usually voting (Weingrod, 1968). The notion of 'machine politics' has long been familiar in political science writings especially those dealing with urban politics in the USA. We shall come back to political machines later on in this chapter.

In addition to their long-standing interest in patronage at the 'centre', that is within governmental and party bureaucracies, political scientists have latterly become concerned with patron-clientelism at the local or village level. Since they are dealing with underdeveloped societies it is with peasant villages and peasant politics that political scientists have become increasingly preoccupied. Peasants are small-scale cultivators who with the labour of their family and using primitive tools and techniques produce mainly for their own subsistence. In addition it is generally agreed that peasantries are contained within larger societies and that peasants are constrained to surrender, in the form of rent, part of what they produce to the holders of political and economic power. Peasants occupy what Teodor Shanin (1973) has termed the 'underdog position'. Because of the primitive techniques they are forced to rely on, the peasant lives at the margin of subsistence. Not infrequently he and his family are driven below this margin by the vicissitudes of their existence: flood, drought, diseases, sickness, death, violence and intimidation by outsiders. The peasant, in short, is relatively powerless in the face of uncontrollable forces that hold sway over his daily life. Nonetheless he may look for tangible assistance and this primarily from two sources: first there are members of his kinship group, neighbours and the wider community to whom he is bound by ties of reciprocity and mutual aid. Second there are important and powerful individuals outside the community, socially if not geographically, who may be prevailed upon to help during times of crisis. It is with such individuals that peasant cultivators attempt to develop patronage relationships. Sydel Silverman gives a nice example, based upon observations in central Italy, of how such a relationship may be established:

> A peasant might approach the landlord to ask a favour, perhaps a loan of money or help in some trouble with the law, or the landlord might offer his aid knowing of a problem. If the favour were granted or accepted, further favours were likely to be asked or offered at some later time. The peasant would reciprocate – at a time and in a context different from that of the acceptance of the favour, in order to de-emphasise the material self-interest of the reciprocative action – bringing the landlord especially choice offerings from the farm produce, or by sending some member of the peasant family to perform services in the landlord's home, by refraining from cheating the landlord or by merely speaking well of him in public and professing devotion to him (Silverman, 1977, p. 296).

The above quotation brings out the enduring nature of the relationship; once established it is perpetuated over time, perhaps even over generations. Silverman notes that the patron need not necessarily be the peasant's landlord but simply rich and powerful, one of the 'signori' who is approached by a would-be client. She also points out a crucial feature of the relationship, the fact that the peasant-client's needs tend to be critical – access to a piece of land or a loan to cover a domestic crisis – whereas the needs of the patron are marginal. He can get along well enough without the esteem and promises of loyalty of the individual peasant and anyway he has a large number of peasant families to choose from. Patrons are always in short supply and hence their bargaining power is much greater.

J. D. Powell has suggested that at the core of the patron-client relationship lie three basic factors which both define the relationship and help to differentiate between it and other power relationships. First the patron-client tie develops between persons who are unequal in terms of status, wealth and influence. Given this inequality, Powell believes Julian Pitt-Rivers' designation of the patron-client tie as a 'lopsided friendship' to be particularly apt (Pitt-Rivers, 1954). Second, the formation and maintenance of the relationship depends upon reciprocity in the exchange of goods and services. Typically the low-status client will receive material assistance in one form or another whilst his patron will receive less tangible resources such as deference, esteem, loyalty and perhaps personal services. Third the development and maintenance of the relationship depends on face-to-face contact between the two parties. Powell means by this that since the exchanges entailed in the relationship are of a personal nature then physical proximity of the type that is found in pre-industrial communities is required (Powell, 1970).

According to this view, then, clientage in peasant societies emerges out of the attempts of peasant cultivators to alleviate their critical situation by attaching themselves to wealthy and powerful individuals. This type of relationship arises, as Weingrod has pointed out, in societies where the state is under-developed, where state institutions are virtually non-existent at the village level so that there is a marked gap between centre and periphery. In normal circumstances tying himself to a wealthy patron is probably the only way in which the peasant can articulate his interests. In fact in some contexts a landowner may be the *only* mediator between the peasant and the outside world. David Lehmann has observed of pre-land reform Chile that the 'latifundia' owners had near monopoly control over any contact that their labourers made with the political system and the state (Lehmann, 1979).

However, as states begin to extend their activities to the periphery the patron's monopoly or near-monopoly situation is likely to be undermined. The extension of state activities is usually associated with the expansion of trade. The expansion of trade requires effective mechanisms of law and order not only to provide stability but also to deal with commercial contracts, sale of land, property and the like. Administration is also needed to ensure the smooth functioning of trade. Licences must be issued, standards maintained, fraud prevented, taxes collected. This means that the peasant cultivator, whether he likes it or not, will have to deal increasingly with bureaucratic situations: to see a lawyer about the sale or purchase of a piece of land, a municipal official to obtain a licence for his shotgun, a tax official about his non-payment of revenue, a co-operative supervisor to obtain his quota of fertiliser. In such dealings the peasant will always prefer to work through an intermediary. The intermediary may be a long-standing landowning patron who, if he is to maintain his monopoly of access to the outside world, must diversify his range of contacts. Or another patron or broker may present himself, a schoolteacher, local businessman, bourgeois landowner, minor official or, as in Chile after 1965, a trades union official, and increasingly likely, a politician. That is to say an individual whose specialised skills and knowledge make him the most appropriate broker for the task in the hand.

But why, when state activities are expanding, even to the extent of providing basic social and municipal services, should peasants continue to depend upon personal mediation in order to obtain services and resources to which they are entitled? The answer to this question is to be sought in the nature of the relationship between the peasant and the outside world. It has already been pointed out that peasantries, by definition, are contained within larger societies and that the peasant is constrained to pay rent in some form to the holders of political and economic power. In other words, the basic feature of the relationship between the peasant and the outside world is one of exploitation. Due to generations of exploitation, intimidation and abuse, the peasant has learnt to distrust everything that comes from the world outside his small community, and wherever possible to avoid it. If he has to deal with this hostile world, he will always strive to do so through somebody who knows the ropes, who is influential, powerful, will therefore command respect, and is unlikely to be cheated or abused. The peasant's conception of the world is very well brought out in F. G. Bailey's article 'The peasant view of the bad life'.

Every society, according to Bailey, distinguishes between different categories of persons giving to some full status as members of the community and relegating others to the position of outsiders. Standards of respect, honesty and consideration do not apply to these outsiders. Conversely one does not expect outsiders to apply these standards to oneself. One justifies cheating government agencies by saying that the officials concerned are bent upon cheating you. Even when behaviour is apparently not exploitative and ostensibly benevolent, it will be interpreted by the peasant as but a hypocritical cover for some as yet undisclosed purpose. On the basis of fieldwork carried out in India, Bailey identifies a villager's moral community as comprising mainly members of his family, sub-caste and fellow villagers. Beyond this category are persons whose culture, the way they dress and speak, places them unambiguously beyond the moral community of the peasant. These are the revenue inspectors, policemen, development officers, health officials and politicians: all people who are to be outwitted, whose apparent 'gifts' are but a bait for involving the peasant in a relationship from which he will undoubtedly come off worse. However, under modern conditions the villagers must deal with outsiders in order to get children into school, his wife into hospital, a prescription from the pharmacist, to register his land or himself as a voter. When he has to deal with bureaucrats, officials, traders who are unknown to him, the peasant will use a broker, an intermediary who, because of his connections, will establish a personal relationship, thereby staving off the anonymous and threatening impersonality of the bureaucratic situation (Bailey, 1971).

The peasant's desire for personal relationships has received much attention from students of political change in the underdeveloped world, for it has frequently been noted that politicians (both national and local) attuned to this need have sought, in the quest for popular support, to insinuate themselves into the ranks of village patrons aiming to build for themselves a network of clients. The role of clientage has for example featured in studies of Indian politics. Patron-client relations are not necessarily incompatible with the caste system, as Gould has emphasised in his discussion of the 'jajmani' system of Hindu patron-clientage as it operates within the local village economy.

He noted a contradiction between the fear that twice-born caste members feel of contamination by other caste or outcaste groups, and their economic interdependence. To facilitate economically necessary contacts with polluting castes, ties that closely resemble bonds of kinship had been cultivated. The patrons (jajmans) acquired particular client families (purjans) with the relationship often continuing over many generations. The jajman provided all kinds of 'considerations' for the purjan – free food, free clothing, free timber or dung – in return for labour and other services (Gould, 1977). As we have seen, the Rudolphs also show how patron-client relationships could be the basis for 'vertical' political mobilisation by locally dominant castes. At other times, however, writers have tended to depict caste and patron-client relationships as alternative bases for political participation.

We can turn once more to Bailey, this time his full-length study of *Politics and Social Change* in the Indian state of Orissa in 1959 to illustrate the importance of clientage in local political mobilisation. Bailey examined how candidates for a seat in the state assembly went about mustering electoral support. In theory they could go for 'mass contact', aiming to transcend traditional loyalties and reach all their potential voters individually but in practice they faced overwhelming obstacles: transport hazards, poorly developed communication media, low rates of literacy. 'In short a candidate who decides to treat his electors as a socially undifferentiated mass of rational minds to be contacted and persuaded of the rightness of his cause is not being realistic' (p. 109). In exceptional circumstances such a candidate could marshall support on the basis of his traditional authority as a prince for instance, or a hereditary tax-collector. Occasionally, but not often in this part of Orissa, he could make use of a well-organised extensive caste association. Normally though he would have to rely on his political party and then not so much its formal organisation – voluntary party work has little appeal for poor people and in such adverse circumstances – but on its informal 'machine' (Bailey warned here against taking the notion of machine too literally: local party machines varied widely in their efficiency and reliability). The machine linked the candidate to the voters not individually but through a chain of bosses or brokers, reaching down to the brokers we have encountered acting as intermediaries between villagers and the outside world of officialdom, and beyond to their clients. The brokers typically were men of local standing but who wanted to reach out beyond the village and traditional ties to, for instance, professional employment or commerce. They did not seek political office for its own sake but for the patronage – a job, licence, grant of development funds, contract – which was their reward for party work and which would help realise their own ambitions. The political party could deliver these rewards through its influence over the administration: this was obviously easiest for the locally dominant party and has been a continuing factor in the strength of the Congress Party. Local brokers in turn could provide support for a candidate's nomination and most importantly votes for the candidate by calling in their favours to their clients.

In its broad sense, clientage then has been a central feature of Indian politics as of the politics of a succession of Third World states. However, in the long term, it is argued, patron-client relationships decline and this decline is inextricably tied up with the onset of modernity in the form of increased prosperity, urbanisation, the spread of literacy, mass education and the emergence of mass politics. This process is particularly well illustrated in Jeremy Boissevain's discussion of the decline of patronage in Malta. Forty years ago patrons, usually wealthy landowners, played a crucial role in village life. These were people who disposed of local housing, credit facilities and had access to important government decisionmakers. Patrons were jealous of the power they exercised and sometimes sought to protect their interests quite ruthlessly. However, economic development since the early 1960s has transformed Maltese society. The need to diversify the economy, making it less dependent on the defence establishment, led to the development of manufacturing and tourism. The emergence of these industries together with the revenue from renting defence facilities to NATO resulted in rising prosperity, increased mobility and permitted the expansion of education and the spread of literacy. As a result, social relationships have undergone a radical change. Family relationships have moved away from their former rigidly authoritarian pattern and the Maltese generally are now much less dependent upon traditional figures to articulate their interests. Needs and interests are now articulated through modern organisations such as trades unions, professional associations and the like (Boissevain, 1977). The notion that the need for patronage declines with the acquisition of full citizenship or 'civic competence' is, as we shall see, firmly entrenched in the literature on political modernisation. Its essence is caught in the following statement from Legg and Lemarchand's conceptual discussion of clientelism, in which the authors state that 'most individuals in an industrialised polity do not require personalised political relationships: affluence and opportunity have diminished insecurity' (Legg and Lemarchand, 1972, p. 169).

From focusing on the political ramifications of local patron-client relationships, let us now return to Weingrod's second type of patronage where politicians distribute jobs and other resources in exchange for political support. The classical location for this type of patronage is to be found in the political machines which formerly dominated city politics in the USA. It is worth while looking briefly at the American political machines as a number of writers have suggested that this form of political bargaining is, for a variety of reasons, particularly apparent in underdeveloped polities.

The term machine used in this sense refers to a political organisation but one which is emphatically not the disciplined, ideological party held together by class ties and common programmes of the kind which developed with the advent of mass politics in Europe. The machine is a non-ideological organisation interested hardly at all in political principle but in securing and holding office for its leaders and in distributing resources to those who run it, work for it, as well as to some of those who vote for it. The machine relies upon what it accomplishes for its supporters in a concrete way and not on what it stands for. The party machine has been likened to a business in which all members are shareholders, and whose dividends are paid in accordance with what one has invested in terms of effort.

In US cities, the 'Boss' of the party machine was the ward committeeman, the party leader of that ward or district. The committeeman received and disbursed party funds, managed campaigns, decided who was to run on the party's ticket to represent the ward in city hall, appointed precinct organisers and dispensed patronage. Of one Democrat boss in the Chicago of the 1950s, William J. Connors, it has been observed that he provided well for his workers not only in the sense of distributing jobs but supplying them with loans when needed. Connors also helped his workers when they were in trouble with the law as well as taking an interest in their family affairs. Connor's relationship with his workers was that of benevolent despot. He had power to withdraw their source of livelihood and banish them from active work in the party.

The Chicago party machine distributed 'gravy' to its officials, its financial backers and voters. The gravy included public jobs – in 1952 Connors had 350–400 at his disposal – contracts, information about potentially profitable land sales, non-enforcement of building regulations, legal restrictions relating to gambling, drinking and prostitution, and ticket fixing (that is persuading police officers to withdraw tickets for parking and other motoring offences). In return for these favours, workers and supporters were induced to get the vote out on election day, to contribute cash and perhaps to threaten: 'The loyalty of the rooming house owner to the Democratic Party was not a matter of ideology: the owner who did not cooperate with the precinct captain could expect a visit from the city building inspector the next day' (Meyerson and Banfield, 1969, p. 177).

During the machine era, local party agents spent their evenings visiting residents in their ward, talking to them, offering to help with their problems, getting them relief, driveway permits, helping them with parking fines, high property assessments, but seldom if ever talking politics, distributing party leaflets, conducting rallies and such like. The relationship between an agent and the ward residents was personal, based, as one agent put it in the 1950s on 'personal friendships between me and my neighbours'.

The personalism of the machine is one of its most salient features and is considered to be particularly appropriate to North American urban politics during the first half of this century. During the early decades of this century American cities experienced massive levels of immigration. Moreover a large proportion of these immigrants were from the peasant societies of eastern and southern Europe. Poorly educated, speaking little or no English and very much disorientated in the urban situation, the immigrant could cope with the multifarious difficulties of city life only through the personal intervention of the machine politician who both literally and metaphorically spoke a language which the immigrant could understand and who could 'fix' things. The need for personal intervention was reinforced by the ethnic diversity of city populations. Each ethnic group had its own particular needs and interests so that lines of patronage tended to radiate from city hall along ethnic lines. In effect it has been argued that, given the deep primordial cleavage within the electorate, the 'giant pay-off' of the machine was the only way of pulling the city together.

It is noteworthy that explanations of the decline of the city machine parallel closely Boissevain's explanation of the decline of patronage in Malta. The machine was a symptom of civic incompetence, of an electorate too poor, too ignorant and too deferential to be able to articulate its needs other than with the personal assistance of the local big man. However, as economic conditions have improved, poverty and helplessness left behind, the sometime immigrant or his children have acquired citizenship and have been incorporated into the mainstream of American life. The vital personal services which the machine offered – the precinct captain's 'hod of coal' – are no longer needed when the citizen's wants can be catered for through alternative channels such as trades unions, political parties, civic and voluntary associations.

There is some dispute as to the relevance of the machine model to the study of underdeveloped polities. Certain writers, notably Aristide Zolberg and Henry Bienen, have argued for its usefulness in relation to politics in Tropical Africa (Zolberg, 1966; Bienen, 1970). This view, however, is criticised by James Scott, for example on the grounds that political machines can only arise where mobilising voters behind particular candidates is essential to the control of government. In Tropical Africa and elsewhere in the underdeveloped world, such electoral competition is either non-existent or subject to manipulation and intimidation. Note that Scott's argument assumes that the US machines involved widespread popular involvement, a point that will be disputed later on in this book (Scott, 1969). In the meantime, Richard Sandbrook has argued against Scott that

machine-like organisations, basing their support almost exclusively on the distribution of particularistic material rewards,
do exist in the non-electoral systems of Tropical Africa. There is
no question, though, that these machines are oriented to the
needs of the masses, since the masses are politically marginalised. The distributive networks of the machines of Tropical
Africa are therefore confined to dominant social classes (Sandbrook, 1972).

Appropriate or inappropriate, a machine-type model is used
with increasing frequency to analyse national (as opposed to
city) politics in the underdeveloped world. The term 'machine'
is less often used than 'patrimonial' or 'patrimonialism'. The
term 'patrimonial' derives from the writings of Max Weber and
was used by him to refer to a type of traditional or pre-modern
bureaucracy whose essential features are highlighted by their
contrast with those of rational–legal bureaucracies. Clearly
defined spheres of competence, subject to impersonal rules, the
rational ordering of relations of superiority and inferiority,
regular systems of appointment and promotion on the basis of
free contract, technical training as a regular requirement and
fixed salaries paid in money: all these are largely absent from the
patrimonial bureaucracy. In place of well-defined spheres of
competence, the patrimonial bureaucracy is characterised by a
shifting series of tasks and powers, commissioned on an ad hoc
basis by the chief or ruler. In the absence of clearcut spheres of
competence and regular fixed salaries there can be no un-
equivocal division between incumbent and office. Accordingly
some degree of appropriation of office is endemic in a patrimonial bureaucracy and, in extreme cases of decentralised
patrimonialism, all government authority with corresponding
economic rights may be treated as a private possession (Weber,
1968, vol. 3, ch. 12).

In 1966 Aristide Zolberg suggested that the party-states, that
is the single party regimes of West Africa, approximated to
Weber's ideal type of patrimonial bureaucracy in a number of
respects. The most important feature of these regimes is the
personal appropriation of office by their leaders and their
followers. This tendency is, for Zolberg, reinforced by the
pursuit of economic policies which, in the name of socialism or
development, have as a major consequence the redistribution of

national income in favour of the incumbents of state bureaucracies. Zolberg did not develop at length his ideas about the relevance of patrimonialism to the study of West African politics, being content merely to refer to the similarity between the party-states and Weber's ideal type. Two years later, Guenther Roth, in an article in *World Politics*, criticised the indiscriminate use of the term 'charisma' by political scientists, particularly in the study of political change in the Third World. The over-reliance on charisma, Roth suggested, had led to a neglect of Weber's concept of patrimonial domination. Pre-modern forms of organisation, Roth continues, may survive into the modern era even though the traditionalist legitimation that once underpinned them is in the process of disintegration. Patrimonialism is one such form and Roth discerns two basic types: the first is to be found in those increasingly few regimes where legitimacy is still based primarily on traditional grounds. Pre-revolutionary Ethiopia is cited as an example of this dying form. The second and much more common type of patrimonialism which Roth terms 'personal rulership' does not require any belief in the ruler or leader's personal qualifications but is based primarily upon material incentives and rewards. Personal rulership is usually subsumed under such terms as 'clique', 'machine', 'faction' and so forth, and is by no means absent from modern societies. In the US, the old political machines have virtually disappeared but personal rulership has not. Behind the alleged charisma of J. F. Kennedy, for example, lay an organisational apparatus which, for Roth, had a distinctly patrimonial flavour. Far from being a vanishing phenomenon, this modern form of patrimonialism has been encouraged by the expansion of state activism in industrial societies, both capitalist and socialist. Examples of patrimonialism amongst officials in the increasing number of semi-public agencies and corporations in the US and Western Europe involve access to various perquisites – expense accounts, residencies, first-class travel tickets – and the partial displacement of universalistic criteria in recruitment patterns.

In the underdeveloped world, personal rulership is probably the most dominant form of government. The Thai bureaucracy, permeated by networks based upon the exchange of material and other rewards, which Edgar Shor (1960) regarded as a deviant case is, for Roth, by no means abnormal. In fact some of the new states are not properly speaking states at all but virtually the private instruments of those powerful enough to rule. A major reason for the survival of personal rulership in the underdeveloped world, Roth believes, is the cultural and political heterogeneity of the new states. This heterogeneity confronts the governments of these states with the task of welding diverse social units into a nation. A bureaucracy run along patrimonial lines, Roth suggests, may be more compatible with the task of nation-building, or perhaps more appropriately given the scale of the diversity in some of these states, the task of 'empire-building' (Roth, 1968).

The Contribution of Modernisation Revisionism

We shall have more to say about patrimonialism in the following chapter, since it features in arguments about the military as an agent of strong government. In this chapter, however, we have been primarily concerned to show, through the examples of caste, ethnicity and clientelism, the way in which modernisation revisionists exposed the simplistic and ethnocentric assumptions about tradition and modernity of the early political development theories. These theories had failed to recognise the variety and tenacity of tradition and the complexity of its relationship with modernity. The enduring contribution of modernisation revisionism has been to awaken us to the specific character and consequences of indigenous social structures and culture. In that respect it has enormously enhanced the realism of subsequent analysis.

At the same time, this approach itself suffers from a number of weaknesses. First, there are still problems about the use of the terms tradition and modernity. Just how traditional *are* such phenomena as caste, say, or ethnicity, as they impinge on 'modern' political structures? In so far as the caste system, modified by the ethos of the market-place and 'democratic' politics, is increasingly one of competition between rather than a hierarchical ordering of castes, is it still essentially traditional? Similarly the relationship between ethnic bases of mobilisation and 'objective' traditional ethnic identities is often tenuous in the extreme (see Wallerstein, 1971; Kasfir, 1979.

Related to this is the tendency for modernisation revisionism to retain political development as a goal and conceptual yardstick. The Rudolphs for instance were remarkably confident that caste, rather than hindering political development, was the agent of mobilisation and integration through which, in the long run, it would be realised. The same has often been argued for clientelism. The assumption is moreover that in the process these 'traditional' residues would be superseded. But it cannot be stated with certainty that such 'reincarnations' of tradition are simply transitional, except in the sense that everything is. And in other contexts the dysfunctionality of such institutions for political development and stability is all too apparent. An obvious example is the role of ethnicity in Nigeria, but clientelism too can have conservative and even destabilising consequences (see Legg and Lemarchand, 1972).

The most serious weakness of this approach is to see the role of such 'traditional' structures as *the* key to understanding Third World politics. In fact on their own they cannot provide a coherent account, but on the contrary only make sense within a wider framework they cannot themselves supply. Anber's analysis of the role of ethnicity in Nigeria's civil strife for instance neglected its context of colonial and neo-colonial economic policies. Similarly, Clapham (1982) has argued that clientelism should be used as a middle-range concept, dependent upon the prior existence of a social class structure and its ramifications in the international economic system. Marxist analysts have in the past been wary of treating 'traditional' social institutions and values as meaningful independent political forces, perceiving them as part of an attempt to 'mystify' underlying social class relations. Recently, however, there has been a somewhat greater recognition of the need to incorporate ethnicity and clientelism into social class analyses of Third World countries. Paul Cammack (1982) for instance argues that in Brazil, at least since 1945, 'coronelismo' or clientelism should be understood in terms of strategies of class control. Thus of the two major political parties founded by Vargas, the Brazilian Workers' Party (PTB) used clientelist practices to mobilise the urban working-classes without allowing them political independence, while the Social Democratic Party (PSD) used them as a means of mobilising rural workers through the landowners rather than on their own account and so as to provide a counterweight to the urban middle and working classes. We return to these issues in Chapters 4 and 5.

However, we must first consider a second and highly influential critique of political development theory. This was not in fact chronologically second but tended to overlap in time, and even in some cases, in exposition (as in Zolberg, 1966). Its most distinguishing feature was its emphasis on the need for political order and stability.

3

The Emergence of a Politics of Order

A basic and usually explicit assumption of the modernisation theories we have been considering was that the 'developing' societies of Asia, Africa and Latin America were in the process of being transformed into stable democracies of the western pluralist type. There can be little doubt that the already-industrialised world, especially the US, provided the model for *political* modernity just as for modernity in general. The democratic ideal, it seemed, had reached its zenith in the West and this was the condition towards which the societies of the Third World were evolving. The traumas and strains of this transformation are frequently intense but they are worth enduring for the goal, once arrived at – and arrival was thought to be inevitable – will be more than adequate compensation. As Huntington has pointed out, these modernisation theories exhibited the kind of evolutionary optimism of early sociologist such as Comte and Spencer (Huntington, 1971).

Unfortunately the course of events during the first development decade of the 1960s gave little encouragement to those who had thought in terms of a smooth transition to modernity. The Congo debacle in 1960 proved to be a harbinger of the violence and instability that reached its apotheosis in the Nigerian Civil War. By the second half of the 1960s the mould of politics, not only in Africa but elsewhere in the Third World, seemed firmly set in the form of communal violence, military coup and secession. Political scientists accordingly had to recognise that the evolutionary optimism of a decade earlier looked a little pale in the face of the violent and uncertain political reality of the late 1960s. So adjustments in concepts and theories were made: 'political modernisation' and 'political development' tended to drop out of academic coinage to be replaced by such terms as 'political decay' (Huntington, 1968), the idea of 'breakdowns' in modernisation (Eisenstadt, 1966), and the notion of 'praetorian' society, a society characterised by the absence of basic consensus and in which social forces 'confront each other nakedly' (Huntington, 1968, p. 196). Gradually political scientists seemed to abandon the democratic ideal of the modernisation theories in favour of a 'politics of order'.

One of the most coherent statements of this re-assessment was provided by Huntington. He argued that in its early stages economic development, far from fostering social stability and the peaceful emergence of a democratic culture, would tend to undermine public order as social inequalities were exacerbated and newly-aroused aspirations were disappointed. This social mobilisation, Huntington maintained, would, as it was frustrated, convert into increasing pressure for *political* participation. But the political institutions of developing countries, whether traditional or 'modern' implants, were often too inflexible or weak to accommodate or withstand such pressure. The result was breakdown or decay. Huntington came to believe, therefore, that before political development as originally envisioned could occur, political stability must be secured. The key factor here is political institutionalisation which essentially refers to that capacity of government to absorb, reconcile and act upon the diverse pressures and demands to which it is subjected. In the famous opening sentence of his book, *Political Order in Changing Societies*, Huntington declares, 'The most important political distinction among countries concerns not their form of government but their degree of government'. The differences between democratic forms in the West and those of communist states were less than between both of these, on the one hand, and many Third World states, on the other, where 'governments simply do not govern'.

Huntington's insistence on looking at what was actually going on in Third World societies was a great step forward in realism from the earlier modernisation approaches. He also headed the recognition that politics or political institutions were not merely passive consequences of social and economic change but could themselves be a determinant of such change. That is, he helped to re-assert 'the primacy of politics'. But there were nonetheless clear conservative and authoritarian implications in his argument which a number of subsequent writers have found disturbing (Kesselman, 1973; Ake, 1974). What really mattered for Huntington was that government was stable and ensured political order. The content of government – whether its policies were progressive – and the openness of government were of secondary importance.

With their new concern for political order as a pre-requisite for political development (sometimes they seemed to be equated and the previous goal of democratic development forgotten), political scientists like Huntington began to look for the key ingredient that would bring Third World governments 'authority', 'strength' and 'legitimacy'. For Huntington the most crucial institution in this process was the political party. This provided the principal institutional means for organising the expansion of political participation. If a society developed reasonably well-organised political parties while participation rates were relatively low (Huntington's examples include India, Chile and Malaya), subsequent expansion of participation was less likely to be de-stabilising.

In early theories of political modernisation, political parties had been seen as agents of democratisation instilling democratic values and habits, and in keeping with this view it was assumed that they would compete for votes within a multi-party system as in developed 'liberal' democracies. As political scientists witnessed the steady trend away from multi-party to one-party systems, particularly in Tropical Africa, they were dismayed. Huntington, however, was not too concerned whether a developing country adopted a multi– or a one-party system. What mattered was not the number of parties but the overall strength and adaptability of the party system. In fact, examining data for 1965–6 he concluded that the one-party system was somewhat less susceptible to military coups. Since this suggested that they were more firmly institutionalised, and since for Huntington military rule was only acceptable in extreme praetorian societies and as a last resort, the one-party option might be preferable.

A number of other writers at this time began to revise their original condemnatory attitude towards one-party systems, now arguing that they were needed in the early stages of political development to provide stability and unity in societies undergoing disruptive change and riven by primordial cleavages. Representative of this re-assessment was Aristide Zolberg's study of five West African one-party states, revealingly entitled *Creating Political Order* (1966). Zolberg, we saw in the previous chapter, portrayed these ruling parties or their leaders operating through a form of patrimonialism, appropriating bureaucratic posts for themselves and their followers, using public resources to which they had access both for personal aggrandisement and to maintain political support. Far from deploring such one-party regimes Zolberg maintained that they were a necessary response to endemic disorder and were the often fragile means of institutionalising some degree of national unity.

To illustrate Zolberg's position we may briefly consider the example of Ghana's Convention People's Party which had been depicted by Bretton as almost 'totalitarian' in the scope and exclusiveness of its political control (Bretton, 1958). Zolberg tells a different story. The first nationalist stirrings in what was then known as the Gold Coast were associated with the emergence of an indigenous elite of high-ranking professionals, often connected with the chiefdom families and typified by their leading spokesman, the lawyer J. P. Danquah, founder of the United Gold Coast Convention (UGC). But long before independence the UGC was being outflanked by a more militantly nationalist movement, supported by the so-called 'young men', like UGC supporters the products of westernisation and urbanisation, but generally of lower status: schoolteachers, clerks and other categories with secondary education. This was the Convention People's Party (CPP) led by Kwame Nkrumah, former secretary of the UGC. As it became clear that the CPP had greater popular support than the UGC, the British administration began to transfer power to its leadership, In 1951 the Gold Coast acquired a new constitution giving the country virtual internal self-rule and establishing a parliamentary form of government. The CPP won the majority of seats in the general election held that year, a victory the more impressive because its vote appeared to cut across the ethnic and regional divisions that were a legacy of colonialism and the boundaries it imposed.

However, it is generally accepted now that the initial success of the CPP had more to do with the absence of any serious political competition than with its own strength and organisation. Even before independence came in 1957, the CPP vote, which never anyway extended beyond about 30 per cent of the adult population, was being eaten into by new parties based on ethnic as well as communal loyalties. Almost immediately after independence the CPP began to restrict opposition. Laws were enacted limiting the rights of opposition. Regional and district party commissioners were created to supervise local government and the Party sought to extend its control over the trade unions and, through the United Ghana Farmers' Council, over the powerful cocoa farmers. These authoritarian trends became more explicit in 1960 with the adoption of the new Republic's constitution. This vested major executive powers in the new office of President naturally assumed by Nkrumah. In 1964, following a referendum that was widely suspected of being rigged, Ghana officially became a one-party state.

Zolberg explains these developments as the logical reaction by the CPP leadership to the growing combined opposition its initial success stimulated amongst old nationalists like Danquah and representatives of different ethnic and communal groupings. Along with this centralisation of political authority arose an ideology to justify the one-party state. It was Sekou Toure of Guinea who first argued that in African societies there was a natural tendency to unity but that unhealthy divisions had been fomented by neo-colonial interests. These divisions could only be overcome by a single unifying party acting as 'the hyphen that binds all layers of the population'. A similar sentiment is encapsulated in Nkrumah's slogan, 'the CPP is Ghana'.

Zolberg, then, was not interested in condemning one-party systems in Africa, seeing them as an attempt to create order in fragmented and unruly societies. The fragility of the CPP's achievement seemed to be confirmed by the military coup which overthrew it so easily in 1966. It was the monotonous regularity of such coups, not only in Africa but in other parts of the Third World, which prompted a number of political societies to look for the guardians of political order not to parties but increasingly to the military itself.

One of the earliest indications of a shift of interest among political scientists away from legislatures and parties towards militaries came in 1962 with the appearance of a collection of essays edited by John J. Johnson. A basic theme running through *The Role of the Military in Underdeveloped Countries* is that independent entrepreneurial elites have failed to emerge in most Third World countries. In the absence of such elites the only sector with the organisational skills and attitudes which render it capable of generating change is the military, that is to say the officer corps. According to Ed Shils, for example, in societies where there is little social mobility due to negligible economic expansion, the army tends to recruit to its ranks the brightest and most ambitious young men of the countryside. Such groups tend to be aware of the distance separating them from traditional oligarchies. Accordingly should the oligarchy get into serious difficulties and appear to lose its way in governing, the military officers, feeling that they have more to offer the country, may be tempted to sweep the civilians from power. According to Lucien Pye, contributing to the same volume, a major problem for underdeveloped countries is that of creating organisations which are capable of mobilising resources in the pursuit of new objectives. The military, however, is in possession of such an appropriate structure founded as it is on hierarchy, a clear demarcation of responsibilities, and incumbency based upon training and qualifications (the model is quite clearly Max Weber's ideal type of rational–legal bureaucracy). Furthermore the background and training of military officers is often such as to make them sensitive to the extent to which their country is underdeveloped. The military officer may have been trained overseas in a developed society, and even if he has not he is likely to compare his own military organisation to foreign ones. If the military like the rest of society is in the hands of traditional elites and therefore dominated by nepotism and corruption, then younger more 'modern' officers may become increasingly impatient both with their superiors and with their paymasters in the government. Impatience may be transformed into implacable hostility in the face of a humiliating defeat which shows up the inefficiency and poor organisation of the army. Such a defeat was endured by Egypt in the struggle over the emergence of the state of Israel in 1948. The disastrous performance of the Egyptian army during this period was widely attributed not just to poor training but also to widespread corruption among senior officers and civilians who had diverted funds earmarked for re-equipment. The subsequent overthrow of the Egyptian monarchy by Gamal Abdel Nasser and his Free Officers in 1952 was very much a reaction to the 1948 debacle.

In effect Nasser's coup remains something of a model for this type of progressive military intervention. Directed against the stagnant and spectacularly corrupt regime of King Farouk, the coup aimed to inaugurate the modernisation and reconstruction of Egypt, eventually (after 1963) along state socialist lines. Nasser himself in terms of social background fits the model very closely. The son of a post office clerk in Egypt's rural heartland, Nasser was one of those bright young men of the countryside who graduated into the officer corps. Certain writers have emphasised the lower middle-class background of progressive junior officers against the upper-class (traditional landowning) background of conservative senior officers (see Dowse, 1969). Behind this line of thinking lies the notion that the military, or sections of it, in UDCs plays the progressive role allegedly played by the bourgeoisie in European societies, most notably Great Britain. The economic situation in UDCs, especially those recently emerged from colonial rule, is one in which an indigenous bourgeoisie has not yet developed. The military, therefore, steps into the breech. Thus we find Huntington suggesting that in the earlier stages of modernisation the military can play a progressive role. Military officers, like the protestant entrepreneurs of western Europe, embrace a form of puritanism attacking waste, inefficiency and corruption, and promoting economic and social reform. Military leaders and military groups, Huntington goes on, played this innovating role in the larger and more complex societies of Latin America in the late nineteenth century. During this period military officers in Brazil and Mexico, for example, embraced modern ideologies such as Comte's positivism and strove to inaugurate the development of their countries. A similar progressive role was played by the military this century in the relatively less developed Bolivia, Peru and Ecuador where army officers have advocated programmes of social reform usually against the entrenched interests of landed oligarchies. Egypt, Iraq and

Syria after the Second World War are also cited by Huntington as furnishing examples of similar progressive military coups (Huntington, 1968, ch. 4). Along similar lines Manfred Halpern has argued in relation to the Middle East, and by implication, to other UDCs, that military officers form a sort of vanguard of what he calls the New Middle Class. In the absence of entrepreneurial elites the historic task of modernisation devolves upon other sectors of the middle class, mainly bureaucrats and professionals. The officer corps, Halpern maintains, as the most cohesive sector of the New Middle Class provides it with leadership. Not only is the officer corps cohesive but it would also seem to be free of the pettiness, venality, internecine rivalry and self-aggrandisement which bedevil civilian politics: 'In civilian politics corruption, nepotism and bribery loomed much larger. Within the army a sense of national mission transcending parochial, regional or economic interests or kinship ties seemed to be much more clearly defined than anywhere else in society' (Halpern, 1962, p. 74).

The Myth of the Unified Military

Halpern's view of the military – fairly typical of writings of this ilk – sees the officer corps as somehow outside society; free of the conflicts, tensions and temptations that afflict other social classes and groups. In this tendency to regard the military as in some way insulated or above the banalities of routine social and political life lies the fundamental weakness of this type of approach. A good deal of evidence indicates that broader societal conflicts and divisions are in one way or another reflected or refracted within the military. The degree to which this is the case will vary from country to country but is probably most apparent in newly-independent societies where the state structure is a relatively recent, and in many respects, an artificial creation. Tropical Africa furnishes the readiest examples of deep-rooted societal divisions manifesting themselves within the military establishment. We have already seen how communal differences in Nigeria in the period leading up to the Civil War were articulated through the military. The coup of January 1966 was carried out by young officers who claimed to have been motivated by national concerns, particularly the desire to end tribalism. However, the fact that most of these officers were Ibos and no prominent Ibo, military or civilian, was killed during the course of the coup precipitated the backlash six months later by northern officers and NCOs. The subsequent fragmentation of the military along ethnic/regional lines removed one of the few obstacles to Nigeria's slide into civil war.

Uganda provides another well-known example of an ethnically divided military. As is often the case, the roots of Uganda's communal problems lie in the colonial experience. Under the British the recruitment of indigenes into the Ugandan army tended to be drawn disproportionately from northern nilotic tribes such as Acholi, Langi, Lugbara, and Amin's own group, the Kakwa. This northern preponderance was partly the outcome of deliberate policy with the British preferring to recruit from northern stateless tribes than from the more unified and dominant Baganda of the South, but it also reflected the economic and social backwardness of northern Uganda where military or police service constituted about the only occupational alternative to traditional herding or agriculture.

During the early independence period tensions in Uganda manifested themselves primarily around the Baganda/non-Baganda division. The Baganda wanted autonomy for the Buganda region and recognition of their own monarch, the Kabaka, while non-Baganda favoured a centralised state. In 1966 Milton Obote took over the government and, with the support of the northern-dominated military, enforced the submission of the Baganda bringing their monarchy to an end. However, during the 1966–70 period relations between northern groups in the military were increasingly characterised by suspicion and growing enmity. A split developed between the Acholi and Langi on the one hand, and other northerners on the other. Obote, a Langi himself, was accused of discriminating in favour of Langi and Acholi in relation to army promotions and generally. Eventually non-Langi, non-Acholi northerners in the army overthrew Obote and installed Idi Amin as Uganda's president. However, tribal conflict within the military continued with Amin moving in 1974 against another northern group, the Lugbara, whose loyalty he had come to suspect. Paradox-

ically Amin came to depend for support on the very Baganda he
had helped Obote to suppress in 1966 (Mazrui, 1976).

It is not only in Tropical Africa that we encounter militaries
riven by primordial cleavages. If we turn to the Middle East, the
locus classicus of Halpern's New Middle Class, it is not difficult to
find examples of this phenomenon with the Republic of Syria
being one of the most apparent.

Syria, in fact, bears some resemblance to Uganda in that
colonial policy favoured recruitment from the country's minorities into the army and the police. Accordingly the French
drew their recruits disproportionately from Druze, Ismaili and
Alawite heterodox Muslim minorities in order to play them off
against Syria's dominant orthodox Sunni majority. In 1966 the
Ba'ath (Arab Socialist) Party seized power but only with the
support of the Syrian military. The Ba'ath's dependence on the
military has placed considerable power in the hands of Druze,
Ismaili and Alawi officers. But, again paralleling Uganda, these
minorities have failed to remain united in the face of long-term
Sunni hegemony. From 1966 until the late 1970s the Syrian
military provided the context for an at times vicious struggle
during which the Alawis have striven to eliminate non-Alawite
officers from key positions. The outcome of this struggle has been
that the Alawis have achieved dominance in the military, the
party and to a considerable degree in Syrian society at large.
This dominance, however, is extremely precarious not only
because in the process of securing it the Alawis have alienated
most other social and economic groups in the country, but also
because the Alawis are not united among themselves. According
to one writer, Nikolaos van Dam, the late 1970s have seen
serious factionalism within the Alawite community. In order to
protect himself from conspiracies, real or imagined, orchestrated by his Alawite brothers in the Party and army, President
Hafiz el-Asad has been forced to rely increasingly on members of
his own clan and village. Interestingly the same writer has noted
a similar process in neighbouring Iraq where the Ba'ath Party is
also in power (although for complex historical reasons strongly
opposed to the Syrian Ba'ath which reciprocates the hostility to
the extent of supporting Iran in the Gulf War). Since coming to
power in 1968 Ahmad Hassan el-Bakr, and his successor in the
presidency, Saddam Hussein, have assiduously filled the most

sensitive positions in the Party (and by implication in the state apparatus), with kinsmen and friends from their home town of Takrit (van Dam, 1983). The need for a network of personal dependants appears to be bound up with the atmosphere of conspiracy and distrust which seems to pervade politics in most underdeveloped countries and which places a premium on personal relations of long standing.

The predominance of sectarianism, personalism and factionalism within the military would seem to call into question one of the fundamental assumptions of those who have proposed it as an agent of modernity: that the military is a unified rationally co-ordinated organisation. In fact in the face of the fragmentation of militaries throughout the Third World more recent commentators have abandoned the rational-legal model and resorted to the notion of patrimonialism in their attempts to comprehend not only military but elite politics generally.

Patrimonialism, the Military and Society

We saw in the previous chapter that a patrimonial bureaucracy is one in which there is no strict separation between office and incumbent and where bureaucratic resources – the spoils of office – may be used by office-holders for their own purposes. So far as the political sphere generally is concerned these purposes usually entail the exchange of resources for political support; that is to say the building up of a following. Followings are as important politically within the military as in other areas.

Thus we find Harold Crouch conceiving Indonesian politics since the coup of 1966 in terms of a series of networks both within and outside the military, most of which radiate in one way or another from the person of General Suharto. Control over a vast patronage machine has been the crucial factor which has enabled Suharto to win and maintain the support of the armed forces. Under the General's 'Guided Democracy' army officers, along with most public officials, have used their positions to further their own interests. In order to reward supporters and, more important, co-opt potential dissidents, Suharto has appointed military officers to civilian posts which give them access to state funds. These funds have been used to start private businesses and, in addition, army officers have been able to use their influence in the government administration to secure for themselves, their relatives and friends, licences, contracts, credits and other resources. But, as Crouch is careful to point out, the arteries of patronage do not circulate throughout Indonesian society, only within the country's dominant groups. Politics is played out in the form of a competition both within and between hegemonic groups, although mainly the military, for political office and corresponding spoils. Because of Indonesia's expanding resource base, due to revenue from oil and an influx of foreign capital, Suharto has been able to widen his sphere of influence through the judicious distribution of patronage. For Indonesia's masses, however, political participation is minimal and that which exists is carefully orchestrated from above. The ritual of elections is celebrated but since such events are dominated by fraud and intimidation the result, a sweeping victory for the government party Golkar, is a foregone conclusion. All forms of opposition to the Suharto regime have been met with successive waves of repression inaugurated, in the wake of the 1965 coup, by the decimation of the Indonesian Communist Party in a pogrom which claimed probably half a million lives. By means of such grisly examples the regime has striven to depoliticise the masses, that is to render them politically passive. Despite such tactics the Suharto government is facing increasing popular disaffection especially from more mobilised sectors of the population such as students, professionals, petty bourgeois elements in the process of being squeezed by foreign capital, and the urban poor (Crouch, 1979).

The model proposed by Crouch is one of a society whose dominant groups are incorporated at the centre through the distribution of bureaucratic resources along clientelistic networks. The mass of the population are excluded from the distributive process through a combination of ideological control and repression. Any form of organisation which might serve to articulate mass grievances is either destroyed or taken over from the centre. Because of the dependence on force, military and para-military institutions, if not actually in formal positions of government, occupy a central place in this type of regime.

This kind of approach informs to varying degrees much

recent thinking about the operation of underdeveloped polities, although the notion of patrimonialism may not always be explicitly employed. However, one study which does attempt to use the term systematically in relation to a specific country, Brazil, is worth looking at in some detail. This is not, we hasten to point out, because we are committed to the concept of patrimonialism as an explanatory device, but because in the process of reviewing its use we will be able to illustrate certain themes as well as draw out others to be discussed in subsequent chapters.

Patrimonialism in Brazil

In his study of Brazil Riordan Roett (Roett, 1972) aims to show how, since independence, a minority has maintained a firm grip on Brazilian society even during the era of so-called democratic politics from 1948 and 1964. The key to understanding the basis of this control lies in the ability of dominant groups to manipulate the distribution of public offices so as to create and maintain networks of personal dependents. Brazil, for Roett, is a patrimonial society, that is to say a society based upon a highly flexible and paternalistic public order in which the spoils of office are used by ruling groups to reward friends, co-opt potential and actual opponents, to satisfy local and regional allies, and generally to incorporate newly-emerging groups into the system. The possibilities of incorporation through a spoils bureaucracy have been enhanced by the rapid expansion of the federal bureaucracy over the last half century. In 1920, according to Roett, one in 195 actively employed Brazilians was working in the federal bureaucracy. By 1940 this figure had become one in 142, and by 1960 one in 65. However, in order to understand Roett's analysis it is crucial to appreciate that support for the regime is not confined to the public sector. Roett brings out very well the fundamental point that the notion of a patrimonial regime involves the idea that personal connections ramify throughout key areas of the society in question. In order to illustrate the pervasiveness of personal networks Roett invokes an extremely perceptive study of Brazilian society by social anthropologist Anthony Leeds (Leeds, 1964).

Of major importance in the Brazilian socio-political system, for Leeds, is the *panelinha*, literally a little saucepan, but metaphorically a relatively closed informal group held together by common interests as expressed in the personal contacts of its respective members. *Panelinhas* exist in all areas of Brazilian life – recreational, cultural, literary, academic – but for the purposes of understanding the patrimonial regime the most important *panelinhas* are those which are avowedly politico-economic. A politico-economic *panelinha* characteristically consists of a customs official, an insurance man, a lawyer or two, a businessman or accountant, a municipal, state or federal deputy and a banker. No formal commitment is made by these people and no formal meetings are held. The cohesion of the group or quasi-group is based upon certain very simple potential sanctions. The member who leaves or who does not conform to group norms risks losing his connections which are usually important if not essential to his work. For example, members may enjoy a good deal of immunity from the law because of pressure that can be brought to bear by associates with connections with the police or judiciary. If the banker leaves he loses the deposits of his peers and these may be substantial. The banker will have difficulty finding replacements as most persons of substance will already be connected with other *panelinhas*. Again the deputy depends to some extent upon his fellows and the votes they can muster for election (and hence for his salary as well as his connections). These votes may come from employees, tenants, debtors or other individuals or groups who are in some way obligated to the other *panelinha* members. Conversely these other members depend upon the deputy, for his connections with the various departments of government are invaluable in solving a host of problems: obtaining import licences, building permits, access to confidential information and so forth. And so Brazilian society is conceived as a reticulated structure of cells whose members are bonded together by the expectation of the benefits which should accrue from their association. But of course not all Brazilians are members of *panelinhas* since membership depends upon the possession of resources: wealth, connections, knowledge and the like. Since the overwhelming majority of Brazilians have very few or none of such resources they will not be included in the patrimonial system. We can be confident that the São Paolo autoworker or the sharecropper in the North East will never, throughout their lives, be invited to join a *panelinha*.

Here we come to the other side of the patrimonial coin: the exclusion of the majority from participation in the scramble for spoils. As in Indonesia the system depends upon the rigid containment of pressure from the masses, both urban and rural. Historically the patrimonial system in both countries was relatively immune from mass challenge primarily because of the isolation and fragmentation of the masses. That is to say the overwhelming majority in Brazil and Indonesia were, until fairly recently, lodged within a peasant, primarily subsistence, economy. Without going into too much detail at this point it is fairly well-established that the socio-economic structure of the peasantry is such as to pose a number of impediments to the development of lateral consciousness. As Marx observed in a much-quoted essay (Marx, in Fernbach, 1973), one of the most basic of these impediments is the very nature of subsistence production which depends primarily on family labour and tends not to draw individual peasant families into manifold relations with each other. The isolation which is inherent in the division of labour is reinforced by geography and poor communications, particularly in countries as vast as Brazil and Indonesia.

However, in the last half century or so most countries in the underdeveloped world have seen rapid economic expansion and social change. Such expansion has been particularly marked in Brazil which embarked upon a concerted programme of industralisation under Vargas in the 1930s. This meant that by the 1970s parts of Brazil had acquired a sizeable urban proletariat employed initially in the production of consumer durables for an expanding middle-class market. It is precisely from such urban elements, primarily because of their concentration as well as efficient means of communication, that the most serious challenge to the regime has arisen. Accordingly since the coup against Goulart in 1964 the military has adopted a strategy aimed at screwing down the lid on pressure from below. For convenience we can identify three main elements in this strategy: repression, co-option and ideological control.

Under the military regime, and particularly since 1968, potential sources of political opposition have been ruthlessly repressed. The Second Institutional Act, 1965, abolished all previous national political parties, replacing them with the pro-government party, ARENA (Alianca Renovadora Nacional), and the official opposition party MDB (Movimento Democratico Brasileiro). At the same time leading opposition politicians were deprived of their electoral mandates by executive decree. Public appointees such as college professors or civil servants were the subject of compulsory retirement orders. According to one source, by January 1978, 4877 persons in leading public positions had lost their jobs, been forced to retire or lost their mandates. A vital role in these purges was played by the new National Information Service (SNI), a vast intelligence agency whose head served in the cabinet and which employed, in Schmitter's words, 'both the most modern techniques of data processing and retrieval and the most mediaeval methods of "data extraction"' (Schmitter, 1973, p. 224). Amnesty International in 1973 listed 1081 persons reliably reported to have been tortured and commented, 'We can say that torture is widespread and that it can be said to constitute administrative practice. It appears to be used in the majority of interrogations, even against people detained for a short period of time or "rounded up" in "sweep" arrests and held because they lacked the necessary identification papers' (p. 186). One feature of the repression was the activity of unofficial para-military groups of off-duty policemen, the 'death squads' estimated by Reuters to have claimed 1300 victims.

Working-class and peasant bases of opposition were systematically repressed. Already under the Estado Novo period of Vargas' rule (1937–45) a legislative framework had been created, and codified in the Consolidated Labour Law 1943 which could effectively prevent the emergence of politically independent trades unions. From the mid-1950s its provisions were applied less rigorously, encouraging the development of a powerful trade union movement. But these same measures, supplemented as necessary and forcibly applied, were used by the post-Goulart military government to eliminate trades union opposition. Unco-operative union leaders were purged, 400 unions were 'taken over', strikes were outlawed and those taking part subject to harsh penalties, wage bargaining was suspended and job security provisions abolished. In reality the determination of wage levels came to reside in the President's office and it is estimated that between 1964 and 1974 the real value of industrial wages fell by 15 per cent. During Goulart's last years dominant groups in Brazil had been alarmed by the mobilisation of the traditionally docile peasants of the North East through the activities of hundreds of peasant leagues. The suppression of most of these leagues was one of the new military regime's earliest achievements.

Repressive measures were, however, accompanied by attempts to co-opt or incorporate the more acquiescent sectors of potential opposition groupings. The MDB could be seen in this light though even so its career was chequered. The Fifth Institutional Act closed down Congress altogether accompanied by a string of executive decrees stripping five senators and 88 deputies of their political rights, but the ARENA–MDB system was revived by the end of 1970. The process of co-option, however, was most apparent in the policies of the regime towards the trades unions. As we have seen, the post-1964 regime could largely rely on the legal framework of the Consolidated Labour Law established under Estado Novo. As Erickson (1972) describes, this had been based on an explicit doctrine of corporatism according to which hierarchically structured corporate organisations were to represent the main economic sectors in society, with the State supposedly playing a residual superintending role. The official unions, or 'sindicatos', were established to replace existing ones. Their primary duty was defined as being 'to collaborate with the public authorities in the development of social solidarity'. They were financed through an annual tax on all trades union members, equivalent to one day's pay. The tax was levied and redistributed by the Ministry of Labour and its use for funding strikes was prohibited. This financial control, together with the assignment of compliant individuals to key union positions – they were called 'pelegos' after the sheepskin blanket worn between horse and saddle making the horse easier to ride – reduced the *sindicatos* largely to the function of administrative agencies distributing various social benefits and leisure services to their members.

This corporate framework notwithstanding, individual labour leaders during the post-war years were increasingly able to exploit certain aspects of their position – the threat of strike action and opportunities for patronage arising from the scarcity of resources to be distributed as social benefits – to gain real political leverage. They were assisted by the opportunities for political bargaining opened up by the restoration of a competitive party system, a relatively sympathetic military and, in 1960, the passage of a social security law which set up separate 'institutes' heading each of the different industrial sectors and on which trades union leaders were given substantial representation and hence further possibilities of patronage. As economic conditions deteriorated in the early 1960s, union leaders grew steadily more militant in their claims for their members. The post-Goulart regime moved swiftly to reinstate the old *sindicatos* system, replacing purged union leaders with reliable *pelegos*. Government control over the unions intensified with the merger of the various institutes into a single National Social Security Institute (INPS) with diminished union representation. At the same time the new leadership succeeded in counteracting the fall-off in trade union membership that ensued by enhancing the economic benefits for individual members. Provisions giving preference to unionists in hiring for work on public contracts were extended. A scholarship scheme for members and their children was introduced in 1966 and in 1970 there were further measures to expand union-administered social services.

Parallel to this reincorporation of the labour movement, the Government worked to replace the previous relatively independent rural syndicates and peasant leagues with new officially sponsored employers' syndicates and peasant associations, the former category, however, greatly outnumbering the latter. Writing in 1973 Schmitter foresaw 'within a relatively short time, every municipio will be tied into this sponsored network and . . . some minimal panoply of social services will accompany it' (Schmitter, pp. 208–9). The last remaining unincorporated arena that caused so much anxiety during the Goulart era would then, Schmitter believed, have been pre-empted and very largely placed beyond the reach of any future radical mobilisation.

The third means by which post-1964 governments have sought to secure control is ideological. Traditionally, as Schmitter notes, authoritarian governments in Brazil have been relatively tolerant and pragmatic in the sphere of dissenting political beliefs, reflecting a political culture in which ideological polarisation was rare. But in response to the growth in radical populist ideologies and working-class consciousness, the post-Goulart governments not only took steps to suppress 'subversive' ideological sources – closing down the Higher Institute of Brazilian Studies, depoliticising existing mass literacy programmes and increasing the range of media censorship – but to an unprecedented degree sought positively to instil new and more appropriate political values. A decree law of 1969 established a programme of moral and civic education throughout the education system under the auspices of a new National Commission on Morality and Civics. In addition a massive government-sponsored literacy programme got under way from 1970 which, though lacking in explicit political content, was instructed to use only materials that 'awake civic responsibilities, combat egoism, rebellion and disobedience, or which exalt loyalty, heroism and fulfilment of duty, respect for the aged and love of country and national historic events' (cited in Schmitter, 1973, p. 217). To complement such programmes the regime has manipulated nationalistic symbols, as after Brazil's victory in the soccer World Cup when, according to Schmitter, it 'deluged the country with flags, hymns, parades, jingles, bumper stickers, and pamphlets exalting the grandeur of Brazil' (Schmitter, 1973, p. 217).

Bearing in mind our theme of the politics of 'order' we have seen that the military is by no means immune to sectarianism, factionalism, personalism and self-enrichment: effectively the range of excesses which the soldiers have habitually laid at the door of the civilian politicians when they have removed them from office. Furthermore those writers who emphasised the military's modernising potential were either not aware of, or turned a blind eye to, the repressive nature of many military regimes. Although economic growth may have been achieved under some military governments (for a negative view see Nordlinger, 1970), it is questionable whether mass arrests, the widespread use of torture and murder squads can be reconciled with the idea of long-term development. However, this should not be taken to mean that the military can *never* act as a progressive force. In fact one of the major weaknesses of much of the writing on the 'military' is a tendency to treat the term as if it signified the same set of arrangements in all Third World countries (a tendency which, incidentally, is implicit in the approach of the military-as-modernisers school). As we have already seen underdeveloped countries vary significantly from each other in terms of their historical development, institutional patterns, resources, involvement with the developed world (capitalist or socialist) and so on. Accordingly in attempting to understand the behaviour of the military in this or that area of the world it would seem productive, if not necessary, to take account of the broader socio-economic context. The next section looks at certain writings which in a general way have followed this type of approach.

The Middle-class Coup

As we have seen a central feature of Brazilian economic strategy during the 1970s was that it was based largely on an expanding middle-class market whilst at the same time holding down the incomes of the working class, other elements and the peasantry. This point we can link up with certain arguments which have attempted to explore the relationship between the military and the class structure. At the beginning of this chapter we looked at some of the writings which imputed a progressive 'modernising' role to the military in the Third World. However, in fairness to one of the writers mentioned in this context, it must be pointed out that Huntington believes that these progressive militaries appear only at the earlier stages of development, that is to say in societies made up primarily of a peasantry and a landed oligarchy; where economic development has not yet reached the stage to produce a working class nor a bourgeoisie (other than a petty bourgeoisie). In this type of society the military may move in to break the economic and political stranglehold of the oligarchy and institute reformist development-oriented policies. But when the stage of what Huntington calls 'mass society' is reached the military becomes a conservative force protecting the existing order against incursions from the lower classes. The military, Huntington tells us, are the 'doorkeepers' of political participation: their historic role is to open the door to the middle classes and to keep it closed to the lower classes.

What Huntington refers to as the 'veto' coup is a direct

reflection of increasing mass participation in politics. It is thus not coincidental that the more active role of the military in Argentina after 1930 coincided with the rapid expansion of that country's industrial proletariat from around 500 000 to one million in little over a decade. A veto coup is likely to take place after civilian politicians have whipped up mass expectations with promises of radical reform. The 1964 coup which overthrew President Goulart in Brazil could be seen in this light. Joao Goulart, when he first entered Vargas' cabinet in 1953 as Minister of Labour, could hardly be described as a radical. Goulart was a cattle-rancher from a wealthy and politically well-connected family, who had used the PTB, the party based on organised labour, to advance his political career. Elected as Quadros' vice-president in 1960, Goulart became president when Quadros resigned the following year. In his election campaign Goulart had stressed his commitment to basic reforms although the nature of these was left somewhat vague. Nonetheless his opponents on the right attacked him as a Peronist or even a communist. As the country's economic difficulties became more acute the left became more vocal and Goulart, in search of a coalition of support, found himself driven into adopting radical policies. He advocated structural reforms including a much tougher line with Brazil's foreign creditors and investors, and in particular a long-needed reform of Brazil's pattern of land tenure. Conservative middle-class opinion inside the military and without, grew alarmed at these policies, or at least their prospect for the coup came too soon for them to be implemented. Goulart seemed to have become the instrument of the radical populist left.

In his article, 'The Middle Class Coup', José Nun (1967) has proposed, although much more elaborately, an argument that follows similar lines to Huntington's. First of all Nun makes an important distinction between a 'middle class' and a 'bourgeoisie'. A middle class is simply a class in the middle of the social structure located between the aristocracy and the lower classes. A bourgeoisie on the other hand, is a self-conscious middle class which is capable of asserting its interests politically and economically. For a middle class to consolidate itself as a bourgeoisie basically two conditions must be fulfilled: it must have help from outside its own ranks; and second, it must develop a *modus vivendi* with the masses. Nun then proceeds to illustrate this transition from middle class to bourgeoisie by looking at the emergence of the bourgeoisie in Great Britain at the time of the industrial revolution.

The British bourgeoisie had help from outside its own ranks from the aristocracy which both adapted to commercial activities and supported the establishment of a political environment conducive to trade as well as conceding political power to the middle class through such legislative measures as the 1832 Reform Act. Second, because the process of industrial revolution in Britain was relatively protracted and because the extension of the franchise was correspondingly gradual, the British bourgeoisie was able to defuse the revolutionary potential of the working class.

> For this purpose it skilfully utilised the deferential attitudes still persisting in the working class; it ceaselessly diffused the values associated with its capitalist, liberal and Christian ethical system; it gave enthusiastic encouragement to a complex of institutions devoted to self-improvement and self-help, and, above all, it proved able from the middle of the last century, to effect a considerable improvement in the economic position of a labour aristocracy which responded eagerly to such encouragement. Without this intermediate process, which made possible the ending of the original identification of the 'labouring classes' with the 'dangerous classes' the electoral reform of 1867 would be incomprehensible: the workers only began to be accepted as citizens when their conformism had extinguished the old Chartist fervour (Nun, 1967, p. 99).

By contrast the position in Latin America, the area of the world with which Nun is specifically concerned, is that the middle classes have been able to work out a compromise neither with traditional oligarchies nor with the masses. The nature of Latin American economic development has been such that an indigenous middle class began to emerge only with the adoption of import substitution policies in the 1930s and this only in the more developed Brazil, Chile, Argentina and Uruguay. Prior to the period of import substitution, commerce was overwhelmingly based upon the export of primary commodities: coffee, sugar, wool, beef, minerals; and this commerce was mainly in the hands of traditional landowning elites. Because of its relatively recent emergence the Latin American middle class has yet to acquire the economic power to consolidate itself politically.

So far as the masses are concerned there exists in the more developed countries of Latin America a situation which differs in one vital respect from European societies at a comparable stage of economic development. At the outbreak of the First World War only 10 to 15 per cent of the population of Europe took part in elections. Even in Great Britain, the first industrial nation, in 1913 only 17 per cent of the population had the right to vote. In the late 1950s and early 1960s, at a level of economic development roughly similar to Europe in 1914, rates of electoral participation were three to four times as great in Argentina (44 per cent of the adult population voted in 1963), Uruguay (36 per cent in 1958), and Chile (31 per cent in 1964). Accordingly these countries exhibited the fundamental disability of all underdeveloped societies: high rates of social and political mobilisation with low rates of economic development, and therefore minimal capacity of the system to absorb the demands placed upon it. For Nun the characteristic response of the Latin American middle classes to this high degree of mobilisation is political demagoguery, the populist politician – Perón, Belaunde, Vargas, Goulart – who whips up mass expectations by promising the political kingdom. When these expectations cannot be fulfilled the middle classes turn in panic to the military for help in restoring stability. The outcome is a type of military intervention that is basically defensive: defending the middle classes from mass pressure.

As examples Nun cites the coup against Goulart in Brazil which we have already considered and in addition military intervention in Argentina. In the case of Argentina, as far back as 1916 fear of military intervention on behalf of the middle class had been a major factor in inducing the Argentinian export-oriented landed oligarchy to allow the free elections which secured the presidency for Hippolito Yrigoyen, leader of the middle-class political party, the Union Civica Radical. Paradoxically it was because Yrigoyen's government was still in power in the late 1920s, when Argentina's economy felt the impact of the Depression, that it was blamed for the ensuing crisis. In 1930 the military staged a coup on behalf of the oligarchy but it was not opposed by the middle class.

In the early 1940s Argentina's economy began to revive as exports of beef and grain were stepped up and industrial production for the home market expanded. Two effects of these changes were to increase the industrial labour force and to increase the money available for state expenditure. This was the background to the much debated phenomenon of Perónism. Colonel Juan Domingo Perón became Minister of Labour in the new military government of 1943 and rapidly seized the opportunity to build himself a power base in the growing trade union movement. Perón was no socialist: earlier in his career he had been much impressed by Mussolini and now, while assisting co-operative unions, he attacked those backed by socialists and communists. Nonetheless the military viewed Perón with growing suspicion and eventually, in 1945, placed him under arrest. However, the main trades union federation, the General Federation of Workers (CGT), staged a strike which secured Perón's release and prepared the way for his election to the presidency in 1946. Once in power Perón stifled the democratic development of the trades unions placing them under centralised bureaucratic control. The constitution of the CGT was altered so as to make its fundamental purpose support for Perón and his policies. Unions which sought greater independence were denied legal recognition and many strikes were suppressed with great severity. Nonetheless the welfare laws passed by Perón and the collective industry-wide contracts he fostered significantly increased the standard of living of the working class during the first years of his government. Between 1943 and 1948 real wages rose by 37 per cent. Perhaps more importantly Perón came to be seen as a champion of the unions and the people. His populist rhetoric and demagogic style, sleeves rolled up to show solidarity with the *decamisados* (the poor, literally 'shirtless'), his attacks on the landed oligarchy and US imperialism, all fuelled the myth of his radicalism.

So long as economic prosperity meant that improvements in working-class living standards were not at their expense, the middle classes and the military were prepared to tolerate Perónism. But this toleration could not survive renewed economic difficulties in the late 1940s. Nun argues that Perón's fundamental mistake was his failure to take the measures needed to increase agricultural productivity. Such reforms would have threatened the interests of the landed oligarchy but had they been implemented in the early years of his rule they could have drawn on middle class and military support. Perón's failure to act left the oligarchy intact and aggravated an economic crisis which stirred up middle-class fears of working-class militancy. For Nun the coup which deposed Perón in September 1955 signified a middle class backing away from its progressive historic mission to become a hegemonic bourgeoisie. Instead it allied itself with a conservative oligarchy against the menace of a politicised working class. The new military regime soon moved to stamp out Perónism in the unions. Their administration was put into the hands of government-appointed officials and the CGT was disbanded.

Brazil and Argentina provide Nun with his primary examples but it is also worth looking at the case of Chile. Nun conceded that the apparent political neutrality of the army in Chile, after its intervention in the 1920s, could be held to contradict his thesis. However, Nun argued that this abstention was dependent upon a specific and fragile set of conditions. Since the time of his writing the coup of 1973 has proved him tragically prophetic.

In 1924 the new President Alessandri, leader of the moderately middle-class reformist Alianza Liberal, faced opposition from the oligarchy, through parliament and particularly through the senate, to the implementation of his programme. The result of military intervention was to push through the necessary social legislation and, following a further coup led by younger officers under Colonel Ibanez, a new constitution was adopted which lasted until 1973. Nun in 1967 observed, 'One should not forget therefore, in considering the subsequent political stability of Chile, that the institutional structure that has governed Chile down to the present day was fashioned by Ibanez between 1927 and 1931' (Nun, 1967, p. 40). But even this stability, Nun suggested, was precarious: every widening of the franchise threatened a political crisis and the success of Eduardo Frei's Christian Democratic government, elected in 1964 on a populist platform, would be heavily dependent upon continuing economic growth:

It is therefore probable that the pressures exercised by the lower strata of the urban and rural proletariat will become stronger in the future and – if the government fails to satisfy their demands – may cause breakdown of the stability which a limited degree of democracy has made possible in Chile. Thus conditions would again favour a middle-class coup (Nun, 1967, p. 108).

Nun could not of course predict the precise way in which a destabilising polarisation of class forces would occur. Although Frei's government did run into difficulties in attempting to implement its modest reform programme against a background of renewed economic stagnation and inflation, the immediate sequel was not a coup but the election of a government far more radical. Chile's constitution did not allow the same individual to serve more than one consecutive term as president. The man who emerged as the Christian Democrat (PDC) candidate for the presidency, Tomic, was too far to the left of Frei to be acceptable to the conservative National Party which had supported Frei in 1964. This temporary division within the middle-class parties made it possible for Salvador Allende, leader of the Socialist Party and candidate of the left coalition Popular Unity, to win the election with 36.2 per cent of the vote.

It would certainly be a mistake to describe the policies of the new government as populist in the Perónist sense. The two main parties were based on the working class and, while divided on questions of strategy, their leaderships were committed to the ultimate establishment of a socialist order. At the same time they believed, for the most part, in a distinct and unprecedented 'Chilean road' to socialism in which working-class parties would gain control, through constitutional means, of the institutions of parliamentary democracy. They argued that certain features of Chilean politics such as its democratic tradition, the conventional constraints on political intervention by the military and the strength and discipline of working-class organisations, made Chile uniquely suited for this pioneering role. The government of Allende, then, was socialist but constitutionalist. Though more revolutionary elements in the Socialist Party might anticipate a direct transition to socialism, as Roxborough *et al.* comment, 'It is not clear that Allende and the Communist Party ever envisaged that a sharp break with the capitalist system might occur during the period of Allende's presidency' (Roxborough *et al.*, 1977, p. 72). Indeed part of their strategy was a calculated bid for the support of the 'capas medias' or middle sectors of society by demonstrating that their interests would not be threatened.

However, despite its moderation and commitment to constitutionality, Allende's government was overthrown by a military coup in September 1973. The reasons for the coup have been much argued over. The effective economic blockade mounted by the US government together with the activities of individual US-based companies were at least an indirect cause through their destabilising impact upon the Chilean economy. Disunity within and between the political parties that made up Popular Unity and Allende's serious errors of judgement have also been blamed. However, Roxborough *et al.* have plausibly argued that Popular Unity was overthrown by 'its own bourgeoisie (and its political agent the armed forces), when it became clear that there was a real threat to bourgeois society' (Roxborough *et al.*, 1977, p. 114). From the start the Allende government planned to create a 'social property area' of nationalised economic enterprises through which it would be increasingly able to control the rest of the economy. Its initial intention was to take over 150 of the largest industrial and mining firms and most of the financial sector; but this would be followed by further nationalisations. The propertied classes and those professionals and petty bourgeois closely dependent on capitalist enterprise were not surprisingly alarmed by such attacks on private property. At first they relied on the institutions of parliamentary democracy – Congress, the Contraloria or constitutional council and the courts – to obstruct Allende's programme. Indeed in return for support from the Christian Democrats, Allende had been obliged to sign a statute of Guarantee as President pledging the freedom from political interference of governmental institutions, the mass media and the educational system. Opposition to the government in Congress repeatedly sought to impeach individual cabinet ministers and, particularly through the Hamilton-Fuentealba amendment to the Constitution, aimed to define the scope of nationalisation in a highly restrictive fashion. While these tactics were fairly successful in delaying the implementation of Allende's programme they could not prevent the increasing mobilisation, often despite rather than because of leadership from above, of urban workers in the 'industrial cordons' and community commands, and of peasants anticipating the promised land reforms. Still the opposition waited to see whether the Congressional elections of March 1973 would finally give them the two-thirds majority they needed to impeach Allende. But in the event Popular Unity won 44 per cent of the vote. Not only the National Party but the increasingly right-wing leadership of the Christian Democrats joined those burgeoning fascist organisations who were calling for a military resolution of the crisis.

As we have seen, one of the reasons why adherents of the 'Chilean road' thought a peaceful transition to socialism was possible was the military's supposed reluctance to intervene in the political sphere. At the outset of Allende's presidency such 'golpista' tactics had in any case been discredited by an unsuccessful attempt to kidnap the constitutionalist General Schneider, the Chief of Staff. As the political situation deteriorated Allende and the Communists continued to believe that a significant section of the military supported them and would defend the government against any coup mounted by the right. Ironically from March 1972 the government increasingly called on the police and the army to restore order, and for a time generals were brought into the cabinet. More ironically still General Pinochet was believed by the government to be a constitutionalist and was thus privy to such plans as existed on how the government should respond to a coup attempt.

Despite the immediate crack-down on all unofficial sources of information about the coup to the outside world, the scale and ferocity of ensuing reprisals are by now well-known. As Roxborough *et al.* wrote in 1977, 'it was the most brutal coup yet in Latin America' (p. 238). A recent Guardian article cites Hans Goren Frank, the Swedish Secretary-General of the international commission of inquiry into the crimes of Chile's military junta, who estimates the toll of ten years under Pinochet at more than 200 000 arrests, almost as many people tortured, 30–50 000 killings by the police and the army, and over 2000 disappearances. Far from being an exception to Nun's thesis Chile would now seem to provide its most convincing example.

It is extremely important to appreciate that Nun applies his notion of the middle-class coup only to the more developed countries of Latin America. Military intervention in less developed societies may be symptomatic of a quite different complex of social and political forces. Nasser's coup in Egypt, for example, is seen by Nun as quite unlike the middle-class coup of Latin America. Egypt in 1952 contrasts markedly with countries like Argentina, Brazil, Chile and Uruguay, having only recently emerged from colonialism as well as possessing only a small middle class. Military intervention under these conditions accordingly signifies something quite different. Here Nun is inclining to the view of Huntington, mentioned earlier in this chapter, which concedes that the military may be a progressive force at certain stages of development.

Recent events in certain countries in West Africa might be taken to support this position. In Ghana at the end of 1981 Flight Lieutenant Gerry Rawlings and a group of young officers and non-commissioned officers returned to power on a wave of popular resentment against a civilian government to which Rawlings had voluntarily relinquished power barely a year before. The Rawlings regime through its executive organ, the Provisional National Defence Committee (PNDC), has been forced to introduce a number of draconian policies to prevent the total collapse of the economy as well as to curb the indiscipline and corruption that was the chief legacy of the previous government. Despite acute shortages of food, petrol and other essential commodities the Rawlings regime has managed to retain a considerable degree of popular support mainly, it seems, because of a genuine attempt to place political and judicial power in the hands of the masses through the establishment of people's defence committees and public tribunals throughout the country. After inspecting the operations of the tribunals in various parts of Ghana a senior British judge, Lord Gifford, claims that they had made substantial inroads into curbing the abuse of power:

> the process is starting of converting a society where the laws were flouted by the powerful, into a society where the laws are obeyed. That can be generalised over the country; an incredible achievement given the background of law-breaking and corruption which existed (*West Africa*, 10 October 1983, p. 2342).

Even the US government, which one would normally expect to be hostile to a radical regime that has fairly close ties with Cuba, recently announced the waiving of restrictions on technical aid to Ghana because Washington is 'impressed with the integrity of the PNDC and effective ways of aid distribution' (*West Africa*, 30 July 1984, p. 1555).

Interestingly Ghana's neighbour Upper Volta, renamed Burkina Fasso in 1984, one of the poorest countries in the world, experienced a coup in August 1983 led by junior officers under Captain Thomas Sankara although in this case one of a succession of military governments was replaced. Sankara retains close links with the Rawlings regime and both leaders have stated their commitment to a revolutionary approach to the problem of underdevelopment. To this end Sankara's National Revolutionary Council has called for the establishment of revolutionary committees throughout the country. It is too early to say whether the proposed Voltaic revolution will be translated from rhetoric into political reality. However, from the point of view of our present discussion the argument centres not on the degree of 'progressiveness' of this or that military regime but on the level of development and its consequences for the society in which the military comes to power. It is extremely difficult to envisage a Rawlings-type coup in Argentina, Brazil or Chile with their long-established officer corps, each with close economic and institutional links with a bourgeoisie which is more developed than its counterparts in Tropical Africa. Even the Buhari coup in Nigeria at the end of 1983 cannot reasonably be assigned to the same category as that which took place in Ghana two years before. Although the coup was directed against the grandiose scale of waste and corruption in the Second Republic (1979–83) and was generally welcomed by the Nigerian masses, the Buhari regime shows no signs of setting up mechanisms of popular power along Rawlings-Sankara lines. Indeed so far as a number of observers are concerned one of the basic aims of the New Year's Eve coup was precisely to pre-empt a more radical thrust by younger officers influenced by the Rawlings model. Whether such an action was in the offing and whether it would have succeeded are extremely complex questions and are beyond the scope of this work. However, any explanation would need to take account of the fact that Nigeria's oil boom has generated a degree of economic expansion which places the country, in terms of basic economic and social indicators, on a par with the poorer countries of Latin America such as Peru, Nicaragua and El Salvador (*World Bank Development Report*, 1980, p. 110). Without advocating an economic determinist argument our general point is that the behaviour of the military in a given country or region needs at some point to be related to the relevant socio-economic context.

Conclusion

We have suggested that the non-emergence of liberal democracies in UDCs led to a shift in focus among political scientists away from democracy as the end-state of political development to an emphasis on stability and order. Donal Cruise O'Brien has ingeniously postulated a link between US foreign and domestic policy pre-occupations in the second half of the 1960s and the abandonment of the 'democratic ideal' by a number of American political scientists (O'Brien, 1972). Strong government was now the order of the day especially in the context of Third World countries.

The need for muscle inevitably threw the spotlight on the military. For a number of writers the officer corps was one of the few bodies in underdeveloped societies with the organisation needed to martial the energies of often disparate social forces in pursuit of the goal of growth. This conception of the military, it has been argued in this chapter, seriously overstated its homogeneity and its capacity for co-ordinated action. In the recently emerged states of Tropical Africa, the Middle East and parts of Asia which are often deeply divided by primordial divisions, it is usually the case that the military also is split along sectarian lines. Even in the older states of Latin America where national armies have existed for over a century, by no stretch of the imagination can the officer corps be regarded as unified. On the contrary a number of writers on Latin America have emphasised the persistence if not predominance of personalism, followings and factions not only within the military but within dominant groups generally (in addition to Roett, 1972, see Schmitter, 1971; Purcell, 1973; Malloy, 1977).

More generally we have seen that a particular model of an underdeveloped polity has been proposed in which some degree of integration at the centre is achieved through the distribution along patrimonial lines among hegemonic groups of the spoils of office. The mass of the population is excluded from this process of distribution while dominant groups attempt to contain pressure from below through a combination of ideological manipulation and repression. (We noted that the repressive side of political order has been conveniently ignored by its leading advocates.) While the patrimonial model has a number of defects which we are unable to discuss here (see Theobald, 1982), it has nonetheless enabled us to develop certain themes, particularly the significance of personal networks in underdeveloped states. To some of these themes we shall be returning in succeeding chapters.

Finally we criticised the over-general use of the term 'military' as if it meant the same thing throughout the Third World. We suggested that the military as well as other political manifestations need to be understood in terms of the context in which they are constrained to operate. A crucial feature of this context for some scholars is the relationship between the economy of a specific Third World state and the international economy including the historical character of that relationship. For those who embrace this 'dependency' perspective the fundamental weakness of the strong government school is its failure to take this international economic dimension into account. The proponents of strong government assume that if power is concentrated at the centre political order will be achieved and development, including economic growth, will ensue. Underdevelopment, therefore, is a consequence of the absence of political order. Dependency theory, to which we now turn, maintains by contrast that underdevelopment is a direct consequence of the inferior terms under which Third World economies were incorporated into the world capitalist system with this condition of inferiority maintained by the ongoing structure of that system. Re-organising the state at the periphery, so far as the dependency school is concerned, is not a solution to the problem of underdevelopment.

4
Dependency Theory and the Study of Politics

Our chief concern in this chapter is with the third major critique of the political modernisation approach, that which arises out of dependency theory. We shall see that the primary focus of dependency theory is the international economic order. No society can be understood in isolation from this order and in fact the condition of underdevelopment is precisely the result of the incorporation of Third World economies into the world capitalist system which is dominated by the developed North. Accordingly the principal weakness of the modernisation approach from a dependency prespective is its total neglect of the economic dimension and its practice of explaining social and political change in the Third World entirely in terms of factors which are internal to the countries in question. In examining the impact of dependency theory on the study of politics we shall not be reviewing the wide range of dependency theories that have emerged during the last ten or fifteen years (see O'Brien, 1975, and Hoogvelt, 1982). We shall start by looking at the earlier writings of one of the most prominent dependency theorists, André Gunder Frank, their implications for the study of politics and certain critical reactions to these writings. We shall then look at briefly at other writers in the dependency school and derivatives of it before making an assessment of the approach from the point of view of our interest in political change. Before actually turning to Frank we need to consider briefly some of the primary influences upon him. These will not only shed light on his writings but provide a number of useful reference points for our subsequent discussion.

Lenin's Theory of Imperialism

In an important sense the roots of Frank's approach lie in Marxism, or rather in the progressive reactions of Marxists and

Marxist-inspired thinkers to social and political changes in both the developed and the underdeveloped world. (This does not necessarily mean that Frank is a Marxist. He himself has never claimed to be one and a number of his Marxist critics would agree with him.) Both Marx and his followers have been very much pre-occupied with two basic features of capitalism: the failure or non-emergence of a proletarian revolution in industrialised Europe and, second, the spread of capitalism to the rest of the world. Marx himself believed that once capitalism was implanted through colonial contact in the non-European world, the result would be the eventual industrialisation of the countries concerned. Furthermore he saw capitalism, and by implication colonialism, as a progressive force, 'regenerating' ancient stagnant civilisations such as that of the Indian sub-continent and laying the material foundations for western society in the East (Palma, 1978, and Warren, 1980).

Both Marx and Engels argued that colonialism would lead to the establishment of more or less autonomous capitalist systems whose development would proceed along the lines mapped out in the *Communist Manifesto*. That is, just as in Europe, capitalism in the East would eventually produce its own proletariat which would ultimately rise up and throw off the yoke of bourgeois domination: in the case of the colonies, western bourgeois domination. Since therefore the liberation of the colonies waits upon the arrival of a proletariat which itself requires the implantation of capitalism from outside, colonialism *per se* is not condemned.

This was the 'orthodox' Marxist position though it must be noted that Marx himself did not always adopt such a determinist line. In his early writings Lenin was an 'orthodox' Marxist, welcoming the increase in foreign investment as a means of developing capitalism in pre-capitalist Imperialist Russia. He took issue with the Narodniks, that section of the Russian intelligentsia who conceived of liberation from Tsarist servitude in terms of a socialism based upon existing peasant communes. The Narodniks were anti-capitalist, regarding capitalism not only as a dehumanising system but as unnecessary for the development of socialism. In fact they seriously doubted whether capitalism could emerge in such a backward country as Russia. While Lenin concurred on the brutalising effects of capitalism he emphasised its essentially progressive role in transforming pre-capitalist socio-economic structures and making possible the formation of a radical proletariat. He maintained that the development of capitalism was well under way, though the process would be much slower than in western Europe. This was due to three main factors (factors which we shall see recur frequently in contemporary literature on under-development). First was the weakness of the Russian bourgeoisie, not only in terms of size but also in its inability to mobilise sufficient capital internally to generate development. Hence Russia's heavy dependence upon foreign investment. The second factor was the effects of competition from the already much more developed West. And third was the capacity of traditional, that is pre-capitalist, structures to survive.

Ironically just as Lenin was insisting on both the necessity and the inevitability of capitalism in Russia, Marx was prepared to concede that 'if the Russian Revolution becomes the signal for a proletarian revolution in the West, so that both complement each other, the present Russian common ownership of land may serve as the starting point for a communist development' (cited by Schapiro, 1971, p. 10). However Lenin's famous pamphlet, *Imperialism: the Highest Stage of Capitalism*, first published in 1916, exhibits a fairly profound shift from the 'orthodox' Marxist position (Lenin, 1966). Two factors in particular are thought to have influenced this shift. There was first the 1905 Revolution in Russia when strikes, urban and peasant revolts and mutinies in the armed forces compelled the Tsar to accept the principle of constitutional government. These events helped persuade Lenin that revolution was possible in a relatively underdeveloped society, in which the proletariat was still a small minority of the employed population. But given the weakness of the bourgeoisie, the task of completing the bourgeois revolution could well devolve upon the proletariat, which could however rely on the assistance of the poorer sections of the peasantry. This meant that the two revolutions, bourgeois and proletarian, rather than being separated by a considerable lapse of time, as in the orthodox Marxist scheme, would run into each other.

Lenin was, second, reacting to the abandonment of the ideal of international solidarity by the European working classes in favour of the frenzied nationalism of the First World War period. He attributed this nationalism to a new opportunism which was in turn a symptom of the capacity of developed western economies to assimilate key sectors of their working classes. This capacity for assimilation was made possible by the high level of profits from imperialism. Lenin went on to incorporate his explanation of working-class opportunism within a broader theory of imperialism. The imperialist expansion of the late nineteenth century reflected a fundamental change in the nature of European capitalism. Competition within the industrial nations had resulted in the concentration of capital and the formation of monopolistic cartels, syndicates and trusts. The level of profits generated by monopoly capitalism exceeded the opportunities for domestic investment and investment outlets had therefore to be sought overseas. The wave of imperialist expansion at the turn of the century was thus stimulated by this quest for investment opportunities, especially in those parts of the world – Tropical Africa and Asia – where labour was cheap, raw materials in plentiful supply, but capital a scarce commodity.

Imperialism, then, lay at the root of the failure of European radicalism, since it enabled the European bourgeoisie to 'buy off' the working class, or key sectors of it. But whilst imperialism diluted radicalism in Europe, it simultaneously intensified the struggle against capitalism in the form of colonial domination in Africa and Asia. However, Lenin had to recognise that the struggle in the colonies was not waged by a proletariat when, as in Russia, this was so tiny, nor by the bourgeoisie, when they were alien entrepreneurs. The struggle was primarily national and at the heart of it, Lenin maintained, stood the agrarian question, the conflict between the peasantry and the feudal landowners who had allied themselves with the imperialist powers. The peasantry would thus be at the centre of the bourgeois (national) revolution and in fact Lenin believed that an indigenous bourgeoisie would develop out of the peasantry. Yet no Marxist could deny altogether a role for the proletariat and Lenin came to accept the view, initially formulated by Trotsky, that the proletariat's crucial task would be to check the bourgeois tendencies of the nationalist revolution once this got under way. But given the underdeveloped nature of the proletariat in the colonies, its vanguard role could only be exercised through a revolutionary party whose hierarchy and discipline would compensate for the proletariat's structural weakness.

In the aftermath of the Bolshevik Revolution, such questions became of more than theoretical concern, for the survival of the new Soviet state was integrally bound up with the anti-imperialist struggle. Since the imperialist powers, mainly Britain, engaged in military operations against the new regime, agitation against British imperialism anywhere in the world, in so far as it tied down British armed forces, must in some way benefit the Bolsheviks. In the longer term, the anti-imperialist campaign was part of the world revolution, as progressive forces throughout the Third World threw off the yoke of imperialism and prepared the way for proletarian uprising. The progressive forces were the peasantry, proletariat and nationalist bourgeoisie. Support for a bourgeois national revolution against imperialism and its feudal allies was, until Stalin consolidated his rule, the line taken by the Communist International (Comintern); it was also the position adopted by many radicals throughout the world.

Towards a Theory of Dependency

Moving forward considerably in time, one development that greatly affected the thinking of those concerned, academically or in a more practical sense, in Third World revolution, and which had direct consequences for the argument of Gunder Frank, was the revolution in Cuba, in 1959. The Cuban Communist Party, at least its leadership, was reluctant to take up arms against the dictator Batista because of disagreements about the character of the coming revolution. Could an immediate transition to socialism be made? The Communist Party inclined to the view it could not and seemed willing to support the idea only of a democratic and anti-imperialist revolution. We need not explore the intricacies of this debate; the crucial point is that it led the Castroites and their supporters in Latin America to question the progressive role of the indigenous bourgeoisie. By 1967, through the Latin American Solidarity Organisation (OLAS), these radicals formally abandoned the notion of a revolutionary role for the bourgeoisie, at least the Latin American bourgeoisie which, because of its social origins and kinship connections, was now deemed quite incapable of formulating a political line independent of the interests of the imperialist powers.

At this juncture we may introduce André Gunder Frank who was clearly influenced by the course of the Cuban Revolution and was producing his first controversial essays about the same time as the OLAS declaration. Frank studied economics at the University of Chicago and initially viewed the problem of underdevelopment through the lens of orthodox, or as he would no doubt now put it, bourgeois economics. Underdevelopment or lack of growth he attributed to such factors as scarcity of capital, traditional institutions which impeded savings and the concentration of power in the hands of rural oligarchies. At this time he encountered the work of economist Paul Baran but on his own admission did not really understand it. However, whilst teaching and researching in Latin America in the 1960s, Frank came to see the problem of underdevelopment in quite a different perspective.

In the formulation of this perspective, Frank owed two particular intellectual debts. The first, which he has perhaps insufficiently acknowledged, is to the United Nations Economic Commission for Latin America (ECLA). As Booth has well recounted, it was the Latin American economists associated with this body, such as Raoul Prebisch and Celso Furtado, who first recognised the inappropriateness of existing orthodox economic frameworks for analysing and explaining the specific economic history of Latin America and especially for evaluating the policy of import-substitution industralisation (ISI) in Argentina, Brazil and Mexico (this policy in the context of Brazil is more fully discussed later in this chapter, see pages 112–13). These economists rejected conventional international trade theory, according to which 'given free trade and certain other conditions, the benefits deriving from trends in productivity in the world economy as a whole would be distributed towards the primary-producing "periphery", since technical progress was more vigorous and widespread in the production of industrial goods' (Booth, 1975, pp. 54–5). They argued that the reverse had been happening and in their explanation emphasised the contrast between economic conditions, and particularly the organisation and employment of labour, in the 'core' industrial countries and primary-producing countries of the 'periphery', which perpetuated and even reinforced the core's trading advantage. Frank, like many Latin American radicals, was to take issue with the ECLA's favoured solutions to this dilemma, first ISI and later increased foreign investment, but the terms of the whole debate had nonetheless been largely framed by the ECLA.

The second major influence was the ideas of Paul Baran. Baran's *The Political Economy of Growth* was published in 1957 and may be regarded as a pioneering attempt, from a Marxist standpoint, to break out of established thinking about economic growth or the lack of it. On the basis of a historical survey of the manner in which capitalism 'broke into' the economies of the underdeveloped world, Baran submits that the nature of this penetration was such as to preclude the materialisation of the classic conditions for growth. Far from serving as an engine of economic expansion, the implantation of capitalism in these countries has resulted in economic stagnation and social backwardness. These outcomes are the effects of the appropria-tion of the surplus generated in colonial economies by the imperialist powers. Baran maintains, in line with Marxist theories of imperialism, that the expansion of capitalism in the West was predicated upon colonisation, destruction of indigen-ous economies and appropriation of their surplus. Accordingly the solution to underdevelopment lies not in the accumulation of domestic capital or the fostering of native entrepreneurial abilities but in socialist revolution. Such a revolution will entail the appropriation of the assets of both foreign and domestic capitalists and will thus enable the masses to assume full control over their economy.

In his first book Frank adopts a similar perspective in explaining the 'development of underdevelopment' in Chile and Brazil. But before turning to this work let us briefly consider an essay Frank first published in 1967, not only because this helps reveal the evolution of Frank's thought but also because it links up with our discussion in Chapter 2. In this essay, 'The Sociology of Development and the Underdevelopment of Sociology' (Frank, 1971). Frank launches into a blistering attack against what he understands to be current sociological approaches to development, though certain of the writers he singles out for special criticism, such as David McClelland and Walt Whitman Rostow, are not in fact sociologists. We do not need to discuss the essay in detail here but suffice it to say that many of Frank's criticisms of the modernisation approach resemble those of the modernisation revisionists discussed in Chapter 2. So when Frank considers the application by Bert Hoselitz of Parsons' pattern variables to the study of modernisation his main line of attack is to point up the logical and empirical weaknesses of such dichotomous approaches. Hoselitz, for example characterises developed countries as being universalist as opposed to particularist (Hoselitz, 1964). Against this Frank uses evidence from Japan, France and other European countries to demonstrate the continued importance of particularist orientations among all social classes, especially the working class. However it is when Frank trains his sights on Rostow's stages of economic growth theory that we see how his perspective moves beyond that of modernisation revisionism.

We have already seen that Rostow delineates five stages in the process of economic growth: the traditional, preconditions for take-off, take-off, drive to maturity and the age of mass consumption. We recall that although the initial stimulus to modernisation in the underdeveloped world arrives from outside through the example of the industrialised world, for Rostow the basic problem of taking off is totally internal to the economies concerned. Essentially the task is to produce enough individuals with entrepreneurial abilities. As with other modernisation theories, Rostow's approach is explicitly teleological: contemporary developed societies represent the end-state towards which the non-industrial world is evolving.

For Frank, Rostow's scheme is to be rejected in its entirety because it does not correspond to historical or contemporary reality. It is impossible, Frank maintains, to find anywhere in the world today a society which exhibits the characteristics of Rostow's traditional stage. This is because such 'traditional' societies have long since disintegrated with their incorporation into the world capitalist economy. This notion of incorporation emphasises the interdependence of developed and underdeveloped worlds, a relationship entirely ignored by Rostow.

Rostow's scheme, Frank points out, implies that the industrialised world developed in isolation whereas in reality this development was predicated on the progressive incorporation of the multifarious economies of Asia, Latin America, the Middle East and Tropical Africa. The economic and political expansion of Europe since the fifteenth century resulted in the now underdeveloped countries being drawn into a single stream of world history. The outcome of this process has been the 'present development of some countries and the present underdevelopment of others'. This is the core of Frank's position, that development and underdevelopment are opposite sides of the same coin: the development of the industrialised world was and is made possible only by the corresponding underdevelopment of the Third World. The approach of Rostow and of other modernisation theorists, with its assumption that the problem of under- or non-development is internal to the countries concerned and that once overcome, these countries can follow the developmental path blazed by the already industrialised world, fails totally to enhance our understanding of the problem of underdevelopment.

Frank's conception of underdevelopment and its causes is elaborated at some length at the beginning of his case study of Brazil, also first published in 1967 (Frank, 1969). Here Frank starts off by inveighing against dualist explanations of underdevelopment. The notion of dualism in the context of Third World societies has been evolved by a number of writers, including the Dutch former colonial administrator J. H. Boeke, J. S. Furnival and most notably the economist, Arthur Lewis. (It also occurs in the writing of some ECLA economists, such as Furtado, despite their emphasis on core–periphery relations, and is one of the grounds for Frank's repudiation of their arguments.) The notion of dualism has been applied specifically to Brazil by the French geographer, Jacques Lambert (cited in Frank, 1969, ch. 3). Dual societies consist of two fundamentally different sectors: a dynamic modern sector, organised on capitalist lines and located around major cities and ports, and a large, mainly stagnant, subsistence sector located in the rural hinterland and containing the mass of the population. Economic and social interaction between the two sectors is minimal if it exists at all. In fact the problem of underdevelopment is understood by dualists as primarily that of creating linkages between the two sectors so that modernity can be diffused from one to the other. The dualist approach tends to imply that the problem of underdevelopment and its solution are largely internal to the economy or society in question. In Lewis' theoretically elaborate model they are depicted as entirely internal (Lewis, 1955).

As may be expected, Frank's main line of criticism against dualism centres upon the idea of a large subsistence sector somehow cut off from the world economy. Against this conception, Frank proposes a model consisting of a world *metropolis*: the US with its governing class; national satellites like the southern states of the US; international satellites like São Paolo which in turn play the role of national metropolises. These national metropolises are further linked to provincial satellites, for instance Recife or Belo Horizonte. Ultimately economic links reach down to the local hacienda or rural merchants. So we have a chain of dependence extending from the very centre of the world (capitalist) economic system down to its furthest periphery. This system is characterised by close economic, political, social and cultural ties between each metropolis and its satellite, with the implication that, contrary to the dualist thesis, outside the socialist bloc there is no area of the world, no matter how remote, that is not in one way or another incorporated.

Now a crucial feature sustaining this system, for Frank, is its monopolistic structure, with each metropolis exercising a monopoly over its satellite. This monopolistic structure leads to the misuse and misdirection of resources throughout the chain. Most importantly, misuse and misdirection involve the expropriation and appropriation of a large part or even all of the economic surplus or surplus value of the satellite by its local, regional, national or international metropolis. For us the most significant aspect of this process is the appropriation of surplus by the developed industrial world from the underdeveloped Third World, a process which has been going on for a considerable period and which began with the incorporation of different areas of the world into the world capitalist system. If we want to understand why a particular country is underdeveloped, we need to analyse its historical interaction with countries in the developed world. Accordingly in seeking to explain the underdevelopment of Brazil, Frank traces the character of that country's involvement with European economies from its settlement by the Portuguese in the sixteenth century to the military coup of 1964.

Frank on Brazil

Frank divides his historical account into two sections. The first dealing with the colonial period up to 1822, when Brazil obtained formal independence, can be reviewed briefly. Frank distinguishes within it a number of stages according to the specific content of the economic relationship with the metropolis.

Even though Brazil had no obvious enticements such as large deposits of gold or silver, as in Mexico or Peru, Portugal was forced to claim Brazilian territory to prevent it falling into the hands of European rivals for Latin America's riches. There was, however, valuable wood useful for dyeing in Brazil's North. And in the sixteenth century came the rapid expansion of European demand for sugar leading to the establishment of plantations based on slave labour in the North East. The sugar economy in turn generated its own satellite livestock industry. Since most of the profit from sugar was transmitted back to the metropolis rather than being invested in Brazil, the socio-economic structure of the North Eastern region was even then impregnated with the logic of underdevelopment.

The sugar economy was hit by the expansion of sugar cultivation in the West Indies towards the end of the seventeenth century. As profits declined, the North East experienced what Frank terms a process of 'passive capitalist involution'. Involution occurs when a satellite's ties with the metropolis are weakened so that the economy turns in on itself. In its passive form the direction of change is towards a subsistence economy and extreme underdevelopment. As we shall see below involution can take an active form. In the North East labour transferred from sugar cultivation to the livestock sector which was closer to subsistence. These economic changes underpinned the spread of 'coronelismo': the extreme concentration of economic and political power in the hands of a few landed magnates. *Coronelismo* was to survive into the twentieth century with major consequences for Brazilian politics. However 'feudal' *coronelismo* may appear, it was the outcome, Frank insists, of capitalist development.

In the eighteenth century the discovery of gold and diamonds in the interior region around Minas Gerais and Goias generated Brazil's own gold rush. A similar pattern of capitalist incorporation followed and after the gold boom receded from 1760, the region went through a parallel process of passive involution. Subsistence agriculture came to predominate accompanied by the rise of *coronelismo*. The Northern region – the third major region of *coronelismo* – experienced a further variant of this pattern of underdevelopment. Towards the end of the eighteenth century the North met with a brief period of prosperity as the wars of American independence together with expansion in Napoleonic Europe stimulated the demand for rice, cocoa and especially cotton. Nearly a century later the North was granted a second short-lived respite when it became a centre of rubber cultivation until this role was taken over by South East Asia. Another crucial feature of this first colonial epoch was the thwarting in the eighteenth century of Brazil's first tentative efforts at industrialisation by decree from the Queen of Portugal fearful of competition with her own country's manufactures.

Frank summarises his discussion of this first period by stressing again how the regions of passive capitalist involution were the most economically underdeveloped and bequeathed the legacy of *coronelismo*. Even by the 1960s, when he was writing, their politics remained the least ideological, dominated as they were by clientelism and directed to serve immediate local interests. These were the regions where the conservative PSD derived its greatest support.

In 1822 Brazil declared independence from Portugal, though with the son of the Portuguese Regent as Emperor Pedro I. But such formal political independence went hand in hand with ever-deepening incorporation into a world capitalist system now dominated by Britain. During the early years of independence Brazil was forced to accept the new principle of 'free trade'. As Frank insists, this did not essentially change Brazil's dependent economic status, only the form and mechanism of dependence. Liberalism ensured Britain's industrial monopoly so long as she could maintain her headstart. Once it could no longer exclude her metropolitan competitors, liberalism was abandoned in favour of a policy of imperialist colonialism.

The effect of free trade together with economic depression in the middle years of the nineteenth century was to 'put Brazil entirely out of the development race', in contrast to less satellised countries like Germany, the US and, above all, Japan. Brazil became a satellite exporter of primary products, dependent on imports for manufactures and luxury goods. The Brazilian bourgeoisie did not seek tariff protection so long as they could pay for these imports with the surplus they exacted from exploitation within Brazil.

Towards the end of the nineteenth century, expanding world demand for coffee generated the coffee boom in the São Paolo region. As in all subsequent periods of economic expansion, this was accompanied by domestic inflation. Moreover though coffee production was initially financed by Brazilian capital, as its profitability was established it was increasingly subject to foreign take-over. By the opening years of the twentieth century Brazil was facing problems of over-production. In 1905 the Government (Brazil had become a republic in 1889) began a policy of subsidising coffee prices and stockpiling, which was still in force in the 1960s. The1880s also saw the consolidation of São Paolo's position as an industrial centre. But, in keeping with Frank's basic thesis, it was during the First World War, when economic ties with the metropolis were loosened, that the real industrial spurt came.

With the recovery of the world capitalist metropolis in the 1920s Brazil's underdevelopment was resumed. Apparent economic expansion was accompanied, according to Frank, by inflation and devaluation, initially improving but then deteriorating terms of trade and growing reliance on external finance. All this damaged indigenous industry and brought Brazil ever deeper into debt and greater dependence on the metropolis, now increasingly the US. But while these developments paralleled those in the second half of the nineteenth century, new mechanisms of satellisation were evolving. American investment in Brazilian industry was tending more and more to take the form of affiliates of major US corporations, although part of the capital they raised came from within

Brazil's own banking system. The political corollary of this economic pattern was a government, under Washington Luis, representing dominant agricultural, commercial and coffee interests and entirely devoted to the cause of the imperialist metropolis.

The next major phase of Brazil's economic history came with the crash of 1929 and its drastic impact on the price of coffee. President Luis's response was to cut government spending and reduce the money supply, in line with American advice and metropolitan interests. The adverse effects on Brazilian industry fuelled the 'Revolution of 1930' which brought Getulio Vargas to power. Vargas represented the protest of the industrial bourgeoisie against the agrarian commercial and metropolitan hegemony embodied in Luis' government. It was not, however, a genuine revolution: the new contenders for power, the industrial bourgeoisie, together with southern agrarian interests, did not oust former dominant groups but simply claimed a share of their privileges.

The economic consequence was a period of very *active* capitalist involution. While the new government continued to support coffee prices this was through internally rather than externally raised finance and it adopted a policy of tariff protection. Above all there was an unprecedented surge in the expansion of domestic industry. This was the era of ISI already referred to in connection with the ECLA economists. The temporary disruption of ties to the metropolis seemed to permit a form of autonomous economic development. However, Frank is careful to point out the limits to this development: industry was still producing mainly consumer goods so that by 1938 domestic iron and steel output covered only one-third of Brazil's requirements. Brazil's dependence was thus not fundamentally altered: the mechanism had simply changed once more. Now the basis of the metropolis's monopoly was shifting to capital and intermediate goods. As a result those satellite countries which had earlier been able to acquire some industrial base and with it the beginnings of an industrial bourgeoisie could seize the opportunity provided by the relaxation of metropolitan-satellite ties to expand the manufacture of consumer goods. The duration of this phase of active capitalist involution was necessarily limited but was prolonged by the impact first of the

1937 recession, and then of the Second World War and its aftermath.

The political counterpart of this stage was the Estado Novo, certain aspects of which we encountered in the previous chapter. Frank's explanation for its emergence runs more or less as follows: the partial recovery of the metropolis between 1934 and 1937, especially in Germany, increased demand for Brazilian exports and led to pressures to raise exchange rates, which Vargas went some way towards meeting. This particularly antagonised the export–oriented landowning and commercial interests, a section of whom in their bid to undermine the regime were increasingly attracted by the fascistic ideas then prevalent in Germany and Italy. The dictatorial powers, which Vargas assumed under Estado Novo, were an attempt to contain this threat from the right as well as to check militant unionist and communist surges from the left. As the repercussions of the Second World War served to prolong Brazil's experience of active capitalist involution, Vargas and Estado Novo grew ever more identified with the interests of the industrial bourgeoisie and the 'sindicatos': the corporatist organisations of labour upon which his new political party, the PTB, was largely based. As we have seen, his government adopted many socially progressive measures such as the establishment of a minimum wage.

But for Frank, these political developments were entirely dependent upon the temporary weakening of metropolis––satellite ties. With the economic recovery of the metropolis after the war this ruling alliance of national industrial bour-geoisie and organised labour, together with the economic policies which expressed their interests, could not survive. However, Frank's explanation of the collapse of Estado Novo is not entirely clear as Vargas himself was ousted from the presidency in 1945 when the metropolitan economies could not seriously be argued to have recovered. Vargas was re-elected in 1951 having adopted a populist anti-imperialist stance. Never-theless, the impossibility of sustaining such a position was dramatically symbolised in Vargas's subsequent suicide. His successor, Cafe Filho, presided over an ultra-reactionary gover-nment which, abandoning the economic policies of the Vargas era, actively favoured foreign over domestically-based enterprise. This approach continued under Kubitschek, President from 1955 to 1960, though Frank conceded that he did attempt to stem the tide of Brazil's reincorporation into the metropolis-satellite system by resorting to externally financed internal expansion. In Frank's graphic phrase, this was simply to seek 'the help of the wolf's paw to protect the Brazilian people from the wolf's ravenous appetite' (p. 204). The short-lived government of Janio Quadros that followed demonstrated again the impossibility of pursuing populist, nationalist policies while Brazil was open to the full blast of a thriving metropolis. As we have seen in Chapter 3, Quadros's resignation left the Presidency in the hands of Vice-President, Joao Goulart. Goulart, through the PTB, had managed to acquire a major following within both the more nationalist sections of the bourgeoisie and the labour unions. This alarmed foreign and Brazilian metropolitan interests but they were unable to oust him so long as he retained this political base. However, the rapid deterioration of the economic situation, as the policies adopted under Cafe Filho and Kubitschek resulted in escalating foreign debt, faced Goulart with a dilemma: whether to yield still further to domestic and foreign commercial interests and hope they would bail Brazil out, or to assert a more independent, nationalist line. In vacillating, Frank maintains, Goulart typified the national bourgeoisie of which he was a member and this time the national bourgeoisie itself did not come to his rescue. The result was the coup of 1964, which ushered in the military government of Castello Branco. Writing in the mid-1960s, Frank's judgement was that this government had finally 'handed over the Brazilian economy to the Americans, lock, stock and barrel' (p. 186), and he elaborated upon the consequent economic difficulties beseiging the new regime: inflation, unemployment and so on.

However, the real point for Frank was that the alternative nationalist policies of Vargas and Quadros were not alternatives at all. He took issue with those like Furtado who believed that if it had not been for the worsening terms of trade, by 1955 Brazil would have reached the point at which its development could be self-sustaining. The phase of active capitalist involution had been by definition temporary, caused by the weakening not the severing of the ties of dependency, and indeed during it new mechanisms of destabilisation were evolving. Brazil's 'national' bourgeoisie remained compromised by its involvement in the capitalist chain of exploitation, never able to break completely with the system from which it benefited and which protected its own privileged position. Truly autonomous economic development could come about only with the politicisation of the Brazilian masses who had nothing to lose and everything to gain from it.

The Limitations of Frank's Approach for Political Analysis

From this brief summary of Frank's treatment of Brazil it will be readily apparent that his approach is conducted very much on the macro-economic level of the world capitalist system. In locating the core of underdevelopment firmly within the structure of the world economy Frank differs radically from the sociologists and political scientists who preceded him and from whose accounts the international economic dimension was virtually absent. And it is important to realise that this applies not only to the modernisation theories that Frank was attacking but to much subsequent political science in the 1970s. In fact many political scientists continued to write about Third World politics paying minimal attention either to burgeoning dependency theory or to the economic context generally. This would be true, for example, of an otherwise very useful survey, Gerald Heeger's *The Politics of Underdevelopment* (1974; see also Dodd, 1972).

However, the converse of this situation was that dependency theory itself tended to marginalise the political. That is to say, from the dependency perspective, at least in its earlier manifestations, the character of governments, parties, bureaucracies, elections, militaries and the substantial variations between countries as well as within the same country at different periods of time all tend to be treated as appendages of the world capitalist system and therefore peripheral to the analysis of change in UDCs. The very terms in which Frank casts his economic analysis of Brazil, for example, have implications for its politics. By denying the possibility of any meaningful economic development, by characterising all apparent development, even industrialisation, as underdevelopment, Frank discounts the significance of Brazil as a nation-state, whether in terms of the independent effect of its internal political alignments and struggles or of the state itself. These are all made simply instrumental to the economic mechanisms of metropolitan domination.

A number of subsequent writers, whilst not rejecting the overall notion of dependence, have found Frank's dichotomy of development and underdevelopment too black and white – curiously paralleling the tradition – modernity dichotomy of political modernisation theories – to be able to describe and explain the gradations of grey, the variations in degree or at least forms of underdevelopment between Third World countries and within countries over time. Brazilian economist Henrique Cardoso, for instance, has argued within the overall parameters of dependency that certain countries, of which Brazil is a leading example, have been apable of 'associated dependent development'. If development is defined, as Frank seems to imply, by the accumulation of capital, then dependent development involves accumulation of capital together with some industrialisation at the 'periphery' itself (Cardoso, 1973). This model has recently been applied in an extensive study of industrialisation in Brazil by Peter Evans, (1979a), to which we return later in this chapter.

Bill Warren, a Marxist economist who in many respects harked back to the old 'orthodox' analysis of imperialism, in responding to Frank went much further, maintaining that in certain Third World countries autonomous capitalist development is occurring. Such factors as political independence, East–West rivalry and growing competition between imperialist powers and agencies have combined to give Third World states greater scope for bargaining and for autonomous development initiatives (Warren, 1973). Warren's argument, in particular the evidence he cites to show that autonomous capitalist development is already apparent in a number of Third World states, has been effectively criticised in turn (see Emmanuel, 1974), and further revision may be necessary in the light of the impact of the current world recession. But the central point for our purposes is that even in purely economic terms the total incorporation and underdevelopment of all 'peripheral' societies is highly questionable. Brazil, specifically, would seem to be one case where, beginning at least with the period of ISI, significant local accumulation of capital and not simply its siphoning off by the metropolitan core has taken place. This would appear to suggest that we should give more attention to the Brazilian *nation-state* as a unit of analysis, to the possibility of *state policies* that make economic development more likely and to the political context in which such policies may arise.

This is not the place for a thorough-going alternative account of Brazil's historical development but a few examples will illustrate the shortcomings of imputing too minor a role to internal political factors. Skidmore, for instance, in explaining; the origins of the Estado Novo, underlines the extent to which it was not so much the mechanically determined outcome of Brazil's economic position, or the political alignments this gave rise to, as 'a highly personal creation' of Vargas himself (1967, p. 32). Again, in seeking to explain the factors that led to Goulart's overthrow, Skidmore demonstrates the importance of the nature of political institutions between 1945 and 1964 and their failure to adapt to changing social circumstances, in particular the fact that no political party emerged adequately reflecting 'centre' middle-class opinion, which continued to express itself 'as it had throughout the history of the Republic', through the army (Skidmore, 1967, p. 120). At the same time the existence during this period of 'democratic' institutions meant that a wide range of interests had to be at least partially accommodated, in ways that 'could significantly affect economic policy making', as in the spheres of credit policy, wage policy and foreign investment. With the imposition of military rule in 1964, 'the independent sources of influence have been progressively eliminated in favour of a technocrat-dominated system that creates a minimum of institutionalised opposition' (Skidmore, 1973, p. 36). All these observations are not incompatible with an emphasis on the constraints arising from Brazil's insertion into the world capitalist economy, but they show how political consequences of changing economic circumstances can then have implicatations of their own for subsequent development. At other times still greater autonomy for the political could be claimed as when the institutions and alliances inherited from the Estado Novo, notably the *sindicatos* and the PTB, thwarted the move to prevent Goulart becoming president, even though in Frank's view the economic situation was 'ripe' for a military coup. So these examples lead us to conclude that an account of specific historical events couched largely in economic reductionist terms as with this type of dependency approach glosses over a significant level of political determination.

But second, Frank does not sufficiently acknowledge the salience of political factors in the more long-term determination of Brazil's development. If we accept the arguments cited above about the possibility of associated capitalist development it becomes necessary to examine the nature and relations of the various social groups and classes within a given country. We return to the question of class later in this chapter, but one particular aspect that is relevant here concerns the formation and role of the national bourgeoisie. Frank, it will be remembered, is not prepared to concede that the bourgeoisie has any significant independent role to play at all. Other writers on Brazil, however, would disagree. Evans (1979a), for example, in his very detailed study of Brazilian development argues that while it can in no way be described as economically or politically dominant, the Brazilian national bourgeoisie has been able to establish a sufficiently firm position in the local economy for it to exert some leverage on the multi-nationals through the mediation of the Brazilian state. How has this been possible? Frank tends to take for granted the existence of a national bourgeoisie that availed itself of the opportunities created by the weakening of metropolis-satellite ties, first during the First World War and then during the Depression, to establish Brazilian industry. But Evans shows how specific features of Brazil's earlier development assisted this process. For instance, the fact that by the turn of the century Brazil's major export crop, coffee, was in the hands of local rather than foreign capital, made possible local capital accumulation which 'found its way into the development of infrastructures and later into industrialisation itself' (Evans, 1979a, p. 61). Another factor was the entrepreneurial role played by Brazilianised immigrants from Europe.

Whereas Frank discounts the independent significance of Third World States, seeing them as mere agents of metropolitan interests, Evans emphasises the complexity of the state's relationship with the metropolis. The Third World state, he agrees, is constrained by metropolitan interests since foreign capital controls a growing share of the most dynamic sectors of the economy but, in Brazil, the state is almost bound to respond to pressures from the national bourgeoisie and has intervened in a number of ways, most notably the implicit threat of nationalisation, to induce multi-nationals to make concessions to local capital, allowing local research and development facilities for instance. The Brazilian state is, though, more than a mere agent or mediator between international and local capital. It has its own interests in long-term local capital accumulation and in extending its control over the Brazilian economy, most obviously through the expansion of state-owned enterprises. Not only have the powerful and relatively successful state enterprises set up under Estado Novo, such as Petrobras, CSN (steel) and the electricity generating companies, been retained and developed by the present military regime, despite the initial economic liberalism of Castello Branco, but the number of new state economic enterprises has increased more rapidly than in the previous era. The State has also engaged in a growing number of joint ventures with multi-nationals. These ventures, Evans believes, have turned out to be a means of involving multi-nationals in local capital accumulation.

Dependency Theory and Africa

So far we have devoted a considerable amount of space to discussing dependency theory in relation to Brazil. This is partly because in focusing on Brazil we can link up with arguments raised in previous chapters, but mainly because a fair amount of the dependency literature is concerned with Brazil. Indeed dependency as a general approach was developed in the context of Latin America, a point to which we must return. For the time being, and bearing in mind the criticisms raised above, we must ask whether it is not possible that Brazil is untypical of the Third World generally. Brazil is after all a highly developed country as evidenced by the fact that it is currently exporting armoured cars to Iraq for use in the Gulf War. A counterpart of this relatively developed economy is a complex social structure with the process of class formation well advanced. In other words do we not here encounter the set of conditions which are most likely to point up the weaknesses of a Frankian type dependency approach? If we turned to other areas of the Third World, Tropical Africa for instance, may we not there discover that the degree of underdevelopment is such that the internal socio-political structure is indeed virtually an appendage of the world capitalist economy?

Interestingly Colin Leys initially regarded state and bourgeoisie in Kenya as entirely subservient to the needs and interests of metropolitan capital (see Leys, 1974). However, Leys has more recently revised this view: by 1977 the Kenyan bourgeoisie, apart from its heavy involvement in commercial farming, had made substantial inroads into real estate, construction, mining, insurance and even manufacturing. This means that capital accumulation at the local level has taken place to such a degree that the interests of the indigenous bourgeoisie may increasingly conflict with those of the metropolitan bourgeoisie. The Kenyan bourgeoisie has used and will continue to use the state apparatus to consolidate its position in relation to social and political forces both inside and outside the country. Leys' main point is that it is in the interests of an analytically sound political economy that we examine the history of specific national bourgeoisies in order to determine how each was originally able to accumulate capital and the extent to which this has led to subsequent opportunities for industrialisation and further capital accumulation at the periphery (Leys, 1978).

If we turn to Nigeria we encounter a bourgeoisie, fractions of which man the state apparatus, which seems to acquiesce readily in the interests of metropolitan capital. The oil industry is absolutely central to Nigeria's economy, accounting for almost one-third of the country's GDP (compared with less than 1 per cent in the late 1950s), as well as for 85 per cent of export earnings. The 1975/80 Development Plan described the oil industry as 'the main engine of growth of the Nigerian economy'. Nonetheless this vital area is still overwhelmingly in the hands of expatriate oil companies. As of 1978 little progress had been made in the transfer of technology to Nigerians. The oil companies have continued to contract work abroad and have managed local operations without government involvement. According to Terisa Turner writing at the end of the 1970s, 'Little has changed in Nigerian oil beyond a much larger transfer of money from companies to the state. The government remains very much a passive tax collector' (Turner, 1980, p. 210).

This government passivity has been very much encouraged by incumbents in the upper echelons of the state bureaucracy into whose hands have flowed millions of naira in the form of kickbacks paid out by the oil companies through local intermediaries (compradors), for access to strategic areas of the Nigerian political and economic system. Were indigenous technical expertise to develop to the point where it could be given an institutional expression then these lucrative channels would be by-passed or cut off. Not surprisingly, then, compradors in the public sector have blocked the emergence of a potentially competitive 'para-statal' (state-run enterprise) and have overridden attempts by Nigerian technocrats to promote the transfer of technology.

Yet to conclude from this that the Nigerian bourgeoisie and the Nigerian state are entirely subservient to the dictates of foreign capital would be simplistic. Such a view would assume that all or most of the Nigerian bourgeoisie, a vast and diverse category in itself, were able to avail themselves of the substantial perquisites which flowed in with the oil money. To be sure, the oil wealth filtered down from the upper layers of the state vastly expanding opportunities for profit in areas ranging from importing luxury goods – videos, colour televisions, Mercedes cars – to the spectacularly lucrative building and renting of houses in the tree-lined ex-colonial suburbs of the major cities. But even under favourable circumstances when oil revenues were at their highest, substantial sectors of the Nigerian bourgeoisie and those with bourgeois aspirations found themselves, at best, on the periphery of the state-sponsored distribution of spoils or, at worst, excluded from it altogether. Accordingly since the early 1970s opposition to the comprador state has expressed itself in the form of a nationalistic drive to loosen the grip of expatriate interests on the economy. The 1972 Indigenisation Decree reserved large areas of economic activity for Nigerians: advertising and public relations, blending and bottling alcoholic drinks, brick and block making, bread making, and retail trading are some of these areas. Foreign companies operating in other specified areas had to meet a minimum size requirement as well as accepting a fixed proportion of local shareholding. In order to facilitate the acquisition of equity by Nigerians the banks, now 40 per cent government owned, were required to allocate at least 40 per cent of their loans to indigenes. A second decree five years later pushed the process further, aiming at whole or part indigenisation of all foreign enterprises in the country. Writing in the mid-1970s, before this second decree, Gavin Williams felt able to talk about the consolidation of Nigeria's 'capitalist class' and was envisaging further conflict between this class and expatriate capital over control of the economy and a greater share in profits (Williams 1976, pp. 32, 33).

The breathtaking dissipation of the country's oil wealth by the politicians and bureaucrats of the second republic (1979–83) alienated all levels of Nigerian society including substantial sectors of the bourgeoisie struggling now to feed off a rapidly shrinking economic pie. Hence the almost total lack of opposition to the military coup of 31 December 1983. Given the military's expressed commitment to cleaning up the public sector, it seems likely that the comprador element will come under increasing pressure, and that, concomitantly, technocrats and other nationalistically oriented fractions will attempt to seize the opportunity to assert greater control over the economy. This does not of course mean that the Nigerian economy, particularly the oil industry, will soon cease to be under the overall dominance of expatriate interests. The point being made is that within this context of dominance there is room for manoeuvre and that an appreciation of the character of the manoeuvrings is as essential to a proper understanding of the nature of underdevelopment as a thorough knowledge of the chains of dependency.

From Dependency Theory to Modes of Production

It is important to emphasise that in reviewing the relevance of dependency theory for the study of political change in the Third

World we have dealt so far only with the work of A. G. Frank and with Frank's early work at that. In what sense is Frank's writing typical of dependency theory generally? May the criticisms we have made so far be applied to other writers working with this perspective? According to one critic, Tony Smith, the answer to this question is in the affirmative. For Smith the chief characteristic of the dependency school's approach to the study of underdevelopment is its basic focus on the international economic system as a 'whole'. This pre-occupation with the whole has led dependency into neglecting the parts, that is to say variations at the periphery, variations between indigenous political forces and traditions. The course of development of the whole system, Smith maintains, is to some degree affected by the nature of its interaction with locally structured forces. A proper understanding of this complex part-whole relationship demands that the prime focus for analysis is the 'organisation of the state' in Third World countries (Smith, 1979, p. 260). Neglect of the state and the course of its development in specific countries has led the dependistas into promoting a simplistic view of underdevelopment.

Somewhat surprisingly the writers Smith devotes most space to criticising are not, strictly speaking, dependency theorists. Frank's mentor Paul Baran is singled out for exaggerating the destructive effects of colonialism in the Indian sub-continent. Baran's analysis, Smith charges, takes no account of the socio-economic conditions that existed prior to the invasion of the Europeans, particularly the weakness of the Mogul state and its excessive exploitation of its peasantry. Special attention, however, is reserved for Immanuel Wallerstein's world system approach. Wallerstein's perspective is basically very similar to dependency theory and his starting point, which is to assert that the world system has been capitalist since the sixteenth century, is the same as Frank's. Wallerstein rejects the analysis of underdevelopment within any specific territorial unit claiming that the phenomenon can be understood only in relation to the cyclical rhythms and secular trends of the world economy as a whole. This world economy is divided fundamentally between a 'core' and a 'periphery'. In core economies are located advanced economic activities such as manufacturing, banking and the processing of primary products. The activities of peripheral economies are more or less restricted to the production of primary products. Between these two poles lie semi-peripheral areas which trade with both core and periphery and occupy a kind of half-way house position in terms of such features as profit margins and wage levels. As with Baran and Frank, Wallerstein's world economy is structured in such a way that surplus flows from periphery to core. But the appropriation of surplus by northern core economies is explained not just by the international division of labour nor by their technological headstart. World inequality is underpinned by political power. Core economies are able to develop strong state structures, strong that is, both internally and in relation to other states. Peripheral economies have weak states which means that these areas are unable to control the terms under which they relate to the international economy. Their subservient economic position is thereby confirmed (Wallerstein, 1974, ch. 7). Again like Frank and Baran, Wallerstein attributes to peripheral elites (compradors) a collaborationist role in the appropriation of surplus by the core. There can be little doubt that the state, for Wallerstein, is virtually a by-product of the international economy. In fact he goes so far as to claim that 'there are today no socialist systems in the world economy any more than there are feudal systems because there is one world system. It is a world economy and it is by definition capitalist in form' (quoted in Smith, 1979, p. 263). The fundamental political reality of this world system is not therefore the state but the class struggle. This is not always, though, unequivocally a *class* struggle as class consciousness articulates with ethnic consciousness, nationalism and internationalism.

Smith is particularly critical of what he sees as Wallerstein's devaluation of the state's importance for development. He points out first of all, citing other critics of Wallerstein, that the latter's historical analysis is quite simply incorrect. The strong states of the sixteenth century were not in the core (England and Holland), but on the periphery (Spain and Sweden). Holland during this period was ruled by a federation of merchant oligarchs while the English state, notably deficient in both centralised bureaucracy and standing army, depended heavily on a mercantile elite and local notables. Neither do the late industrialisers, sometime peripherals like Germany, Russia and

Japan, conform with Wallerstein's paradigm. In all of these a crucial role was played by a strong state during the actual process of industrialisation. These countries, furthermore, have their parallels in the contemporary Third World where the strong 'bureaucratic authoritarian' state seems to be associated, according to a number of writers, with a specific state of capitalist development: 'Such regimes are linked to a particular phase (or crisis) of capital accumulation encountered in the maturation of dependent industrialising countries' (Smith, 1979, p. 265). In other words we appear to encounter strong states at the periphery, a phenomenon which Wallerstein's model finds it difficult to explain. The explanation of the existence of strong states in the periphery, according to Smith, must be based around the pattern of historical development specific to the country in question. For example, bureaucratic authoritarianism in contemporary Latin America can only be understood as a reaction to the upsurge of populist nationalism from the 1930s on. At this point Smith presents an argument which is very similar to that of Nun which we encountered in the previous chapter. The First World War and the Great Depression propelled on to the political scene populist leaders like Vargas and Perón firmly opposed to foreign domination and internal compradors, mainly landed oligarchs. Determined to develop their respective countries along nationalist lines the populists forged an alliance between the middle classes and the masses. By the 1950s, however, ISI was running out of steam and the boom in primary product prices was coming to an end. The populist coalition, now no longer able to promote growth or ensure political stability, disintegrated. In order to contain mass pressure dominant groups opted for a military authoritarian solution. So for Smith the explanation of authoritarianism in Latin America lies not in the dependent status of the continent, but in the 'internal evolution of its social and political forces' (Smith, 1979, p. 267).

Smith's criticisms of Wallerstein seem to carry considerable force although it must be said that Wallerstein's 'theory' is couched at such a level of generality and, in the words of one critic, 'with such elegant imprecision' (Evans, 1979b, p. 17), that it is virtually impossible to refute. Nonetheless Wallerstein's explicit rejection of the nation state as a datum of analysis inevitably marginalises the political as we understand it. However, can Wallerstein's position be taken to be representative of dependency theory in general? Smith's implicit view is that it can. Smith, though, is not entirely fair to dependency theory of which there are a number of exemplars. For example he mentions only in passing the work of F. H. Cardoso and does not consider what is a major contribution to our understanding of social and political change in Latin America, Cardoso and Faletto's *Dependency and Development in Latin America*, written in the late 1960s and first published in English in 1976. Smith's neglect of this work is especially puzzling in the light of his observation (quoted above) about the internal evolution of social and politial forces as Cardoso and Faletto's aim is precisely to examine in considerable detail these forces within an overall dependency perspective.

It would be impossible in this context to give more than an indication of Cardoso and Faletto's extremely sophisticated survey. For them the structural dependency perspective focuses on the interrelationship between three levels: the international economy, the nation state and the alliance of social classes within the state. The writers are very clear that the state in Latin America is in no sense a passive agency 'mechanically conditioned by external dominance' (Cardoso and Faletto, 1979, p. 173). The state is a system of domination which relates dialectically to external factors and one of the tasks they set themselves is to develop concepts which will enable them to explain 'how internal and external processes of political domination relate one to the other'(Cardoso and Faletto, 1979, p. xviii). Essentially their position is that the process of economic expansion in the more developed countries of Latin America – Argentina, Brazil, Chile and Mexico – has posed the problem at the level of national politics of the incorporation of new social groups: the industrial and commercial bourgeoisie and elements of the popular sectors. The quest for a stake in the system on the part of such groups, together with the need of the state to reconcile economic expansion with political stability, led to the emergence of varying patterns of alliance. The variations from country to country depended upon their respective resource bases before the period of ISI, the nature and degree of foreign involvement and the consequent balance of social forces.

In Argentina, for example, the path of development was such

that there had emerged a dynamic indigenous agro-exporting sector before the Great Depression. The existence of this exporting sector permitted the creation of an industrial sector based upon it as well as a strong financial constituent. These were the groups who spearheaded economic expansion in the 1930s and 1940s taking advantage of the crisis in world markets. Their main problems were to keep control of the expanding economy and contain pressure from below. For a variety of complex reasons efforts at containment were unsuccessful. New social groups that were being mobilised and incorporated into the labour force could not be incorporated at a political level either from above along corporatist (that is, state sponsored) lines, or within the old trades union structure, dominated as it was by skilled immigrant workers. The outcome was a break-down of the existing system of bourgeois domination as well as the old-style union structure. Perónist populism is seen as an attempt to break out of the impasse without losing the impetus of economic growth; growth, it should be noted, based firmly on private enterprise. The problem of the further incorporation of the masses was dealt with by the state which undertook the role of arbitrator in the class struggle as well as redistributing income (through wage increases, establishment of welfare services and so on) to white-collar workers and sections of the working class. This process of incorporation, however, could continue only so long as terms of trade remained favourable. The end of the export boom after the Korean War presented the dominant sectors in Argentina with two alternatives: to hold down wages and public expenditure at the expense of the masses; or to reorganise and raise the productivity of the agro-exporting sector using it to finance further industrial expansion. The fall of Perón in 1955 represented a victory for anti-populist forces with their preference for containment of mass pressure. However, the agro-exporting sector was insufficiently powerful to impose such a solution even in alliance with a weak industrial bourgeoisie. Hence frequent appeals for assistance from the military have been an enduring feature of Argentinian politics since the fall of Perón. But continuing resistance to the authoritarian solution from the popular sectors already mobilised during the populist phase has impeded growth and the attainment of political stability.

The path taken by Brazil within the same overall international context has been quite different. In contrast to Argentina Brazil did not have an indigenous entrepreneurial class powerful enough to neutralise the 'traditional oligarchy' ('various segments of the exporting sector and of the non-exploiting latifundista groups', Cardoso and Faletto, 1979, p. 138). So when Brazil entered the period of ISI power was still largely in the hands of this traditional oligarchy. Because of the absence of a powerful entrepreneurial class industrialisation did not follow the liberal course taken by Argentina but one characterised by extensive economic regulation by the state as well as the creation of state enterprises. Not only did the Brazilian state promote basic industries such as transport and electric power but participated in the development of consumer durable sectors such as automobiles. Industrialisation policy in Brazil was therefore characterised by 'economic nationalism'. But how could such an orientation succeed in a context containing such diverse elements as traditional landowners, urban popular sectors, middle classes and entrepreneurial groups in industry and commerce? Because, answer Cardoso and Faletto, those groups who gained control of the state after 1930 'were influenced more by political than by economic considerations in pursuing industrialization' (Cardoso and Faletto, 1979, p. 139). Economic considerations appear to be an interest in creating a domestic market which would become the engine of self-sustained growth. A 'political' option was forced on the Brazilian government by the creation of a large, unemployed and potentially volatile urban sector, forced out of agriculture by declining opportunities. Since the (private) capitalist sector was unable to respond quickly enough to the exigencies of mass employment the state was compelled to step into the breach. The alliance upon which economic nationalism was based comprised the most backward (that is, traditional latifundist) groups of landowners, farmers who produced for the domestic market, the urban middle class, industrial sectors and the urban mass. Excluded were the agro-exporting coffee growers who had controlled the state before 1930. Also excluded was the peasantry since its inclusion would have alienated the latifundists. The populism of Vargas was the somewhat vague expression of this attempt to incorporate the urban masses. Cardoso and Faletto suggest that it differed from Perónist populism in that it was not based upon the creation of strong trades unions: 'It was less an economic definition of workers' rights than a political movement in favour of the "humble" ' (Cardoso and Faletto, 1974, p. 141).

Although this phase of Brazilian development was based on substantial state involvement in the economy this did not exclude the participation of private capital. In fact initially the private sector needed the state for credits. But as Brazil's economic base expanded and capital became available from the export sector and from abroad, opposition to statism began to emerge. The policy of state promotion of industry was carried forward from the Estado Novo through the Dutra dispensation (1946–50) into Vargas's second term (1950–4). The commodity boom during the Korean War enabled Brazil to accumulate foreign exchange which could be used to give a further boost to industrialisation. Although opposed to state intervention, especially to exchange control, the export sector accepted protectionism and domestic expansion so long as its incomes were maintained by the price of coffee. The deterioration of the coffee market after 1954 threw the coffee farmers into an alliance with elements of the middle-class opposition along with domestic and international financial groupings. When internal opposition was augmented by pressure from the US uneasy at the nationalist direction of Vargas's policies, the populist alliance fell apart. It was revived briefly, however, under Goulart who attempted to broaden its base not only by extending participation and economic benefits to the masses, but also including sections of the peasantry. Such a policy obviously, alienated the landowners. It also alienated sections of the national bourgeoisie since further incorporation of the masses must divert capital from accumulation. Acting largely on behalf of bourgeois and landowner fractions the military moved in 1964 to bring Brazil's populist phase of development to an end.

Argentina and Brazil represent two modes of dependent industrialisation, with the former following a 'liberal' path dominated by private capital, and the latter a 'nationalist-populist' path where the development impetus comes from various social groups linked through the state apparatus (Cardoso and Faletto, 1979, p. 133). In fact Cardoso and

Faletto outline a third mode which they refer to as the 'developmentalist state'. This path is more typical of 'enclave' economies where there is considerable foreign domination. In order to overcome a weak domestic capital situation as well as combat a powerful foreign presence, the state must not only promote industrial development but in addition forge an alliance between already mobilised popular sectors and the middle classes. This is the path taken by Chile and Mexico. It differs from the liberal path through the absence of an indigenous entrepreneurial sector and from the national – populist by the prior mobilisation of the masses. It must be said that Mexico with its incorporation, especially under Cardenas (1934–40), of the popular forces into the single mass party, Partido Revolucionario Institucional, seems to fit this model better than Chile.

Overall development in Latin America depended on an improvement in the terms of trade and the extension of benefits to broader sectors of the population. The period of expansion under ISI and during the favourable circumstances of the 1940s and 1950s permitted some degree of mass incorporation through some form of populist alliance (Argentina and Brazil) or the developmentalist state (Chile and Mexico). However, the incorporation of the peasantry and the further extension of benefits to the urban masses was incompatible with the interests of landowners and, after the collapse of the post-war boom, with those of the urban bourgeoisie. With the breakdown of the populist alliance the pattern that has emerged with varying degrees in Latin America is modernisation in an authoritarian context. A new kind of oligarchy in association with foreign capital manipulates the state for its own benefit at the expense of an increasingly marginalised (un- or under-employed) population. Cardoso and Faletto, though, do not see this as an inexorable and unalterable trend. Although the possibilities for action are hedged around by external constraints, various kinds of social and political movements can arise. The character and performance of such movements will depend 'not on academic predictions, but on collective action guided by political wills that make work what is structurally barely possible' (Cardoso and Faletto, 1979, p. 176).

This is not the context in which to engage in a detailed

critique of Cardoso and Faletto. We will instead make a few general observations which will help our argument forward. *Dependency and Development in Latin America* is set at a high level of generality, although to be fair this is probably inevitable in a survey of this scope. Nonetheless Cardoso and Faletto's argument does depend for its validity on the analytical viability of certain rather general categories. For example it will be apparent by now that the notion of 'populism' figures prominently in their developmental scenario. This would be fine if the ideological content of populism were unproblematic. Cardoso and Faletto indeed seem to regard the term as unproblematic since they introduce it without feeling the need to specify its contents in any detail. In fact populism is an extremely difficult term, at worst a 'sponge' concept (Worsley, 1970), a catch-all which can accommodate an extremely diverse range of collective behaviour. The employment of populism thus in our view demands some discussion of its allegedly distinctive features (see Ionescu and Gellner, 1969, and Laclau, 1977). Populism apart, Cardoso and Faletto's analysis rests fundamentally on the existence and activation of certain socio-economic categories: the traditional oligarchy, agro-exporting sectors, middle classes, commercial and industrial sectors, the masses, the 'humble' and so on. This position depends upon a number of assumptions: first, that these groups may in reality be differentiated from each other and that they have some kind of social identity vis-à-vis themselves and each other. Second that the interrelationships between these groups constitute the most appropriate metaphor for understanding the competition or struggle for national resources in Latin America. And arising out of this, third, that other forms of social relationship, for example feudal, clientelistic, ethnic, regional, parochial and so on, are at best marginal to the analysis of political change in Latin America. The above turn on the basic assumption that Latin American states have been very largely penetrated by capitalism and that class analysis constitutes the most suitable approach. This indeed may be a reasonable assumption but it needs to be looked at critically. In fact there exists a debate which deals precisely with this question and which is worth looking at not only because it relates to our present discussion but also because it will serve to introduce themes which will be treated in our next chapter.

In 1971 Ernesto Laclau published an essay, 'Feudalism and Capitalism in Latin America' (Laclau, 1971), which has had considerable influence on the study of change in the Third World. It is interesting to note, first of all, that this essay deals with an argument which is not just an academic debate over concepts and terms. In common with much of the writing discussed in this chapter, fundamental questions are being raised about political tactics. Debate on the Left in Latin America during the 1960s had centred around the question of whether the continent should be seen as feudal or capitalist in structure. If feudal then socialists should be seeking an alliance with the national bourgeoisie, forming a front against the landed oligarchy and their imperialist patrons. The opposing view saw Latin America as already capitalist and hence ripe for socialist revolution. As we have seen this was the position adopted by Frank, rejecting entirely the claim that Latin American societies are still feudal. Latin America, according to Frank, has been capitalist since it was incorporated into the world capitalist economy during the colonial period. The struggle therefore must be *against* the national bourgeoisie, which is anyhow a *comprador* bourgeoisie. The task in hand is then to 'defeat capitalism, not feudalism' (the title of one of Frank's essays, Frank, 1970).

In seeking to understand the debate between Laclau and Frank it is essential to appreciate that in Frank's view to maintain that Latin America is still basically feudal is, in effect, to adopt a dualist position. That is, it is to see Latin American economies as being split between a dynamic capitalist sector and a stagnant subsistence or feudal sector: feudalism is equated by Frank with a natural closed economy. Now even before Frank's writings had made their appearance, critics of dualism had attempted to show that the two sectors, far from being rigidly separated, were linked through manifold social and economic relationships. In effect they sought to demonstrate that the backwardness of the traditional sector was in fact a consequence of the dynamism of the modern sector. This was an argument that differed little from Frank's notion of the development of underdevelopment, although for Frank both sectors are un-equivocally capitalist; or rather there is only one, capitalist sector.

Laclau's thesis is really an extension of what one might call this critical dualist position. Laclau does not deny that the backwardness of one sector of any economy may be the result of the dynamism of another sector. What he does maintain, however, is that the emergence of a capitalist sector does not *ipso facto* entail the elimination of pre-capitalist forms. Part of the problem, as Laclau sees it, lies in Frank's inadequate conceptualisation of capitalism. Frank sees the essence of capitalism as consisting of production for profit for the market and so is able to argue that the expansion of the world market from the sixteenth century was basically capitalist in character. The difficulty with this approach, says Laclau, is that it does not enable us to distinguish between a wide range of producers operating in quite different socio-economic contexts. The Peruvian peasant, the Chilean or Ecuadorian serf, the slave on a West Indies sugar plantation, the Manchester textile operative: all are deprived of the economic surplus which they have helped to create and which is destined for the market. In all these and numerous other situations, the fundamental economic contradiction is indeed that which opposes exploiter and exploited. But to argue that each of these signifies capitalism would ultimately lead us to insisting that capitalism has existed since the neolithic revolution. We have ended up in this analytical impasse, Laclau believes, because we have ignored what for Marx is the fundamental feature of capitalism, the appropriation of labour power through the mechanism of the market, a condition made possible only by the separation of the producer from the means of production. Only with the appearance of 'free' labour may we properly speak of a capitalist mode of production.

If we accept that free labour is an indispensable component of capitalism, then capitalism could not be said to have existed in sixteenth-century Europe let alone the colonised areas of the New World. Whilst a powerful commercial class producing for an expanding market certainly was discernible in Europe at this time, its economic basis was predicated upon the appropriation of surplus through labour relationships that were pre-capitalist, that is relationships of feudal dependence. This means that the accumulation of capital and production for the market can co-exist with pre-capitalist forms of labour. Laclau goes on to show how in Latin America feudal relationships – relationships based on extra-economic coercion such as enforced labour obligations – occurred alongside production for the market. In fact he discovers in Latin America a parallel with what Engels referred to as the 'second servitude' in Eastern Europe when, from the sixteenth century, landowners intensified feudal obligations in an attempt to step up production for an expanding cereal market. Laclau documents a similar process of intensifed feudal exploitation in Chile at the end of the seventeenth century and again in the nineteenth century. As in Eastern Europe, the stimulus to increased exploitation was the expanding demand for cereals, in this case from Peru. This pattern, in which servile relations were reinforced in order to augment production for the external market, was repeated, with variations, throughout Latin America. Although such conditions were gradually modified, especially during the present century, semi-feudal characteristics, according to Laclau, are still to be found in the Latin American countryside.

Thus, concludes Laclau, to maintain that relations of production are feudal in nature does not necessarily imply support for the dualist thesis. Strict dualism asserts that there are no connections between the modern and the traditional sector. Laclau, on the contrary, is suggesting that the dynamism of the modern sector, its ability to respond to the market, is premised precisely on the maintenance, let alone the intensification, of pre-modern forms of exploitation in the traditional sector. In other words there is no question of the two sectors being cut off from each other. In the final analysis Laclau finds himself, paradoxically, in agreement with Frank that development does indeed generate underdevelopment, except that Laclau is arguing that exploitation is between two modes of production rather than within one capitalist mode of production.

Conclusion

In this chapter we have been concerned with the implications of dependency theory for the study of political change in the Third World. From a dependency perspective the fundamental weakness of the modernisation approach was its total neglect of the economic dimension, particularly its international aspect. In focusing attention on this level and on the process of incorporation of different areas of the world into the world capitalist economy, dependency theorists have undoubtedly given a valuable lead in the study of underdevelopment. However, from our point of view dependency's macro-focus has two principal weaknesses: first – a tendency to gloss over the degree of diversity at the periphery (Smith's internal evolution of social and political forces); and, second – and relatedly, a tendency to concede too little impact to these forces and especially to the state. These tendencies are particularly apparent in Frank's early writings (cf. Frank, 1978), and in Wallerstein's world systems approach. Cardoso and Faletto's study of Latin America is a laudable attempt to overcome the homogenising drift of the dependency perspective. Cardoso and Faletto demonstrate how a fundamental structural problem – the need to reconcile the creation of an industrial base with political stability – generated different responses and varying patterns of alliance in respective Latin American countries. Yet despite Cardoso and Faletto's explicit commitment to dealing with the political level, politics is conceived entirely in terms of the class struggle. This means that the state has only a shadowy existence; is at best merely an instrument which is used by this or that class or alliance of classes. The notion that the state may have some degree of autonomy, be above social groups and classes, is nowhere apparent in Cardoso and Faletto's study. Furthermore the overwhelming concentration on social class runs the risk of neglecting other patterns of association especially those arising out of pre-capitalist modes of production or their remnants. The assumption, implicit in Cardoso and Faletto's work, that Latin American social structures have been thoroughly permeated by capitalism seems to conflict with Laclau's thesis on the survival there of pre-capitalist forms (shades of Lenin on Imperialist Russia!). We should also bear in mind that Latin America is much more developed than the rest of the Third World. Accordingly when dealing with Asia, the Middle East and especially Tropical Africa, we need to be conceptually attuned to the likelihood of pre-capitalist relations continuing to play a significant role at all levels of political activity. In fact precisely the value of Laclau's contribution is that in sharpening up the distinctions between pre-capitalist and capitalist forms of labour it allows us better to understand the process of transition from one to the other; especially the way in which classes emerge or form out of pre-class structures.

Significantly Laclau's discussion of feudalism and capitalism in Latin America coincided with a massive upsurge of interest in Marxism, inspired in no small measure by leading exegete, Louis Althusser, and based upon a close reading of Marx' own writings. This outpouring has resulted in an extensive literature on modes of production and particularly on the interaction or articulation of one mode with another. It is not possible here to delve into the modes of production controversy (for a useful survey see Foster-Carter, 1978). Suffice it to say that this debate has focused very largely on the economic level, concentrating on the process of production and corresponding relations of production. This has usually meant that, as in the case of dependency theory, the political and the ideological have been somewhat marginal to modes of production analysis. Fortunately, however, the same source from which the modes of production debate derived – a close reading of Marx – has more or less simultaneously given rise to another stream of thought which has been concerned with the essential nature of the capitalist state. This is the starting point for our discussion, in the following chapter, of the new interest (and not only among Marxists) in the character and role of the state in the Third World.

5

A Politics of Class and State

The approaches we have been considering so far arose directly as a reaction to early modernisation perspectives. In the present chapter we turn to a more recent literature, written from a Marxist standpoint. While implicitly critical of the assumptions of modernisation theory, this literature is more specifically a response to the dependency debate. Such 'neo-Marxist' writers generally accept the main thrust of dependency theory's critique of 'classical' Marxism: that the possibilities of autonomous capitalist development in peripheral societies are severely limited by relations of economic dependency. But they also incorporate, to a greater or lesser extent, arguments of what could be called dependency 'revisionism', whether based on the feasibility of dependent capitalist development or asserting the survival of pre-capitalist modes of production, which imply a degree of freedom for Third World politics. They emphasise, therefore, the need to examine indigenous social structures: the nature and extent of social class formations, the 'projects' of different social classes, their conflicts and alliances. In so doing they have come increasingly to focus on the political role of the state not simply as a passive reflection or instrument of class struggle but possessed of sufficient 'relative autonomy' to be a significant, sometimes crucial participant in its own right. In this chapter we are primarily concerned to introduce the central themes and controversies of this often densely-argued literature, but we also note that a growing interest in the state as a key to understanding politics in the Third World is not confined to Marxists. It is emerging as a focal point for much current non-Marxist writing as well.

We are not, it should then be clear, suggesting any abrupt hiatus between the dependency perspectives discussed in the last chapter and those of the neo-Marxists, the more so since dependency theory itself retained much of the political orientation and even vocabulary of Marxism. Perhaps most important they share a belief in a progressive historical development (in some ways the counterpart of 'political development'?), achieved through social revolution and leading ultimately to a world-wide socialist order. The arguments, whether previously between classical Marxists and exponents of dependency theory or more recently between 'orthodox' dependency theorists and their new Marxist critics, have, in the last analysis, been about strategy: such questions as must there be a bourgeois revolution before the socialist, can an authentic bourgeois revolution or acceptable substitute be achieved within the constraints of economic dependence, and which alliance of indigenous social classes or fractions thereof holds out the best hopes for revolutionary change? This could be seen as a unifying thread running through the whole debate. What distinguishes the neo-Marxists is first their insistence on a meticulous social class analysis, in contrast to what Higgott (1983) has called the frequent 'banality' of dependency theory's class categories. Second is the emphasis on the state, itself strongly influenced by the increasingly sophisticated Marxist analysis of the modern capitalist state emerging by the late 1960s, in the writings of Nicos Poulantzas and others.

Class Formation at the Periphery

In the previous chapter we saw that critics of dependency theory, such as Laclau, did not accept that the introduction of capitalism in the peripheral economies simply wiped out pre-capitalist modes of production. The capitalist mode was dominant but 'articulated' with other pre-existing modes. Rather as in the modernisation revisionist thesis, it was argued that indeed the capitalist mode could strengthen, if temporarily, aspects of pre-capitalism: the actual term used was 'restructuration' or 'conservation'. This further implied that one 'social formation' at the periphery (often though not always standing for 'nation') could differ significantly in its structure from another. The political implications received less attention at this stage.

At the same time, Shanin (1982) suggests that Marxist hopes for a socialist revolution in the West had been raised and then dashed by the events of 1968. A search began for alternative agents of social revolution. One could even speak of a debate between traditional 'proletarianists', still faithful to the western working class, and 'Third Worldists', inspired by the revolutions in China, Cuba and elsewhere. To quote the introduction to a recent collection of essays on 'the struggles of Third World workers', 'the working classes in the metropoles (with some notable exceptions in Japan, France and Italy) appear to be quiescent, if not totally supine' (Cohen *et al.*, 1979, p. 9). In this context, interest grew in the nature and extent of social class formation in underdeveloped countries, from a more specifically political perspective.

Classical Marxism had contended that such countries *were* experiencing capitalist development, that their indigenous bourgeoisie, with the support of the nascent industrial proletariat, would achieve a bourgeois revolution, through the national struggle against neo-imperialism and that the industrial proletariat would then form the vanguard of the drive towards socialist revolution. Dependency theory maintained that such societies were already capitalist but not due to the independent struggle of the national bourgeoisie. Moreover the agents of the next, socialist revolution would not be the industrial proletariat but those at the very bottom of the social pile: the 'masses'.

The new Marxists are united more by their cautious, methodical approach than by a consensus view on these issues. They are less ready to pronounce on whether individual Third World countries have or have not yet undergone bourgeois revolution (see for instance Roxborough's discussion of bourgeois revolution as a 'disaggregated' process in Latin America, 1979, pp. 146–8). They are also less certain about the role of the national bourgeoisie, or perhaps one should say the possibility of generalising. As we shall see it is this interest in the political 'project' of the bourgeoisie and its relationship with other classes, class fractions and classes in formation, which could all be contenders for political dominance, that has contributed to concern with the state and the uses made of 'state power'.

What we are calling the neo-Marxist school, third, has undertaken a much more rigorous analysis of the structure of the lower tiers of rural and urban society, and this is where we shall begin. Of course their analysis is still uncompromisingly in terms of social class. We cannot engage here in a lengthy discourse on the meaning, for Marxists, of 'class' though, not surprisingly given its pivotal place in Marxist thinking, this is a much disputed question. Traditionally class has been understood as a social category based upon relations within the process of economic production. But while individuals may 'objectively' belong to the same class, it does not necessarily follow that they are either 'class-conscious' or share a common political vision. There are perennial problems in Marxism about the relationship between objective class membership and degrees of consciousness, the extent to which a given class has a 'class project': 'an historically grounded vision of itself, its place in society and a vision of future society, together with a more or less defined programme of action to implement this change' (Roxborough, 1979, p. 71). These problems are compounded in the Third World context where, if we accept the 'productionist' critique of dependency theory, several modes of production, each with its own social structure, can co-exist, and where, as will be suggested, the state has increasingly emerged as an additional locus of control of the means of production and therefore of class formation. Class structure is extremely fluid, with many of the most strategically placed classes still only in the process of formation. For these reasons, too, classes tend to be relatively 'weak'. Whether it is therefore appropriate to insist on the primacy of class however sophisticated its conceptualisation, in the analysis of Third World politics, is a question we shall return to.

To repeat, the traditional Marxist view was that the industrial proletariat, assisted by the poorer peasants, would be the main bearers of social revolution. But the 1960s, partly due to the influence of dependency theory, saw a general demotion of the industrial proletariat, expressed in what came to be known as the 'aristocracy of labour' thesis. We met this thesis in its original formulation as applied to the industrial workforce of western capitalist countries by Lenin: subsequently it was extended to the Third World. As Cohen points out, this low estimation of the indigenous proletariat's revolutionary potential was espoused by revolutionary leaders in all three continents: Mao Zedong in Asia, Che Guevara in Latin America and Frantz Fanon in Africa (1982). One of the most systematic academic accounts of this position was by Arrighi and Saul, in reference to Africa (1968). Their basic argument was that, beginning in the colonial period, a section of the African labour force had come increasingly to share in the wasteful consumption by indigenous elites of the economic surplus extracted from the peasantry. They described how

> the higher wages and salaries (established during the colonial period) foster the stabilisation of the better-paid section of the labour force whose high incomes justify the severances of ties with the traditional economy. Stabilisation, in turn, promotes specialisation, greater bargaining power, and further increases in the incomes of this small section of the labour force, which represents the proletariat proper of tropical Africa. These workers enjoy incomes three or more times higher than those of unskilled labourers and together with the elites and sub-elites in bureaucratic employment in the civil service and expatriate concerns, constitute what we call the labour aristocracy of tropical Africa (p. 149).

The political implication of this economic complicity was that the 'proletariat proper' would have little incentive to seek revolutionary change in a system which, through the monopolistic powers it conferred on their employers, preserved their own privileged position.

The corollary of this downgrading of the industrial proletariat was a tendency to re-evaluate the political contribution of the peasantry and to see them, with the support of the 'lumpenproletariat' as the true vehicles of revolution. In a sense the peasantry inherited the revolutionary mantle of the proletariat. Marx, as is well known, generally professed a very low opinion of the peasantry and its capacity for revolutionary class action. He spoke of the 'idiocy of rural life', and saw the virtually self-sufficient peasant households, individualistic and conservative, as resembling 'potatoes in a sack' (p. 239) incapable of coming together as a cohesive class at all, despite their objectively shared class position (1973). Among early Marxists there was too a widespread assumption that with the spread of capitalism into the countryside the peasantry would rapidly disappear, through a process of differentiation into capitalist farmers and landless labourers. But beginning with Lenin, there was a progressive reassessment of the peasantry as a political force and an enduring social entity. Eric Wolf in his famous study of what he called 'peasant wars' (1969), argued that the peasantry played a crucial part in the revolutions of Mexico, Russia, China, Vietnam, Cuba and Algeria, though the strength of his case in the last two instances is particularly disputed.

With this heightened appreciation went a growing interest in precisely which sectors of the peasantry were the most predisposed to rebellion. The peasantry, as we indicated in Chapter 2 (see pp. 52–3), is a broad category. Shanin has defined it as follows: 'The peasantry consists of small agricultural producers who, with the help of simple equipment and the labour of their families, produce mainly for their own consumption and for the fulfilment of obligations to the holders of political and economic power' (1971, p. 240). Clearly within this definition peasants can vary markedly in terms of wealth and independence. Wolf himself suggested that it was the 'tactically mobile' peasantry, which included both the 'middle peasants', sufficiently secure to take risks but not too rich to fear change, and those peasants living in areas where external controls were weakest – for instance the southern provinces of China or northern Mexico – who were the most prone to rebel (Wolf, 1969, p. 291). Other studies stressed the importance of the poorer peasants, either as a supplement to or as an alternative to the middle peasantry (Alavi, 1965; Zagoria, 1974).

Neo-Marxist intervention in this debate has been above all concerned to inject greater rigour into the analysis of urban and rural social structure. It looks for categories of analysis which are both clear and logical and do justice to the complexity of actual social phenomena as it perceives them. Such writers stress the intricacy and fluidity of urban and rural class formations and the interconnections between them. They are reluctant to generalise. Even so there is a perceptible tendency to reaffirm the old Marxist faith in the industrial proletariat, or at least the proletariat broadly conceived, and a corresponding scepticism where the peasantry is concerned.

In the first place the new Marxist writers insist on a much

more careful conceptualisation of the 'peasantry'. Some indeed deny that such a category can be accommodated within a modes of production framework. If there is no such thing as a peasant mode of production and, on the other hand, the peasantry is not a conceptually autonomous unit transferable from one mode of production to another, then perhaps the term should be abandoned altogether. But as Shanin (1979), who provides a useful summary of this controversy, convincingly reasons, it is throwing out the baby with the bathwater to drop the notion of a peasantry because it sits awkwardly within an abstractly derived frame of reference, when the peasantry or 'peasant syndrome', despite the inevitable heterogeneity of its forms, represents such a central datum of Third World experience. Other neo-Marxist contributions simply hold that efforts to distinguish different types of peasantry have not gone far enough. The peasantry must be examined in the context of differing modes of production and their articulation with capitalism. Even then their propensity to revolt can only be explained by reference to wider national, and of course international, political processes.

A good example of this approach is Lionel Cliffe's discussion of peasant mobilisation in East Africa (1982). In order to explain the variety of patterns such mobilisation has followed, he begins by looking at the interaction of different pre-colonial modes of production with the various ways in which they were incorporated into the capitalist economy. Colonial policy tended to impose a division of labour between the different regions of East Africa, with some designated as sources of minerals, others as areas of plantation farming, European settlement or peasant production of cash crops. To illustrate the range of outcomes possible from these different combinations, Cliffe contrasts the experience of the Kikuyu in Kenya and the Buganda in Uganda.

Originally the Kikuyu were small farmers, access to land was determined through the kinship system and there were few marked economic and political inequalities. By the turn of the century, European settlers were restricting the scope for bringing further land under cultivation and simultaneously recruiting, often by brutal methods, a Kikuyu labour force. The eventual effect was to greatly increase stratification within the

Kikuyu. Three broad groups emerged: the big farmers (including many former lineage heads and colonial servants), small peasants, and the landless, many of whom unsuccessfully sought work in the towns. An attempt to repatriate landless migrants in Nairobi to the already overcrowded native reserves triggered an armed uprising directed against not only the colonial regime but the privileged Kikuyu. This uprising had at least the passive support of the small peasantry. The colonial response was to shore up the economic and legal position of the small peasantry, with the result that when, after Independence in 1966, a tentative challenge was mounted to the continuation of these policies, it found support only amongst the landless Kikuyu minority.

In the kingdom of Buganda, by the era of colonisation, something close to a feudal mode of production prevailed. Here the object of British policy was to induce the peasantry to produce cash crops for export. Initially, bypassing the king, they appealed to the feudal chiefs, providing them with large estates where it was hoped they would establish cotton plantations. The chiefs, however, found it easier to allow peasant cultivation as before and extract a money rent. Accordingly the colonials switched to a policy of encouraging commercial peasant farming. A continuing labour shortage also eventually generated a substantial migration into the area. From this process a complex rural class structure emerged: at the summit were the big landowners, below them capitalist farmers and a kulak-type peasantry. The poor peasantry were divided between free landholders and tenants. Moreover – a point that Cliffe mentions but could perhaps give more weight to – they were divided between the indigenous Ganda and immigrant peoples. Given this social structure, the chances of peasant rebellion were remote (Cliffe, 1982).

It is apparent from Cliffe's analysis that the peasantry cannot always be relied on to rally to the cause of revolt. Elsewhere accounts of the peasantry's political role are still less confident. To say that peasants are 'always victims' (Roxborough, 1979, p. 94) is neither new nor all that easy to refute (though for a dissenting voice see Hyden, 1980). But recent Marxist writings have revived the notion that the peasantry will disappear, through a process of differentiation, even if this is longer and more complicated than previously supposed. A partial exception is made for Africa where, as Post (1972) argues, the currently dominant trend may be increasing 'peasantisation' of the previously primitive cultivators. Even while they are around, the general view is that peasants on their own or inspired by a radical intelligentsia, cannot make a revolution. As Roxborough (1979) states firmly, 'The peasantry, unlike the bourgeoisie or the proletariat, is not a potential historic class; it has no hegemonic mission and its vision of society is limited to a reproduction of peasant social structure' (p. 94). The peasantry has to be led and it has to be in alliance with the proletariat. Otherwise it can be subverted, as in a number of African countries where the ruling bourgeoisie (of which more later) collaborates with the peasantry in order to keep the industrial proletariat at bay (see Sklar, 1979, p. 549). However, the pendulum of appreciation has not swung all the way back. It is now generally recognised that a necessary though not sufficient condition of a successful revolution is the support of the peasantry. Petras' formulation is often cited with approval in this connection:

It appears that in most of the socialist revolutions the original impetus, organization, leadership, and ideology of the revolutionary struggle began precisely in the more 'advanced' sectors of the peripheral economy . . . In all cases, however, the *success* of the revolution which began in the advanced enclaves depended on joining efforts with the bulk of the social forces (peasants) located in the 'backward' areas of the economy (1975, p. 307).

If the peasantry has been downstaged, the notion of a revolutionary 'lumpenproletariat' has found still less favour. For one thing, the lumpenproletariat as originally depicted by Marx, consisted of the predominantly rootless, criminal urban element, and far from being the inflammable tinder of social revolution, was manipulated by counter-revolutionary movements. But as used by Fanon (1967) and others, the term covered the very numerous group of the urban poor who were not regular wage-earners. As Sandbrook (1982) points out, in African cities this would include 'the petty producers, along with their apprentices and journeymen . . . the petty traders and providers of petty services, casual labourers, urban cultivators' (p. 156). Such a heterogenous social aggregate would be unlikely to develop a common class consciousness. Not only would individuals within it often be recent or even temporary migrants form the rural hinterland, but within the city they would be subject to various forms of 'vertical' political mobilisation, as clients of petty capitalist patrons or through the ethnic or communal associations.

On the other hand recent Marxist writings cast serious doubt on the labour aristocracy thesis. They criticise first the frequent inconsistencies and problems with the way the concept is defined or delimited, but more basically they question how far it really does constitute an economic elite. In the specific context of Africa, where this issue has received especial attention, we are reminded that statistics on income need to be interpreted in the light of information about the cost and standard of living of these workers and in the recognition that many of them remit a substantial portion of their income to rural relatives and urban dependants. Sandbrook further notes that the general effect of trades union activity and government legislation is the post-independence period has been to narrow income differentials between skilled and unskilled workers. But even if one could demonstrate real material differences this would not necessarily imply that skilled workers have a distinct consciousness of their own superior status and separate interests. The similarity in life-styles of wage-earners and non–wage-earners in African cities is regularly commented on. Moreover, in so far as the urban poor as a whole has upward aspirations, the role model appears to be not the wage-earner but the small self-employed individual who makes good.

The extent to which this section of the proletariat forms part of or identifies with the political elite is therefore debatable. As Roxborough (1979) points out, there is considerable counter-evidence in Latin America: the Chilean nitrate and copper miners who have been staunch supporters of left-wing parties and the Brazilian and Argentinian working class who followed relatively progressive leaders in Vargas and Goulart, and Perón respectively. One study of the urban working class in Lagos concludes that it is best viewed as the locally-based political elite of the urban masses, 'a reference group in political terms for other urban strata who substantially rely on the prevailing wage structure for satisfaction of their own interests in the urban arena, and, furthermore, look to the wage-earning class for expression of political protest against a highly inegalitarian society' (Peace, 1979, p. 134), though this might seem to contradict the earlier suggestion that the urban poor looks to the petty capitalists for its model and political leadership. One of the chief exponents of the labour aristocracy thesis has more recently acknowledged that while it was for a time valuable in checking 'proletarian messianism', it may have become less relevant in later years, though he still maintains that what Peace and others are describing is essentially *populist* politics, not socialist leadership. 'Revolutionary classes must be made of even sterner stuff' (Saul, 1979, p. 345).

But there has also been a tendency to move away from a narrow focus on the classical core of the urban proletariat, the skilled industrial wage-earners, to a wider definition of the working class. As Cohen writes, this needs to include not only fulltime wage-earners in establishments employing over ten persons, as in the traditional literature, but more marginal categories such as seasonal and temporary wage-earners. At the same time, he and others have stressed the growing importance of wage-earners in the countryside. Into this category fall not only the increasing number of agricultural labourers in India, for instance, or the 'plantation proletariat' of Latin America, but those employed in rural factories. He cites the example of the California-based multi-national, Del Monte, which by 1967 owned canneries and plantations in 20 countries. In the Bajio valley of Mexico alone, 5250 workers were employed in the field factories. The terms 'peasantariat' has even been coined for this hybrid type of worker. The working class conceived in this broader way is rapidly expanding and has already and repeatedly demonstrated its capacity for militant action, for instance in Africa and Asia workers' organisations have usually been to the fore in anti–colonial and nationalist, if not yet socialist struggles (Cohen, 1982). Sandbrook (1982) sounds a similar cautiously optimistic note: in Africa the peculiar patterns of peripheral capitalist development have largely prevented the emergence of an organised labour movement, the working-class, elsewhere the lynchpin of social reform, is small and relatively recent, only semi-proletarianized, and mainly non-industrial . . . Nonetheless, national working classes are growing in size and stability and sections of these have, under special conditions, developed a radical, though non-revolutionary, class consciousness. Their influence on development strategy in the future may therefore not be negligible. (p. 218).

The Struggle for Class Dominance and the State

Whatever their estimation of the respective merits of peasants, workers and the urban poor, the new Marxists would agree with Roxborough that 'the political behaviour of any class, group or category is not an inherent function of the class itself but rather a result of its interaction with other classes, in the context of the overall political system' (1979, p. 87). The nature of the class or class alliance, which dominates a political system, occupies a central place in their analysis, and it has emerged as a question inseparable from an understanding of the character of the 'state' in Third World societies.

In the cruder versions of dependency theory, these issues were seen as unproblematic. Whatever its social derivation, the political elite was an agent of the international capitalist class, and the state was simply the instrument of its rule. The revisions to dependency theory we have outlined implied however an altogether more complicated range of possibilities. On the one hand, once it was conceded that in certain countries associated, or even autonomous, capitalist development was feasible, the nature of the state and its policies became a significant variable.

On the other, the productionist critique implied that indigenous social structures would vary and that accordingly the composition of the dominant class or classes could not be predicted but had to be separately investigated in each case. The implications went further. For as we have seen the picture that now emerged was of a society in which distinct dominant classes or classes aspiring to dominate could co-exist. Beside the representatives of metropolitan capital could be found for instance feudal or quasi-feudal classes and the indigenous bourgeoisie, and these indigenous classes might be at different stages of formation, weak and internally divided. No single hegemonic class could be assumed to dominate the political system: certainly no fully-fledged national bourgeoisie, secure in its control of the domestic means of production, in the form encountered in western industrialised societies. Instead the indigenous bourgeoisie as such tended to be weak, and its ascendance over the 'middle class' of urban professionals and even the petty bourgeoisie (whether very small-scale capitalists or occupying intermediate state managerial roles) was by no means established. All these categories of class analysis and still more the way they are applied to underdeveloped societies are of course themselves highly problematic. Our main point here is, however, that the complexity of dominant class composition in the Third World context meant that the character of the state, from a Marxist viewpoint, could not be taken for granted. And neo-Marxists were the more inclined to recognise this in view of recent developments in Marxist theorising about the state in advanced capitalist societies. At this point therefore we need to consider the evolution of Marxist theories of the state and to begin with how the state was originally conceived of by Marx and Engels themselves. The problem here is that it is not easy to derive a systematic theory of the state from Marx's own writings. Such a theory was projected to take up a substantial part of *Capital* but never materialised, so instead we must rely on the observations scattered throughout Marx's writings supplemented by those of Engels.

However, from these emerges one fairly consistent line of interpretation, what Miliband (1965) has termed the primary view of the state. Actually this takes two forms: first, the form and function of the state reflects and is largely determined by the economic base of society. That is, the state forms part of the 'superstructure'. Alternatively the state is seen as an instrument used in its own interests by the economically dominant class. The classical statement of this position in regard to the capitalist state is in the *Communist Manifesto*: 'The executive of the modern state is but a committee for managing the common affairs of the whole bourgeoisie'. It was this primary view that long dominated Marxist thinking about the state, especially as it was incorporated wholesale by Lenin in his influential pamphlet, originally published in 1917, *The State and Revolution* (1970).

There is however a secondary, more intermittent theme of interpretation that accords the state rather more autonomy, at least under special circumstances, and some would argue by inference much of the time. One of the earliest Marxist thinkers to explore aspects of this alternative construction was Antonio Gramsci. He was not only a theorist but actively engaged in revolutionary communist politics in the Italy of the 1920s and 1930s. As such he sought the political strategy most likely to achieve revolution in the more advanced capitalist countries, which seemed to require a more complex analysis of the political level of the class struggle than that provided by orthodox Marxist–Leninism. While therefore he accepted the fundamental role of economic relations in determining political change and an eventual socialist revolution, he stressed their mediation by relatively autonomous political forces and ideologies. He understood the state in capitalist societies as essential to maintaining the dominance of the bourgeoisie, securing its long-term interests and unification. The state embodied two 'modalities' of class domination; the use of force but also the exercise of cultural 'hegemony', that is the active consent of the ruled. To achieve such hegemony was not simply a matter of instilling 'false consciousness': it required, for instance, concessions to popular interests and appeal to 'national' objectives and values which apparently transcended class interests. Nor was the achievement of bourgeois dominance automatic but a constantly vulnerable process (for a useful discussion of Gramsci's theory of the state, see Jessop, 1982, ch. 4).

Much of Gramsci's writing, due to censorship within the communist movement, only became common knowledge in the late 1950s but then it played a seminal part in stimulating and directing interest in the nature of the capitalist state. Roughly a decade later, two Marxist political theorists, quite different in their methodology but sharing a considerable debt to Gramsci, Ralph Miliband and Nicos Poulantzas, engaged in a well-known argument on just this question. Each criticised the other for taking an excessively limited, determinist view. Miliband was accused of 'instrumentalism', in the specific sense that, notably in *The State in Capitalist Society* (1969), he made use of a sociological analysis of those holding key state positions to show how the (economically) dominant class controls the state apparatus. Miliband has, however, made it clear that he does *not* subscribe to the view of the state simply as a passive instrument of class rule (see Miliband, 1977, pp. 66–74). At the same time Miliband charged Poulantzas with determinism in that he espoused, especially in his first full-length analysis of the capitalist state (originally published in 1968) *Political Power and Social Classes* (1973), the 'structuralist' approach developed by Louis Althusser, depicting the state as a series of structures which were of their nature bound to function in the ultimate interests of the dominant class. Poulantzas, though, was concerned to show that precisely in order to promote these ultimate interests, the state could not be the instrument of the short-term interests of the bourgeoisie, or even one fraction of it. Both Miliband and Poulantzas were in fact pushing towards an analysis of the state in capitalist societies that allowed it in some sense more autonomy.

As we have said, in so doing they could claim to be building on a secondary interpretative theme in Marx's writings, of which the *locus classicus* is generally held to be *The Eighteenth Brumaire of Louis Bonaparte*, first published in 1852 (1973). Admittedly, even here Marx does not provide us with an explicit and extended analysis of the state and, as Miliband has pointed out, the relationship between the Bonapartist state and the different social classes is not made entirely clear. Marx seeks to explain the emergence of the Second Empire, in which power was concentrated in an extensive state apparatus under the sole executive authority of Napoleon, out of the seemingly revolutionary upheavals of 1848. The relative autonomy of this ensuing Bonapartist state is a consequence of the weakness of the bourgeoisie. The bourgeoisie comes to abandon its own characteristic commitment to representative democracy because of the political disorder that threatens from the politicisation of the lower urban classes. It turns for protection and political order to an unprincipled dictator who at the same time stands for the political power of the other major social class, the peasantry. There is a paradox then, that Bonaparte safeguards the order necessary to preserve the economic and social interests of the bourgeoisie by being permitted to break its political power and to base his executive supremacy on the numerically preponderant but atomised peasant class. At any rate, what is clear is that the state does not function directly as the instrument of a dominant class, in this context, even if in some sense it preserves that class's long-term interests. The very precariousness of the bourgeoisie's political position obliges it to accord the state greater than usual state autonomy.

Marx describes the French state apparatus, which arose in the era of absolute monarchy. Until the Second Empire it remained the instrument of the ruling class 'however much it strove for power in its own right', but now it has become seemingly autonomous. With its army of over half a million officials at its call, it is a 'parasitic body, which surrounds the body of French society like a caul and stops up all its pores'; it 'acquires through the most extraordinary centralization, an omnipresence, an omniscience, an elasticity and an accelerated rapidity of movement which find their only appropriate complement in its real social body's helpless irresolution and its lack of a consistent formation' (p. 186). Marx incidentally here suggests a subsidiary aspect of the complicity of the bourgeoisie in the consolidation of state power, of particular relevance to Third World societies. The state provides the bourgeoisie's surplus population with jobs and so enables the bourgeoisie to make up 'through state salaries for what it cannot pocket in the form of profits, interests, rents and fees' (Marx, 1973).

While such observations may have stimulated and ideologically legitimised the attempt to define and explain the relative autonomy of the state in capitalist society, they remain only suggestive and have given rise to widely differing inferences and extrapolations. Perhaps most far-reaching in this respect has been the contribution of Poulantzas. For Poulantzas the most fundamental, objectively necessary, function of the state is to maintain the cohesion of the social formation as a whole, thereby ensuring the conditions for the reproduction of the dominant mode of production. Indeed, in his earlier writings at least, he tends to follow Althusser in defining the state as whatever serves that function, rather than in terms of specific institutions. This does not mean, of course , that the state has no other functions. It is in capitalist societies that the state is most able to specialise in its defining social cohesion function. This is because it is in capitalist societies that the political, as opposed to the economic, 'region' has a particular degree of autonomy. In pre-capitalist societies the state is directly involved in economic class struggle since extra-economic compulsion is required to appropriate the surplus from labour, but under capitalism this can be left largely to 'market forces'. The state can develop specialised and cohesive institutions that appear to be public, impartial, and standing above the struggle between private economic interests. This in turn makes possible the formation of a cohesive 'power bloc'; while the bourgeoisie, or a fraction of it, exercises overall hegemony, the power bloc includes several politically dominant classes or fractions. The state, given its institutional autonomy and cohesion, need not simply be the instrument of any one class or fraction but has relative autonomy from them all (Poulantzas, 1973).

Poulantzas has considerably influenced Marxist analysis of the Third World state. Even he, though, always assumes that the state operates in the ultimate interests of the economically dominant class, in the case of the capitalist state, the bourgeoisie. This is despite his debt to *Eighteenth Brumaire* where we have seen Marx indicates a rather more ambiguous relationship between the Bonapartist state and the bourgeoisie: a state strong in the same measure that the bourgeoisie was weak, which is particularly relevant to Third World countries where the weakness of the indigenous bourgeoisie, in terms of its economic base, is generally the rule rather than the exception.

Neo-Marxism and the Post-colonial State

One of the earliest discussions specifically addressing itself to these questions was Hamza Alavi's essay first published in 1972 on 'The State in Post-Colonial Societies' (1979). He begins by suggesting that to explain the post-colonial state even the framework used to analyse Bonapartism is insufficient. Taking as his model the state of Pakistan since its creation in 1947, he argues that it enjoys a still greater degree of autonomy from economically dominant social sectors for two main reasons. First, these economically dominant interests comprise three distinct social classes – the landowners, the national and the metropolitan bourgeoisies – albeit under the hegemonic

'patronage' of the metropolitan bourgeoisie, not simply fractions of the same class. These three classes have short-term
conflicts of interest though they are not fundamentally antagon-
istic to each other. The state promotes their mutual long-term
interest but in so doing it cannot be the exclusive instrument of
rule of any one of them. Second, post-colonial society has
inherited from colonial times a state apparatus, the combined
bureaucracy and military, that is 'overdeveloped' in relation to
the indigenous social structure. Let us look at his argument more
closely.

Alavi identifies not one but three dominant classes in post-
colonial societies such as Pakistan. In his original essay, it is not
really explained why there should be three but recently he has
been more explicit (1982). It is not necessary to enter into this
part of his argument in detail. Suffice to say, while Alavi rejects
the world systems view as oversimplistic, neither can he accept
that pre-capitalist modes survive essentially intact, though
subordinated to the capitalist mode, at the periphery. Rather he
argues that the original pre-capitalist modes of production have
been *modified* by the impact of capitalism and survive as
elements of a distinct 'peripheral capitalism'.

Alavi's account of the three classes so derived remains
nonetheless somewhat sketchy. There are first the landowners.
Although, in his original article, Alavi characterises this class as
'feudal', it is always in inverted commas. And in his later
writing, he suggests they are no longer strictly feudal in so far as
they are increasingly owners of capitalist landed property and
exploiting the labour of dispossessed peasants, a process reinforced in parts of South Asia by the 'Green Revolution' strategy.
The second dominant class is the indigenous bourgeoisie. As
Alavi notes, classical Marxist theory assumed that in the
colonies there would be both a native 'comprador' bourgeoisie,
merchants working closely with the metropolitan bourgeoisie,
and a growing 'national' bourgeoisie opposed to these same
metropolitan interests as well as to the indigenous feudal class
that allied with them. But, Alavi argues, while it is true that the
national bourgeoisie initially plays an anti-imperialist role,
there is a significant realignment after independence. The
national bourgeoisie no longer needs to combat pro-imperialist
'feudal' elements since the task of winning national political

independence has been achieved and since 'the structure of the nation state and the institutional and legal framework necessary for capitalist development, products of the bourgeois revolution, already exist, for they were established by the metropolitan bourgeoisie' (pp. 57–8). On the other hand, as the national bourgeoisie seeks to expand its economic activities, it finds itself increasingly dependent on the metropolitan bourgeoisie for access to advanced industrial technology. The comprador element, in the meantime, comes to oppose the expanding activities of the metropolitan bourgeoisie with which it cannot compete but, Alavi implies, it becomes of less political significance. Third, there is the metropolitan bourgeoisie itself. While it is not exclusively dominant, 'Neo-colonialism is . . . probably the greatest beneficiary of the relative autonomy of the bureaucratic-military oligarchy' (p. 53). It influences bureaucracy through a combination of private corruption and pressure by metropolitan governments, especially the US. It fosters developmental ideologies within the bureaucracy, partly through its training programmes, that favour metropolitan interests. And it works through the various international and aid administering agencies who guide and fund development projects.

These then are Alavi's three dominant classes. In his later essay, he explains why they cannot be considered different fractions of the same class. In capitalist societies, the different fractions of the bourgeoisie are essentially complementary in that it is only by their coming together that capital as a whole is constituted as a process. But under peripheral capitalism the economic roles of these three classes are mutually exclusive (1982). There are real short-term conflicts of interest between these classes. For instance, in Pakistan, the landowners, through their influence in the bureaucracy, have been able to preserve the exemption of agricultural incomes from income tax, despite the concerted pressure of the indigenous and metropolitan bourgeoisies for an agricultural tax to help fund the larger development plans in which their own interests lie. They also receive generous subsidies. On the other hand the landowners' interests have sometimes been overruled; pricing policy for raw cotton has penalised cultivators to the advantage of the big textile mill owners. Despite such short-term conflicts of interest, the context of peripheral capitalism ensures that there are no fundamental long-term antagonisms. As we have seen, the national bourgeoisie has not needed, in the post-independence era, to oppose the survivals of feudalism in that it has been presented ready-made by the colonial regime with a set of 'bourgeois' state institutions suitable for its capitalist project. This is in contrast with western experience, where the indigenous bourgeoisie had to create its own nation state and corresponding legal and institutional framework, following a forceful revolution. Similarly the national bourgeoisie, following national independence, becomes increasingly dependent on the metropolitan bourgeoisie while the latter values collaboration with the national bourgeoisie, 'because that provides a channel through which they pursue their economic interests without political risks attendant on direct investments by themselves, (1979, p. 60), though Alavi is careful to stress that the relationship between these two bourgeoisies is an unequal one.

It is, in sum, this combination of short-term conflicts of interest between the three dominant classes and a long-term shared stake in the preservation of the existing social order – 'the institution of private property and the capitalist mode as the dominant mode of production' – which is the first important reason for the relative autonomy of the post-colonial state. The other leg of Alavi's argument concerns the 'overdeveloped' nature of the colonial, and thus post-colonial, state apparatus. His point here is that the metropolitan bourgeoisie, in imposing colonial rule, needed not only to establish a bourgeois state structure on the model of the state in the metropolitan economy itself, but in addition to ensure that this state apparatus was powerful enough to subordinate *all* the colony's indigenous social classes. The colonial state was in this sense 'overdeveloped' in relation to the social structure in the colony. And this is the state apparatus, centred on the institutions of the bureaucracy and military, which the newly-independent nation inherits. It is true that the very leaders of the nationalist movement it was the function of this colonial apparatus to repress, after independence became its nominal masters. But, at least in the case of India 'the experience of the partial transfer of power by stages in the twenties and thirties had . . . already institutionalized procedures by which the bureaucracy could bypass the political leaders who had been inducted into office, on sufferance, under the umbrella of British rule' (Alavi, 1979, p. 44). These institutional procedures have subsequently been reinforced by the proliferation of bureaucratic controls.

A subsidiary factor in the degree of institutional autonomy of the post–colonial state, Alavi notes, is its economic role. Given the weakness of indigenous private entrepreneurship, it is the state which appropriates a very large part of the economic surplus to be deployed, together with often even more substantial funds borrowed from abroad, by the bureaucracy in the name of economic development. This is in contrast to the limited economic role of the classical bourgeois state, though Alavi concedes there may be closer parallels with the state's role in contemporary metropolitan societies.

Alavi does not confine his discussion of the state apparatus to the bureaucracy and the military but recognises it may also include political parties and other representative institutions. He further concedes that in so far as political parties should ideally articulate demands from their potential supporters and seek their implementation, they could act as some counterweight to the military-bureaucratic oligarchy, but he is sceptical as to how far in practice this actually occurs. Although a political party based on the movement for national independence inherits its mantle of legitimacy, there is a tendency for its power vis-à-vis the executive wing of the state apparatus to attenuate over time. 'We have yet to see a clear case of unambiguous control of state power by a political party in a capitalist post-colonial society' (1979, p. 43). Recent events in India, he suggests, make even the Congress Party a doubtful candidate. Instead the real function of political parties is to legitimise the military-bureaucratic oligarchy and to manipulate public relations on its behalf.

Alavi's discussion centres on Pakistan but initially he suggested it would have much wider application. More recently he has conceded that this particular class alignment might correspond to societies which the pre-capitalist era had been highly stratified, as in India or the latifundia of Latin America, but that a different alignment could emerge from a pre-capitalist society of small peasants, as in parts of Africa (1982). Despite the many theoretical problems with his analysis, it has helped to stimulate a wide ranging debate.

One set of critical reactions has been to his assumption that the *apparatus* of the post-colonial state is 'overdeveloped'. It is worth noting that several 'bourgeois' political scientists have presented a very similar argument. Riggs, in particular, maintained that the state bureaucracy has inherited an organisational strength and authority from colonial times which are supplemented, after independence, by its central role in the national economy, as an agent of 'planning' and regulation, administrator of foreign aid and director of state enterprises. In so far as the politicians in nominal authority over the bureaucracy – what Riggs calls the 'constitutive' element in government – pursue interventionist policies, they are moreover dependent upon it both for information and for implementation. For instance bureaucrats may collude with particular social groups in tax evasion. This is so even when post-colonial bureaucracy exhibits such 'modern' features as regularised salaries, tenure, and promotion on the basis of 'merit'. Indeed Riggs argues that, where it occurs, the very impermeability of the higher bureaucratic echelons to pressure from party politicians deprives the latter of a vital source of patronage. And these characteristics of post-colonial bureaucracies cumulatively serve to hinder the development of effective independent political parties (1963).

Colin Leys, as a contributor to the 'neo-Marxist' perspective, has on the other hand questioned how far this kind of institutional overdevelopment *was* typical, at the time of gaining political independence, especially in parts of Africa. It is more likely, he argues, that the colonial state, once it had overcome initial native resistance, used less military force than it would have needed to if it had not been able to call on military assistance from other parts of the empire. In Tanzania, the colonial state did not meet with great local resistance and it could hardly be described as particularly strong in relation to its tasks. But even in the Indian sub-continent, it was not until after Independence that the civil service and armed forces really began to expand more rapidly than either national income or population (Leys, 1976).

It might then be wiser to reserve the argument that the post-colonial state *apparatus* is overdeveloped for particular cases, of which the Indian sub-continent would seem perhaps the leading example. Even then, in as much as Alavi associates the institutional overdevelopment of the bureaucracy with an essentially secondary, instrumental role for political parties, it is paradoxical that it is in India that, on Alavi's own reckoning, a political party has come closest to directing the bureaucracy. Alavi of course argues that the Congress Party in India has become increasingly the creature of the bureaucratic-military oligarchy, but such an interpretation seems highly questionable (see Wood, 1977).

The second and much more well-aired criticism of Alavi's thesis focuses on its analysis of social class formation and its relationship to the state. These critics share Alavi's conviction that such questions must be separately examined, not simply subsumed in the dependency perspective. They further agree that the frameworks elaborated for analysing the modern capitalist state will not do, but they find his own proposed framework either misconceived or at least unsuited to the experience of all Third World societies. It is in the context of Tropical Africa that this line of criticism has gone furthest and forms part of an extensive debate on class-state relations.

Before we look more closely at this complex and sometimes rather introverted debate, it may be useful briefly to summarise the main directions it has taken. Alavi, we have seen, imputes to the post-colonial state a significant degree of relative autonomy vis-à-vis its three ruling classes. In so doing he does not suggest any basic conflict with the interests of metropolitan capital, only short-term differences. Moreover, while he acknowledges the relative autonomy of the state apparatus that results, he does not indicate that this apparatus can itself become the basis of a new ruling class or ruling stratum. Although he does touch on the ways in which high-placed state functionaries use its resources for their own private or institutional purposes, whether they be bureaucrats extracting bribes or the military draining public funds, there is no implication that these are manifestations of a distinct class or potential class interest.

A number of studies of the state in Tropical Africa, while in no way dissenting from Alavi's view that it acts in the long-term interests of metropolitan capital, see its relations with internal social classes rather differently. In fact they suggest that the weakness of internal classes increases the state's autonomy and may even permit the emergence of a new ruling stratum, and eventually class, based on the state itself. Others have moved still further away from the determinist dependency perspective to entertain the possibility at least that such a 'petty bourgeois' ruling 'class in formation' might, precisely because of its indeterminacy as a class, show greater ideological volatility to the point of instigating socialist policies; that is, the state might display greater autonomy from metropolitan interests. At the same time a different kind of argument has arisen, reflecting perhaps the particular experience of countries like Kenya and Nigeria. Here it is argued that the national bourgeoisie *is* emerging as a significant political force, increasingly able to influence the state and pursue its own developmental 'project'. Again the implication is that the state acquires a degree of relative autonomy in its dealings with the metropolis.

To begin with, Marxist writers on African politics tended to adopt a position closely derived from dependency theory. The post-colonial state was depicted as still, after formal political independence, essentially an instrument of metropolitan capital accumulation. This task was made easier in many African countries as there was neither a distinctive feudal nor post-feudal landowning class (compare, for example, Alavi's Pakistan) nor any significant national bourgeoisie, especially where colonial policies had encouraged an Asian monopoly of local commerce. Under such conditions the state could be seen as directly serving one class interest, that of the metropolitan bourgeoisie, with minimal competition from indigenous classes. In this situation such writers tended to ascribe a central role to the state bureaucracy itself. An example is Claude Meillassoux's description of the emergence, in the West African state of Mali, of a dominant state bureaucracy. French colonial policies had undermined the traditional Malian aristocracy, while an indigenous commercial bourgeoisie comparable to that found in Ghana or Nigeria had failed to develop by the time of political independence. It was the 'colonial crisis', that is the French decision to pull out, which catapulted the existing native bureaucratic stratum into power. The French had to find a reliable group to transfer power to if their interests were to continue secure. The bureaucrats, with their political party, the US–RDA, were the only obvious candidates. After independence the newly-enthroned state bureaucracy moved swiftly to consolidate its position vis-à-vis other potentially dominant social classes (though it should be noted that Meillassoux hesitates ever to call the state bureaucracy a 'class', preferring to term it a dominant social 'body'). The seizure of state power by the bureaucrats was the true motive behind the creation of a nationalised economic sector achieved 'under the label of "socialism"', which provided them with a convenient ideology to bring the economy under their control, supposedly of course on behalf of the entire population' (Meillassoux, 1970, p. 106).

Issa Shivji's interpretation of Tanzanian political development in many respects parallels that of Meillassoux. Tanzania, one of the world's 25 poorest nations, has since Independence (and especially with the adoption of the Arusha Declaration in 1967) provided a leading prototype of African socialism as formulated and overseen by its President, Julius Nyerere. Shivji is one of the Maji–Maji group of radical intellectuals within Tanzania which has questioned the government's claim to be socialist. His criticisms have in turn been challenged by such fellow Marxists as John Saul and Lionel Cliffe, more prepared to give Tanzanian socialism the benefit of the doubt, at least in the short term. In this argument attention has centred on Tanzania's rulers. Tanzania's only political party, initially the Tanzania African National Union (TANU) and after 1977 Chama Cha Mapinduzi (CCM), was founded in 1956 and prior to Independence in 1961 met with remarkably little opposition either from indigenous groups, including the Asian community, or to any great extent from the colonial authorities. Shortly after Independence what was already *de facto* a one-party state became so *de jure*. At the same time there had been a rapid defection of party leaders into the lucrative commanding positions within the state apparatus. Already by 1962 more than half the district party secretaries and all the provincial party secretaries had moved across in this way. In Kenya a similar process was widely interpreted by critics as leading to the withering away of the ruling party, KANU, as an independent political force (see for example Waiguchu, 1974). Nyerere, however, appears to have been awake to the dangers of such a development in Tanzania. This could at least be one interpretation of procedures introduced into the selection of party candidates for elective office that provided for a genuine element of competition and input from the district level, as well as the provision in 1967 of a 'Leadership Code' which proscribed those in leading party or government positions from retaining any personal interest in profit-making concerns (see Cliffe, 1972). The key question is how far Nyerere actually succeeded in maintaining the Party's vitality, socialist conscience and control over the state bureaucracy.

One of Nyerere's central contentions, elaborated in his writings on 'Ujamaa socialism', has been the irrelevance of the concept of class to African societies and of class struggle to African socialism. Africans never had a word for 'class' in their indigenous languages and traditional social organisations tended to be communalistic. In post-colonial Tanzania, the real problem was not 'redistribution between rich and poor, but a fair distribution of wealth, and of contribution to national expenses, between the very poor and the poor, between the man who can barely feed himself and the man who can barely clothe himself' (quoted in Hill, 1975, p. 219). For Shivji, on the other hand, Tanzanian politics can only be understood in terms of class struggle.

Before and after independence, according to Shivji, the metropolitan bourgeoisie has been the dominant class. While, therefore, no true 'national' bourgeoisie has been able to emerge, the metropolitan bourgeoisie fostered the growth of an Asian commercial bourgeoisie as its subordinate partner. In addition, by Independence, an indigenous African petty bourgeoisie had begun to form. Shivji in fact insists that the essential relationship between Asians and Africans 'is to be found in the sphere of production relations rather than in the area of ethnicity or culture' (Shivji, 1976, p. 40). He argues that while on the basis of such criteria as income the Asian community could be divided into four strata, since members of the Asian petty bourgeoisie either resembled the commercial bourgeoisie, acted as a complementary group, or were active on its fringes, they could all be subsumed into a single class category. The African petty bourgeoisie, for its part, was not socially homogeneous but was overwhelmingly urban, since a sizeable 'kulak' element had failed to develop in the countryside as it had, for instance, in Kenya. There was also, by Independence, a wage-earning class, small in number but capable of militant action, and there was the peasantry. Tanzania's subsequent political history can be explained in terms of the struggle between these classes.

While the achievement of 'Uhuru' or independence was not in itself a phase of the class struggle, it was its necessary prelude. The African petty bourgeoisie was the only class able to lead this movement and in so doing played a progressive role. As a result, the petty bourgeoisie, through TANU, seized state power. Thereafter the state played a central, 'almost omnipotent' part in the ensuing class struggle. This was for two particular reasons. First, Shivji points to the relative independence of those in charge of the state apparatus, in contrast say with Kenya where an important other section of the petty bourgeoisie, yeoman farmers and traders, had its own economic base and was able to exercise some restraint on the ruling group. Second, precisely because this Tanzanian petty bourgeoisie lacked an economic base it needed to create such a base through its control of the state. (None of this incidentally means that the African petty bourgeoisie was independent of the metropolitan bourgeoisie, simply that it had its own additional interests to pursue.) Not only therefore did the Tanzanian bureaucratic petty bourgeoisie consolidate its hold over the administration by preferential recruitment of Africans but, following the Arusha Declaration, it moved to 'nationalise' a series of economic enterprises, which effectively meant breaking the economic power of the Asian community. Here the petty bourgeoisie was again playing a progressive role since, in Shivji's rather chilling phrase, 'the liquidation of the inherited racial structure was condition sine qua non for "purifying" the class struggles' (p. 98). These measures cleared the way for the emergence, at least potentially, of a new 'bureaucratic bourgeoisie', though Shivji, like Meillassoux, hesitates to call this a distinct class, suggesting instead that it may be a class in formation. As in analyses of 'state capitalism' in the Soviet Union and Eastern Europe, it approximated a class in so far as while it did not own, it effectively controlled the means of production.

This bureaucratic bourgeoisie made further progressive contributions in denouncing imperialism and, through the Arusha Declaration and for whatever self-interested motive, putting the issue of socialism on the political agenda, but thereby exhausted its progressive potential. Shivji goes on to trace the embryonic beginnings of a new revolutionary class alignment in opposition to the bureaucratic bourgeoisie and its metropolitan masters. One element of this alignment may be a section of the petty bourgeoisie itself, another the poor peasants whose position has been worsened not improved by the 'ujamaa' system of villagisation. But Shivji's strongest hopes are pinned on the urban working class and here he takes issue with the labour aristocracy thesis.

While he accepts that in the early post-Independence period, petty-bourgeois trades unionist attitudes prevailed within the organised working class, he finds a recent change. Initially TANU policy was unambiguously aimed at controlling labour – the labour aristocracy argument indeed formed part of the rationalisation for this policy – but subsequently the party leadership appeared to favour greater worker participation. Shivji admits this may have reflected the influence of the party's left wing, but attributes much more importance to the fears of the right wing of Tanzania's petty bourgeoisie, fuelled by the January 1971 coup against Obote in Uganda and the invasion of Guinea by Portuguese mercenaries, that working-class discontent could be fomented against them. Worker participation was encouraged by two particular measures: first, following Presidential Circular No. 1, management in the para-statals or national enterprises were directed to establish advisory workers' councils and to promote workers' participation in the existing governing committees and Boards of Directors. The Mwongozo, or TANU guidelines of 1971, went further in forbidding management conduct that was 'arrogant, extravagant, contemptuous and oppressive' (Clause 15) and the corrupt use of profits (Clause 33). These measures, and the management's obvious reluctance to comply with them, sparked off a series of strikes which entailed not only downing tools but lock-outs of officials and even the physical take-over of enterprises. Shivji interprets this as evidence of growing worker militancy and the harbinger of its future revolutionary role.

Saul's principal criticism (1979) is of what he sees as Shivji's excessive determinism. Shivji assumes first that those in charge of the Tanzanian state apparatus have continued, as before Independence, to act almost automatically as agents of metropolitan capital. Second, he presents as almost inevitable the process whereby an indigenous petty-bourgeois ruling stratum seeks first to secure its own control over the state apparatus and then to use this political power to create an economic base for itself, eliminate the (Asian) commercial bourgeoisie and outflank its indigenous rivals for economic power and thus constitute itself as the new ruling bureaucratic bourgeoisie. While Saul agrees that there may be some evidence of such a bureaucratic consolidation in the longer term (though he is less convinced that the Tanzanian bureacratic bourgeoisie does not have private entrepreneurial aspirations), he maintains that in the early post–Independence period, the nature of class formation and alignments and their relationship with the state were much more fluid and indeterminate. To develop his refutation of Shivji, Saul first turns to the work of Roger Murray on the CPP in Ghana (1967). According to Murray, the leadership and cadres who acceded to state power with Independence were drawn from the petty-bourgeois salariat, such occupations as clerks, primary-school teachers, store-keepers and messengers, 'a mixed stratum which concentrated many of the political and cultural tensions of colonial society' and did not express or reflect a determinate economic class. This gave the CPP 'political class', as Murray somewhat confusingly terms it, a relative autonomy and volatility that meant that the way it exercised power could not, at this 'uncertain historical moment', be predicted. As Murray wrote, the post-colonial state, or in the famous phrase of Nkrumah 'the political kingdom', must be viewed 'simultaneously . . . as the actual instrument of mediation and negotiation with international capitalism, and as the possible instrument of a continuing anti-imperialist and socialist revolution' (p. 31). Given the relative autonomy of the ruling petty-bourgeois stratum, it could go either way. Further, a decisive aspect of this struggle would be played out at the level of ideology.

In the same way, Saul wants to emphasise the indeterminate class character of the 'petty-bourgeois' stratum which, through TANU, came to dominate the post-colonial state in Tanzania, and to argue that its progressive wing has had a real effect on state policies. For instance, he takes issue with Shivji's inter-pretation of the political motives behind the Arusha Declaration. Shivji, as we have seen, contrasts the attitude of the bureaucratic bourgeoisie towards the private sector in Tanzania and in Kenya. He gives moreover as one reason for the more favourable attitude in Kenya the greater strength of its non-bureaucratic entrepreneurial petty bourgeoisie. Saul finds this contrast exaggerated and points out that the entrepreneurial element in Kenya had correspondingly more powerful European and Asian commercial rivals to contend with. He also cites evidence to suggest that important sections of Tanzania's bureaucratic bourgeoisie would be very happy to expand their private entrepreneurial roles. For Saul, it is difficult to avoid the conclusion that

> the Arusha Declaration package of policies – the opting for collective solutions to the Tanzanian development problem – represented, first and foremost, an initial victory for a progressive wing of the petty-bourgeoisie (and the announcement of its continuing commitment to the interests of the workers and the peasants), rather than some cold-blooded fulfilment of the class interests of that stratum's bureaucratic core (p. 184).

Most unacceptable of all, for Saul, is Shivji's explanation of the increasing militancy of industrial workers. One has to show where this high level of consciousness came from, and that means recognising the important contributory role of initiatives by a section of the party leadership, in particular the Mwongozo, 'in crystallising worker consciousness and legitimizing, even demanding, the unleashing of popular pressures against oligarchical tendencies on the part of the wielders of state power' (p. 186).

Saul's point is not to insist that this progressive wing will continue to oppose oligarchic bureaucratic tendencies, simply that it symptomises the indeterminate class character of the 'petty-bourgeois' ruling stratum in newly-independent Third World states, such as Tanzania, and the possibility therefore at this early stage of a sincere attempt to pursue socialist development. The need to be more precise about the character of the petty bourgeoisie and the stratum within it that inherits political power is again the theme of Saul's discussion (written subsequently) of what he calls the 'unsteady state' in Uganda (Saul, 1976). A number of writers, including Shivji, had tended to

depict this petty bourgeoisie as consisting of two main, econ-
omically-based 'fractions': on the one hand small capitalists
(traders, 'kulak' farmers), on the other, the educated, primarily
state-employed salariat. They were to be seen as two wings of
the same social class because as Poulantzas had argued, despite
their different positions in the economic sphere, they had the
same 'effects' at the political and ideological level. That is, they
both tended to be associated with values that were individualistic, conservative and aspired to bourgeois status. Saul takes this
analysis further. Given its intermediate position between the
bourgeoisie and the proletariat, it is also the case, and again
following Poulantzas, that the petty bourgeoisie is politically
unstable and capable of swinging towards either main class. He
invokes, in addition to the two fractions already identified,
Murray's 'political class' as distinct and not necessarily exclusively derived from either. Indeed, within this political class,
one will find reflected a whole range of 'fractions', in keeping
with the fluid character of the petty bourgeoisie as a class in
formation. These will not all be based in economic divisions;
some may exist only at the political level, since competition
within the petty bourgeoisie for control of the state, and the
economic advantages it brings, will tend to activate a diversity
of fractions, as its members seek to build alliances and mobilise
support. Here the 'ethnic-regional card' will be a tempting one
to play – 'After all there do exist cultural differences' (p. 20) –
providing a lowest common denominator of trust and communication. But fractions can also form based on institutional
interests, such as those of the military or bureaucracy. Finally
they can crystallise around different ideologies of national
development.

Saul is clearly going a long way beyond the determinism and
relatively simple class analysis of the earlier dependency-orien-
ted approaches here. In so doing he claims to offer a perspective

which, in the realms of theory, can lend to the diverse ethnic,
religious, institutional and ideological alignments of Africa's
petty-bourgeois politics, the reality they so clearly possess in
practice – while at the same time situating them in such a way
as to validate the claims of class analysis to be the crucial key
to an understanding of African social formations (p. 19).

While there is no question of the increased realism of his analysis, it is equally apparent that it has required him to leave mainstream Marxism far behind.

The attempts we have so far reviewed to produce a theory of the post-colonial state which accurately reflects the cirumstances of sub-Saharan Africa concentrate on the role of the bureaucratic petty bourgeoisie. But a second kind of revisionism in the context of Tropical Africa applies the concept of 'associated' dependent development discussed in the previous chapter, and centres instead on the indigenous or national bourgeoisie. Leys's analysis of political development in Kenya, already briefly referred to, exemplifies this new approach. As we saw, Leys originally subscribed to the dependency view which 'sees the state as the more or less independent *mediator* between foreign capital and local capital according to some conception of a "balance" which, since foreign capital is evidently much stronger, can only provide minor gains and compensation for local ("dependent") capital' (Leys, 1978, p. 251). More recently, however, he has come round to the view that since the mid-1960s Kenya's development has been primarily determined by the class project of its indigenous bourgeoisie.

Leys emphasises two 'exceptional' circumstances of Kenya's history that have helped to make this possible. First, before colonisation, in what is now Kenya's Central Province, a class of primarily 'primitive' accumulators of capital, in the form of land and livestock, had already begun to emerge. While colonisation prevented further accumulation in this form, except in so far as some pre-colonial accumulators were appointed 'chiefs' and thus given new opportunities to 'loot' their subjects and increase their holdings through litigation, the main entry route to accumulation for Africans shifted to wage income, based on education, and to commerce. Second, though, colonialism in Kenya involved a substantial white settler community which itself helped to create, for instance through the appropriation of a large part of the means of production and the partial proletarianisation of most of the population, the preconditions for continuing *domestic* capital accumulation. Following the Second World War, the colonial state began to lift many of the restrictions on indigenous African accumulation with the result that what could be termed an indigenous capitalist class had come into being long before Independence was achieved in 1963. This class was concentrated in the dominant ethnic group, the Kikuyu and, because of its heavy investment in education, was strongly represented in the state apparatus and therefore 'exceptionally well-placed to convert its natural dominance in the nationalist movement into a position of strategic control over the post-colonial political realignments needed for the next phase of capital accumulation' (p. 250). Already by 1966, an effective power bloc, under the hegemony of the Kikuyu bourgeoisie, had been established. And thenceforth the state apparatus, which Leys underlines was *not* acting autonomously but under the direction of the indigenous bourgeoisie, enacted a series of measures, including trade licensing, the creation of state monopolies, provision of state finance capital, state direction of credit and state enterprise, to expand indigenous capital accumulation further. Leys cites data indicating the extent of Africanisation of the economy by the late 1970s. Even in those sectors requiring advanced technology and large amounts of capital, such as finance servicing and manufacturing, substantial inroads had been made.

What was this indigenous bourgeoisie in Kenya like? By the 1950s distinct fractions were becoming evident within it. According to Leys, these were based on economic differences, corresponding mainly to the distinction between merchant, agricultural and industrial capital, but not exhausted by these. Clashes between the interests of these different issues focused on such recurrent issues as state protection for manufacturing and wage controls. At the same time the bourgeoisie was developing its own class consciousness, through a series of struggles with other classes. With the banning of the Kenya People's Union in 1969, that section of the petty bourgeoisie which made populist appeals to trades unions and the rural landless had been largely neutralised as an independent political force. Increasingly the unionised working class was brought under state control, through centralised state-directed organisation, a ban on strikes and a system of wage controls. The middle and poor peasantry were incorporated into ethnically-based clientage networks, which might seem 'transclass' but were actually a means of bourgeois control. This indigenous bourgeoisie then, could not be considered 'progressive' in the classical, Leninist, anti-imperialist sense. Nor was it about to generate its own nineteenth-century style bourgeois-democratic revolution. It was progressive in its victory over a petty bourgeoisie which for all its populist and even socialist rhetoric was essentially conservative in its development objectives, but in its relations with the Kenyan working class it was oppressive and exploitative.

The differences between Leys's account and those emphasising the role of the bureaucratic bourgeoisie are partly a function of the societies to which they refer. Leys's model may be more appropriate for economically more developed nations such as Kenya or Nigeria. It may also apply to some of the Latin American states, although problems are posed here by dissimilarities in rural social structure, and specifically the continuing political importance, in a number of Latin American countries, of a quasi-feudal landowning class. At any rate one implication of Leys's analysis must be noted. He attributes a dominant position to the national bourgeoisie, while it is the absence or weakness of such a class that is seen by Alavi, Shivji and others to underlie the relative autonomy of the state. Thus, in Leys's account, the state appears to resume its more classical Marxist role as the instrument of the dominant indigenous bourgeoisie. In this sense the relative autonomy of the state diminishes. At the same time the state's room for manoeuvre in the face of metropolitan interests may be greater.

We have suggested that the consensus among neo-Marxists examining the post-colonial state is confined to the method of analysis to be employed rather than the conclusions to be drawn. Different verdicts reflect both actual variations between Third World societies and different assessments of the correct political strategy for practising socialists to pursue. Nonetheless certain generalisations are possible. A recurrent theme is the 'exceptional' autonomy of the state, due to the weakness of the indigenous bourgeoisie, and the way in which members of the state apparatus – whether Alavi's military-bureaucratic oligarchy, Nun's Latin American military (see Chapter 3), or in Africa a bureaucratic petty bourgeoisie or fully-fledged bureaucratic bourgeoisie – have themselves emerged as rulers or potential rulers.

The question then arises as to how such rule is to be characterised. Generally it is depicted as a kind of incomplete or arrested bourgeois revolution. The influence of metropolitan capital continues to weaken and distort economic and class development. The old landowning class, where it is significant, cannot be dispensed with so long as its support is needed to offset the weakness of the bourgeoisie. And as economic development of a sort does persist, and a larger, more class-conscious working-class emerges, the regime moves to restrict those 'liberal' political freedoms traditionally associated with bourgeois hegemony. In some cases, it is true, the new rulers present themselves as socialists. As Roxborough (1979) points out, one problem here is what is meant by socialism. Through the distortions of Stalinism, and more latterly through the arguments of dependency theorists, socialism has come increasingly to mean simply the process of achieving a state committed to state ownership, some form of economic planning and economic growth. Even then, such claims rarely appear justified. Such socialist revolution 'from above' (Gramsci's 'passive revolution') is more likely to spawn a repressive, patrimonial state, where indeed elements of private enterprise will soon start creeping back once bureaucrats are confident that a substantial portion of the profits will accrue to them. Even Leys, in his later writings on Kenya seems to agree that genuine socialist revolution has to come from below, spearheaded by the working class, including the rural proletariat, and the struggle will be bitter and protracted. We return to this question in our conclusion, when we discuss the radical or Marxist equivalent of political development.

Convergence on the State?

While this chapter has been primarily interested in developments in Marxist theory, we noted at the outset that an emphasis on the state is a feature of recent studies of Third World politics, from a number of other theoretical perspectives. This is not to say of course that writers increasingly agree; they retain their distinctive assumptions and concerns. The degree of convergence on the state as an object of inquiry is nonetheless striking. It reflects the growing general recognition of the importance of political, as opposed to economic and social, determinants of development, and of the national state as the point at which political power is concentrated and can most effectively be deployed to resist metropolitan pressures, promote development or at least shape the kind of economic and social changes that occur.

Without wishing to impose a spurious tidiness in the categorisation of these different approaches, two trends currently in favour lay particular emphasis on the state. The first, though sharing neither Marxism's value system nor its assumption of an inevitable revolutionary process, draws heavily if often clumsily on its political and social analysis. Its method is primarily that of comparative history. Among the writers who could be mentioned here are Philippe Schmitter, Alfred Stepan (for instance, 1978), Guillermo O'Donnell, Ellen Kay Trimberger (1978) and Theda Skocpol.

Much of this writing has centred on Latin America. And it is in this context that discussions of the state have frequently acquired a distinctly authoritarian overtone, linking them with the earlier strong government school. Though statements of outright approval for authoritarian rule may be rare, there is a clear indication that it may be historically necessary.

Perhaps the precursor to this authoritarian statism was the interest, in the early 1970s, in state 'corporatism'. The concept of corporatism first became fashionable as a tool for analysing the politics of such western democracies as Britain and the Scandinavian countries, but then was increasingly applied to certain of the industrially more advanced societies in Latin America, and notably Chile and Brazil. Corporatism in Schmitter's much-cited definition is

> a system of interest representation in which the constituent units are organized into a limited number of singular, compulsory, noncompetitive, hierarchically ordered and functionally differentiated categories, recognised or licensed (if not created) by the state and granted a deliberate representational monopoly within their respective categories in exchange for observing certain controls on their selection of leaders and articulation of demands and supports (1974, pp. 93–4).

The interests represented were assumed to be based on the major economic sectors; thus the model implied a certain level of economic and social development.

Within this broad model of corporatism, a continuum was distinguished, at one extreme of which lay 'natural' or 'evolutionary' corporatism, in which interest organisation was spontaneous and the state's role largely confined to arbitration, and at the other 'state corporatism', in which power and initiative were concentrated in the state itself. The state might actually sponsor interest organisations but would certainly license and regulate them. This was the type of corporatism most prevalent in Latin America. As an example we saw how the post-Goulart regime in Brazil sought not only to repress political opposition but to incorporate the labour movement, making use of the CLT legislation from the Vargas era and offering further inducements to membership in the official 'sindicatos'. Similarly it used employers' syndicates and peasants' associations to incorporate the rural population and pre-empt more radical mobilisation.

In discussing state corporatism in Chile, Paul Drake made a further distinction between 'inclusionary' and 'exclusionary' variants. While under inclusionary forms of corporatism the state sought to undercut the independent emergence of workers' and peasants' organisations through its own process of controlled mobilisation and co-optation, exclusionary corporatism required the deliberate demobilisation of already politicised groups. Elements of corporatist thought and practice go back some way in Chilean history and inclusionary corporatism reached its full flower in Frei's attempt, in the late 1960s, to create an organic society in which intermediate organisations – interest groups, regional bodies, municipalities, families – would link the individual with the state. Later, when General Pinochet came to power in 1973, his new government took up corporatist themes but in reality adopted an extreme exclusionary version in which even the 'gremios' or employers' associations were allowed only a limited political role (Drake, 1978).

More recently, the vogue for corporatism has given way to the concept of bureaucratic authoritarianism (already referred to briefly in the previous chapter). This draws on Juan Linz's account of Franco's Spain (1970) and is a response to the emergence of apparently stable and economically 'successful' military regimes in Brazil after 1964, Argentina after 1966 and more latterly in Chile and Uruguay after 1973. In his discussion of authoritarian rule in Brazil after 1964, Schmitter suggests there may be an 'elective affinity' between delayed dependent development and protracted authoritarian rule. He cites the *Eighteenth Brumaire* as a text ignored by orthodox Marxists and which indicates that when aspiring ruling classes are weak and divided a relatively independent state can result. The experience of Brazil suggests that Marx was only wrong in assuming that the Bonapartist state had to be transitional (1973). The most influential exponent of the bureaucratic-authoritarian model is O'Donnell who outlines a sequence of development stages. In the first, 'oligarchic' state, political competition is restricted to an elite consisting of representatives of the primary product export sector. In the second, 'populist' phase, the new industrial elite enters a tacit alliance with the increasingly moblilised urban popular sector, against a background of economic nationalism and a policy of ISI, which means expanding the domestic market, and with it working-class incomes (the Vargas era in Brazil, or Peronism from 1946 to 1955). The third stage, of 'bureaucratic authoritarianism', arrives when the limits of this form of industrialisation have been reached, and the new elite of military and civilian technocrats invite and work closely with foreign capital. The corollary of these new economic policies, demanding stringent sacrifices from the working-class, is inevitably political repression (1973). O'Donnell's model has been much criticised for both its economic determinism and its tacit condoning of authoritarian rule (see Collier, 1979). However, its chief interest for us here is the crucial role it accords the military and bureaucratic establishment.

While corporatist or bureaucratic-authoritarian models emphasise the state, they still tend to take it for granted, rather than asking what the state is and to what extent it has separate interests of its own. Perhaps the most original recent contribution to this question has been from Skocpol. She points out that even the latest refinements of the Marxist theory of the state never go so far as to suggest that the state can be potentially autonomous in regard to the entire class structure or mode(s) of production. We need first to define what the state is. Skocpol defines it as 'a set of administrative, policing and military organisations headed and more or less well co-ordinated by, an executive authority' (1979, p. 29). As such, she argues, it has its own distinctive functions or imperatives, namely to maintain political order and to deal successfully with other states. In carrying out these functions it requires resources for which it must compete with the dominant class(es). Moreover, at times – in periods of crisis, when it enforces concessions to the lower classes, or in response to external military pressures or opportunities – the state may actually hinder the interests of dominant social classes. In this sense it is potentially autonomous from them. The specificity and realism of Skocpol's conceptualisation of the state seem to offer a promising tool for future analysis. It was, however, developed primarily in the context of the *anciens régimes* of France, Russia and China and has yet to be extensively applied to a Third World state (Skocpol, 1979).

The second currently influential stand, which focuses if not on the state as such, then on policymakers, is the 'public choice' approach. In Chapter 1 we traced elements of this approach back to modernisation theory. It also incorporates arguments from the strong government school; in fact this approach is characterised more by its micro-policy orientation than by its own theory, however loosely that term is understood, of what causes political change in Third World societies. It is for this reason that we devote little attention to it in this book. Nonetheless, since it represents probably the most distinctive and central development in current 'liberal' thinking on the subject, its focus on public authority is worthy of note.

The policy orientation of this approach stems from increasing disillusionment with earlier macro-theories and their sociological or historical underpinnings on the one hand and what is perceived as the 'growing urgency of coming to grips with social change in the Third World' (Migdal, 1977, p. 241) on the other. From the late 1960s a number of former modernisation theorists paved the way: Almond, Coleman, Apter and Easton. They were influenced by general developments in political science: the growing popularity of rational choice models and the introduction of economic concepts, and more latterly the burgeoning of the somewhat vaguely defined field of 'policy studies'.

One factor inspiring this turn to political economy and public choice analysis in the context of the Third World, however, was the sharpening recognition of the 'primacy of politics', specifically of state intervention in economic development. And while no new set of theoretical conclusions has been generated by this approach, its exemplars emphasise the state in at least two ways. First, simply through their concern with policy, they place statesmen, politicians and bureaucrats centre stage and assume that they can and should *choose* correct policies and programmes for their implementation. As Higgott comments, policy and state activity appear synonymous. But second a number of such studies stress the need for power to be concentrated in the state. Migdal, for instance, examines the effect of levels of political institutionalisation on policy success, but in practice largely equates institutionalisation with central-isation. 'Policy successes will depend, in great part, on mobiliz-ing a high proportion of the very scarce political resources of the central authorities in order to attack isolated problems' (p. 259). Grindle (1980), introducing a series of case studies of the problems of policy implementation, concludes that only central authorities able to concentrate extensive amounts of power and thus ensure that implementation remains within their broad policy guidelines can afford to decentralise responsibility for implementation.

In this chapter our main concern has been to trace the emergence of a neo-Marxist literature of the post-colonial state. We have seen how this literature incorporated a number of themes: the reaction against dependency theory's oversimplified class analysis, the quest for revolutionary strategy and agencies in the Third World and the increasing refinement of concep-tualisations of the capitalist state in the wake of Gramsci and the French Marxist structuralists. While neo-Marxist writers are united more by their method and underlying political values than by their provisional conclusions, we observed first a trend towards reinstating the proletariat as the chief bearers of revolution. Second, this school emphasises the state itself as the site in which indigenous ruling classes may initially take form and through which they will ultimately seek to consolidate their economic dominance, whether this reflects the interests of international capital or, to the extent that these are separable, their own class 'project'.

We have also seen how simultaneously writers approaching the subject from rather different theoretical perspectives and value positions have similarly come to focus on the Third World state. Our Conclusion takes up some of the implications of this convergence. What scope is there for a fruitful synthesis of these approaches? And what do the different approaches suggest about the utility of some notion of 'political development', either as originally formulated by the modernisation theorists or according to some new set of criteria? We shall argue in particular that recent aproaches are all characterised by a more or less explicit authoritarianism. How is this to be reconciled with the emphasis so central to early political development theory on the democratic process?

6

The Study of Political Change

We began this book by looking at the first attempts of political scientists to conceptualise the changes that were taking place in what had become known in the post-war years as the Third World. We saw that early attempts to formulate theories of political modernisation and development borrowed liberally from the discipline of sociology, especially from functionalism. The two principal defects of this modernisation approach were first, that they were informed by evolutionary notions of change, being founded upon a naive faith in a smooth transition to 'modernity', modernity being the happy condition in which the developed nations of the 1950s and 1960s found themselves. The second principal defect was that modernisation theorists made no attempt to relate their formulations to what would now be regarded as the heart of the condition of underdevelopment, the character of Third World economies. Indeed the economic dimension was simply seen as irrelevant to the study of 'politics', a stance that was to a considerable degree informed by the academic division of labour between political science and economics.

Modernisation revisionism sought to eliminate the cruder assumptions of modernisation theory, particularly the simplistic dichotomies of tradition and modernity. By exploring the diverse facets of tradition and particularly by demonstrating the survival and adaptation of traditional institutions to the modern situation – the state and political parties – modernisation revisionism emphasised the continued salience for political change of such phenomena as caste, clientelism, tribalism and other forms of communalism; phenomena which modernisation theory had considered to be obsolescent. Whilst modernisation revisionism certainly confronted the major conceptual shortcomings of modernisation theory it was never able entirely to liberate itself from the latter's evolutionary perspective. Behind modernisation revisionism's advocacy of the staying power of tradition lurks the assumption that ultimately tradition *will* decline; caste-based forms of association, for example, will eventually recede into the background in favour of modern, rational-legal patterns. More importantly modernisation revisionism did not begin to tackle the problem of the relationship between the political and the economic.

A second line of criticism of modernisation theory was embodied in the strong government approach. Rather than focusing upon the conceptual weaknesses of tradition and modernity, on the basis of what was actually happening in the Third World in the second half of the 1960s, these writers questioned the viability of western-style democracy in such societies. The high rates of mobilisation associated with early experiments with multi-party systems had led to serious instability, frequent intervention by the military and, in some cases, civil war. Political order rather than democracy was now the immediate goal of political development and political development usually entailed, *inter alia*, the institutionalisation of mass participation within a single party that had been created from above. In exposing the unrealistic assumptions of modernisation theory the proponents of political order undoubtedly advanced the understanding of political change. The principal defect of this type of approach was that the less desirable aspects of strong government were largely ignored. However, we shall be returning to these later on in this chapter.

At about the same time that the modernisation revisionist and strong government critiques emerged dependency theory was also beginning its move to the centre of the social science stage. In effect a number of the criticisms made by the revisionists appear also in early statements of dependency, especially Frank's *The Sociology of Development and Underdevelopment of Sociology* (Frank, 1971). However, dependency theory derived its main impetus not from emphasising the conceptual deficiencies of modernisation theory but from exposing its total neglect of the economic dimension, particularly the alleged exploitation of the underdeveloped by the developed world. Whilst Frank was explicitly directing his onslaught against sociology his darts effectively administered the *coup de grâce* to a mortally wounded politics of modernisation given that it drew much of its inspiration from sociology. Whilst dependency theory undoubtedly made a crucial contribution in pointing up the indispensability of a global world economic perspective, in its cruder versions it exhibited two major defects: its exceedingly 'macro' orientation rendered it conceptually ill-equipped to cope with the range and diversity of Third World societies. And, second, the logical force of dependency, at least in its earlier manifestations, drew heavily upon polarities: development-underdevelopment, centre-periphery, metropole-satellite and so on. Ironically, as certain writers have pointed out (such as Bernstein, 1979), dependency shared two basic characteristics – an overly high level of generalisation and a reliance on dichotomies – with the very modernisation theories it sought to discredit. From our point of view the most important defect of dependency was its tendency to devalue the role of politics and the state at the periphery.

The later 1970s have seen the rehabilitation of the state as a focus for the analysis of political change in the Third World. The political has been put back into political economy. In fact Richard Higgott (Higgott, 1983) has talked of two quite distinct political economies: the first is a Marxist-inspired political economy which seeks to counter the homogenising tendencies of dependency theory by focusing on the formation of social classes as pre-capitalist modes of production dissolve, and the relationship of these classes (as well as extra-territorial groupings such as the metropolitan bourgeoisie) to the state apparatus. Higgott's second school of political economy emphasises the process of formulation of public policy and draws much of its inspiration from a long-established policy studies tradition in which the economics of choice plays a central role. Like the Marxist or radical political economy, the policy studies variant involves a shift from the macro-perspective of modernisation and dependency theories to a much more 'micro' approach. In fact the policy studies approach is a good deal more micro in its orientation than radical political economy in that it confines itself to decisionmaking and the formulation of policy within the state apparatus. The historical structuring of the economy, its ramifications for the process of class formation and the unfolding of the class struggle – central foci for the radicals – figure hardly at all. Furthermore, whereas the radical perspective exhibits an overt commitment to change, usually some form of revolutionary change, the public policy approach with its emphasis on the evolution of long-term policy explicitly or implicitly entails a commitment to political stability. In this respect the politics of public policy shares a basic pre-occupation with the strong government school.

Higgott's dichotomy is a little simplistic as there are a number of writers – prominent political scientists like those mentioned at the end of the previous chapter (Schmitter and Trimberger for example) – who could not unequivocally be assigned to either of the two schools. Nonetheless accepting these as two polar approaches it might be possible, through a critical appraisal of each, to arrive at a methodological position which combines the best features of both.

Central to the radical perspective is the notion of the emergence of social classes as capitalism gradually penetrates and eventually dissolves pre-capitalist modes of production. Whilst the term mode of production has the ostensible advantage of providing a conceptual tool capable of encompassing the wide range of social forms to be found in the Third World, its employment does raise a number of problems. It would be inappropriate to embark upon a lengthy critique of the concept in this context and at this point as this would involve an unacceptably wordy digression, and anyway this task has already been performed quite adequately elsewhere (see especially Foster-Carter, 1978). As far as we are concerned there still seems to be a fair amount of confusion as to what range of phenomena actually constitute a mode of production and, second, as to the number of modes of production which are empirically observable. It is not clear, for example, what unequivocally forms a feudal mode of production or whether an Asiatic mode actually exists or has any explanatory value (see Anderson, 1974, and Melotti, 1977). In addition to feudalism and the oriental mode we encounter in the literature Germanic, Slavonic, African, lineage, communal tributary and other varieties (see for example Coquery-Vidrovitch, 1978, and Crumney and Stewart, 1981). To add to our difficulties different labels are not infrequently attached to the same pattern of phenomena. It is thus ironic that an approach that has its origins in Marxism seems to have fallen into the trap of excessive empiricism with a mode of production for virtually every situation in the real world. If the advocates of modes of production analysis are arguing that in understanding social and political change at the periphery it is vital to examine the ways in which economic organisation translates itself into other levels, then we would find it difficult to disagree. Furthermore many of the observations made by those who have used this approach have significantly enhanced our appreciation of the intricacies of social organisation at the periphery. However, the view that modes of production analysis furnishes us with a distinctive, technically superior methodological approach seems highly questionable.

There can be no doubt that with the penetration of capitalism in the form of markets and market relationships into the recesses of Third World economies, the foundations of pre-colonial and pre-capitalist forms of organisation are undermined. The notion that some form of class structure is emerging in both town and countryside is in a very general sense true if by that we mean that changes in the division of labour are reconstituting people into social categories which differ from those to which they were assigned in an economy based upon peasant and artisan production. However, the drawback of an analysis based solely upon class is that no matter how sophisticated its presentation there invariably lurks in the background the conception of increasing polarisation between a working class and a bour-geoisie leading ultimately to some kind of revolutionary up-heaval. The basic problem with such an outlook is that it is derived from the experience of European societies during an incredibly brief period of their history under conditions – the rapid expansion of labour-intensive factory production – which are extremely unlikely to be replicated in the Third World. Even in developed societies class analysis is not without its difficulties. It is questionable, for example, whether class analysis contributes much to our understanding of politics in the most industralised society in the world, the USA. In most Third World societies only a small minority is regularly employed in wage labour and an even smaller proportion are members of trades unions and other class-based organisations. Trades unions, where they exist, are often outgrowths of the state – Stalin's conveyor belts – rather than independent vehicles of mass interests. In addition the workforce is frequently compartmentalised by ethnic and other parochial attachments. Unfortunately much of what passes for analysis of political change in the Third World has been too much under the sway of the revolutionary optimism of the late 1960s, regarding revolution as a normal phenomenon and dominated by the question, 'Which class is the most revolutionary?' As Teodor Shanin has pointed out, this type of approach severely underestimates the capacity of societies to maintain and re-adjust their systems of domination. For Shanin the question we should be asking is, 'How do revolutions take place and succeed at all?', rather than, 'Why do revolutions not take place more frequently?' (Shanin, 1982, p. 313).

The difficulties of class analysis may be further highlighted by reference to the question, considered in the previous chapter, of the precise character of the indigenous bourgeoisie in colonial and post-colonial societies. The whole discussion is predicated upon the assumption of the occurrence of a bourgeois revolution in the now-developed countries. That is to say that at some stage a class which had acquired economic power through entrepreneurial activities was able to wrest political power – control of the state apparatus – from the landed classes. First with regard to England, the *locus classicus* of the bourgeois revolution, it is by no means evident that the term 'revolution' is the most appropriate to describe the transformation that took place. Without in any way denying that there was a shift in political power in the late nineteenth century from landed to industrial interests, to see this as the outcome of a struggle whereby a bourgeoisie outside the state eventually defeats the landed classes would be little more than a caricature of capitalist development in England. The evidence is that the landed classes themselves readily adapted to entrepreneurial activity, that part of the impetus behind the reforms which permitted bourgeois access to public institutions, such as the civil service, came from these classes. Indeed the very notion of clearly defined 'bourgeois' and 'landed' classes does not accord with the English experience. The whole point about the stability of the transition from an agarian to an industrial society in England is the fluidity of the boundaries between the two classes and the relative ease with which rising entrepreneurs could acquire gentlemanly and even aristocratic status (see especially Perkin, 1969, pp. 61–3 and Anderson, 1979, pp. 126, 127).

If we look at other developed societies the timing and nature of the bourgeois revolution becomes even more difficult to pin down. The political phase of France's bourgeois revolution was inaugurated by the upheavals of 1789, but capitalism as an economic system did not really take root until over a century later. Even in 1939 the peasantry still made up the largest class in France (Zeldin, 1979, p. 131). In both Germany and Japan the bourgeoisie apparently needed a good deal of help from the state in consolidating its ascendancy which would seem to suggest that this class was not powerful enough to make it on its own. What, we might ask, are the essential differences between the 'weak' bourgeoisies of the Third World and their precursors in France, Germany and Japan and other countries which to varying degrees experienced a 'revolution from above'. The difficulty of interpreting the German and Japanese examples within a Marxist framework may be illustrated by referring to one leading Marxist historian who speaks of a 'Prussian way' with a curiously voluntaristic bourgeoisie 'reluctant to make a bourgeois revolution'; and whilst agreeing that the Meiji restoration was not a bourgeois revolution in any real sense, claims that it was 'the functional equivalent of part of one' (Hobsbawm, 1975, pp. 150, 151). It is possible that the American Revolution of 1776 and the Civil War represent two phases of the nearest thing to a bourgeois revolution in the Marxist sense (see, for example, Moore, 1973, ch. 3).

However, we are not historians and our purpose in citing, necessarily briefly, these cases is merely to point up the problematical nature of the bourgeois state. We might also refer at this juncture to the unresolved difficulties in the Marxist conception of political power in the capitalist state. We saw in the previous chapter that because of a reluctance to subscribe to the somewhat crude notion of the capitalist state as the mere instrument of the bourgeoisie (as put forward in the *Communist Manifesto*), most Marxists would now concede a degree of autonomy to the state in the sense of independence of social classes including the bourgeoisie:

the capitalist state asumes a relative autonomy with regard to the bourgeosie. This is why Marx' analysis of Bonapartism as a capitalist type of state is so significant. For this relative autonomy allows the state to intervene not only in order to arrange compromises vis-à-vis the dominating classes . . . but also to intervene against the long-term economic interest of one or other of the dominant classes: for such compromises and sacrifices are sometimes necessary for the realization of their political class interests (Poulantzas, 1975, pp. 284, 285).

The basic problem with such a position is that if the capitalist state enjoys a degree of autonomy, unless we can specify the actual *degree* of autonomy, which would be almost impossibly difficult, then it is not clear how the capitalist state differs from other types of state; the absolutist state for example (Anderson, 1979, ch. 1), or the neo-colonial state which, we recall from the last chapter, enjoys a degree of autonomy because no one class is powerful enough to dominate it.

We wish to emphasise that the above criticisms are not made in the spirit of the currently modish drive to discredit Marxism, nor to devalue the undoubtedly major contribution that Marxist scholarship has made to our understanding of social and political change. We simply wish to highlight an important point, already made by Bernstein, that theories of class and state in the Third World are often, if not usually, based upon the untenable assumption that capitalist development in the West is non-problematic (Bernstein, 1979, p. 94).

Turning now to the public policy approach, we have in previous chapters supported the position that imputes to Third World states the ability to determine policy within their borders, albeit subject to what are often very severe constraints. If this position is accepted then the process of policy formulation and implementation, and the individuals and groups who take part in this process, must be a proper object of study for political science. However, we would differ from the established policy choice position at least in emphasising the relevance of a much broader context to the process of policy formulation than is usually encompassed by this school. First all public policy decisions are to some degree affected by the international economic and political environment. This is a fact of life even for industrialised nations; much more so is it the case with dependent economies: that is to say economies that are dependent on a single export or a narrow range of exports, which must import technology and raw materials to keep their manufacturing industries operating, which must increasingly import food to feed exploding urban populations, where multi-national companies usually play a highly strategic role, and which increasingly find themselves in a condition of chronic indebtedness. The ability of the current military government to implement Nigeria's fourth development plan will obviously be constrained by such factors as the world market for oil as well as for the other commodities which Nigeria exports; the outcome of the protracted negotiations with the IMF and the conditions which the IMF attaches to such loans as are forthcoming; as well as on a range of other factors which are extraneous and largely out of the control of the incumbents of the Nigerian state apparatus. Not only would we insist that the scope of a satisfactory analysis of Third World politics be broadened to take in such factors, but further that an historical perspective is essential. In order to grasp the complexities of Nigeria's current foreign exchange crisis we need to know a good deal not only about the rapid increase in oil revenue and its disbursement during the 1970s but, equally important, about the structure of the economy before oil became the country's major export. Effectively we need to be aware of the general pattern of Nigerian economic development both under and since colonialism.

In addition to external factors the actions of government in all societies are constrained by the structuring of social forces within them. Whether the Nigerian military eventually agrees to 'strings' being attached to an IMF package such as devaluation of the naira, removal of import restrictions, and further cuts in public spending, will depend *inter alia* on its estimation of what Nigerian society can sustain in terms of increases in unemployment, inflation, scarcity of necessary food and household items, an increase in black-market activity, smuggling and general criminality, and the social unrest that would probably ensue, the forms that this unrest might take and the likelihood of the state being able to contain it. Naturally we are not suggesting that Nigeria's military rulers run through a checklist like this or that they will always form an accurate appraisal of the costs and benefits of the policies to be applied. The course of political change in the Third World abounds in examples of governments and leaders who have grossly miscalculated the impact of price or tax increases or the introduction of repressive measures and the like, often with disastrous consequences. What we are saying is that the formation and implementation of policy proceeds in some kind of dialectical relationship with the articulation of social forces within a given country. This articulation is itself a manifestation of underlying economic changes and the consequences of these for the re-ordering of the social structure. Therefore an historical appreciation of these changes is crucial to a proper understanding of the policy-making context.

In summary we are saying that insights from both political economies, radical and conservative, can be drawn together to produce an orientation for the study of political change. This orientation is one that focuses upon the state apparatus, the groups and individuals who control this apparatus and their relationship with social forces both outside and inside the country. The three levels on which we focus, the international economic and political environment, the national state and the internal economic and political environment, makes our approach not unlike that of some of the proponents of the radical political economy school, Alavi for instance. The major difference is that we would be reluctant to rely solely on class analysis for the reasons stated earlier. We would add here that one of the most serious problems of class analysis is that it cannot take account of ethnicity and other forms of communalism except by writing them off as aspects of false consciousness. It is undoubtedly the case that socio-political analysis in the 1960s tended to over-emphasise ethnicity to the neglect of class, a point made in our critical remarks on Paul Anber's treatment of the Nigerian Civil War in Chapter 3. However, in order to correct this tendency and to rehabilitate and in some cases enthrone the notion of class, the drift in the early 1970s was to treat communalism as something of a marginal phenomenon. Whilst this tendency has to some extent been corrected in more recent literature which has sought to explore the dialectical relationships between class alliances and various types of communal attachments, it is nonetheless difficult to get away from the assumption that evolution in the direction of class politics is a normal process (see, for example, Leys, 1971, p. 307 and Johnson, 1977, p. 207). The widespread existence of such an assumption is borne out by explanations of the alleged decline of clientelism in industrial societies (Theobald, 1983).

It is undoubtedly the case that communal allegiances are often, perhaps normally, exploited by dominant groups for their own ends and are in this sense an ideological mask obfuscating underlying economic interests. However, the fact that such attachments are real enough to inspire collective outbursts running from demonstrations and riots on the one hand to revolutions and civil wars on the other would seem to indicate that they cannot be written off as mere delusion. It would be facile to interpret the Lebanese conflict since the Civil War of 1975 solely in terms of Christian–Muslim primordial hostility. But equally facile would be an analysis based solely on class ignoring the confessional divisions which have been at the heart of the struggle for the Lebanese state since the break-up of the Ottoman Empire.

If our approach seems to be egregiously eclectic we make no apologies. We are concerned with understanding political change in the Third World and this requires us to draw upon ideas and methodological approaches from various streams of thought. The conviction that there exists some definitive set of concepts, a distinctive methodological approach that is complete within itself, more scientific and therefore superior to all other approaches – a conviction that lurks behind a fair amount of the writing on development – must be regarded with some sceptism.

Political Development?

The terms political development and political modernisation figured predominantly in the pioneering studies of political change in the Third World over two decades ago. The terms are now no longer employed in the rather specific sense that they were used in the 1950s and early 1960s: that is, signifying movement towards western-style political systems. However, since they still appear in the literature we must end by asking the

question of whether political development and political modernisation retain any analytical utility? In attempting to answer
this question we would suggest that these terms are typically used
in one of three ways, each signifying a distinct set of characteristics. First there is the original meaning, movement in the
direction of western-style democracy; second, a radical variant
which emphasises 'liberation', self-reliance and an end to
dependency, and in some cases, revolution. And third there is
the view which sees political development or modernisation as
synonymous with political stability and economic growth. We
now discuss each variant in turn.

Western-style democracy

We have seen that development for the modernisation school
entailed a transition from a traditional undifferentiated and
authoritarian political system to one that is differentiated,
integrated and democratic. By democratic the proponents of
this perspective had in mind the social or 'bourgeois' democracies of western Europe and North America. That is to say
pluralist democracies characterised by free elections and open
competition between interest groups to exert influence on the
state. The state acts as some kind of neutral arbiter or referee
over this competitive process. The competition between interest
groups is supposed to approximate to the economists' perfect
competition with no single group powerful enough to corner the
market in public resources.

Few political scientists would now argue formally that
political development or modernisation means the evolution of
this type of system. Nonetheless there remains a deep-seated
belief popularly, and no doubt in the hearts of many political
scientists, that social democracy is desirable and that authoritarian systems are undesirable and inappropriate for the
'modern' age. Since the overwhelming majority of Third World
states are run along authoritarian lines, and since there is a
pronounced strain within political science which appears to
condone such arrangements, we feel we must address ourselves
to the question of the prospects for western-style democracy in
UDCs.

Let us begin by looking at the impediments to the establishment of bourgeois democracy. First, a point made by a number of writers, the phasing of economic and political change in Third World states has been such as to impose severe strains on their social fabric, especially their political institutions. In most parts of the developed world (two significant exceptions are the United States and Sweden) an industrial base had been firmly established before the masses were admitted to the political arena; that is before the working classes were permitted to participate in politics or were subjected to political appeals and promises, in short were granted citizenship and came to expect things of the state. As Michael Lofchie has put it, the political environment in western societies during the early stages of industrialisation was such 'as to insulate fledgling state institutions from the social misery generated by the incipient industrialization process' (Lofchie, 1971 p. 5). By the time welfare policies were adopted and eventually taken for granted the industrialisation process was well advanced and many of its worst consequences had been eliminated. In Third World societies, by contrast, the masses have been granted access to the political arena when their economies are much more underdeveloped than was the case in the developed world. This means that the vast majority in these societies, in addition to having low incomes, have little or no access to very basic social and municipal services – schools, hospitals, potable water, a regular electricity supply and so forth – and yet have been encouraged to expect and demand these things by the politicians during the phase of political mobilisation. The fact that in most of the countries of Africa, Asia, the Middle East and Oceania mass mobilisation has been highly concentrated into a relatively brief period of time, as well as being linked with the struggle against colonialism, has greatly heightened expectations of the imminent realisation of the 'political kingdom'. As a result the sheer volume of demands vastly exceeds the poorly endowed state's capacity to deliver the goods. The meagre size of the national cake in underdeveloped states induces not the sedate competition of the western democracies but a frenetic scramble which can often be extremely vicious. Scarcity and instability promote an atmosphere of insecurity: with inflation running at over 60 per cent will you be able to afford a tin of powdered milk or a bag of rice at the end of the month? With import controls and consequent hoarding will these and other household essentials actually be available at the end of the month? Will you receive your salary anyway or will it have been spirited away by corrupt bureaucrats or appropriated by the state governor to help finance his re-election campaign? This kind of ambience promotes a state of mind which suggests that it is rational to grab what you can regardless of the long-term consequences. Those powerful enough grab on a spectacular scale and have no compunction about using violence to achieve their ends. The use of hired thugs to intimidate and if necessary kill political opponents and their supporters is a normal feature of the political process in many Third World states. The fact that possibly a majority of these states are riven by deep primordial divisions makes it that much easier for unscrupulous 'big men' to pursue self-aggrandisement by exploiting them. Hence the profound civic strains – riots, 'rampages', burnings, communal violence and soaring urban crime rates – which seem to be a normal feature of underdeveloped societies. Hence also the frequent resort of dominant groups to authoritarianism as the only way of containing pressure from below.

Does this mean that democracy, at least in its western guise, cannot be operated in an underdeveloped economy? The record of existing Third World states regrettably gives little grounds for optimism, for the moment. The basic reason lies not in the apparently high propensity of UDCs for social disorder, itself a symptom of the condition of underdevelopment, but because of the major impediments to the masses having any real influence over the political process. We must bear in mind that in most UDCs the majority of the population, sometimes over 80 per cent, live in isolated villages. The rapidly increasing minority who live in the towns are, like its rural counterpart, poor, ill-educated and, probably most important, poorly organised. As we have already pointed out, few of them are members of trade unions, and trade unions, anyway, are frequently an arm of the state. Because of the absence of a strong independent trade-union movement, genuine mass parties along European social democratic lines have failed to emerge in most countries of the Third World. Where parties exist they are usually either organs of the state – for instance, the late Sekou Toure's Democratic

Party of Guinea, Houphoët-Boigny's Democratic Party of the Ivory Coast, the Ba'ath parties of Syria and Iraq – or they are merely factions or cliques of 'big men' devoting most of their energies to the scramble for spoils, (such as in Nigeria's First and Second Republics, pre-Civil War Lebanon, Morocco). Even in the relatively developed countries of Latin America – Argentina, Brazil, Chile, Mexico – where trade unions and other forms of popular organisation are more firmly rooted, hegemonic groups, through a combination of repression and patrimonialism, have achieved a remarkable degree of success in depoliticising the masses. It is the very lack of accountability of dominant groups in the Third World which means that democracy, in the form of parties and elections on western lines, is often little more than window-dressing designed more to impress the aid donors of the North than to afford real political influence to the masses.

Political scientists have to face up to these real and formidable obstacles to a western-style democracy in the Third World. They and policy-makers should be sceptical of the facade of democratic forms that may conceal systematic repression and oppression. Nor should they confine their appraisal of such regimes to questions of participation and accountability, but also consider how dominant groups use their power, however achieved, whether they promote economic and social reform or simply suck up and squander national resources.

To acknowledge the prevalence of authoritarian regimes, however, is emphatically not to condone authoritarianism *per se*. While, as we shall see, an argument can be made (see, for instance, Nehru, 1979) that extensive political participation is incompatible with capital accumulation or economic growth, it clearly does not follow that authoritarian regimes will either seek or attain these latter goals. And in the meantime we have indicated the forms of political persecution they can instigate. It would be cavalier to dismiss without examination such mechanisms of accountability, for instance a relatively free press, a relatively independent judiciary, as may exist, however far short they fall of western ideals. Nor can all political parties be written off in advance as mere means of legitimising state power or mobilising the masses behind self-centred elites. Exceptionally parties have been channels of pressure by more progressive social forces and even afforded some minimal protection to the poor. As Morris-Jones writes, 'the poor have at least one thing in their favour – their numbers', and given a chance as in Brazil after Vargas, Chile before Pinochet and in particular states and localities in India, they have made effective use of their vote (Morris-Jones, 1979, p. 41).

What we are arguing, then, is that genuine mechanisms of accountability and representation are to be welcomed where they occur, though we should be open-minded as to what form they may take, instead of anticipating a relentless movement in the direction of western liberal-democratic institutions. But second we should recognise that democracy of any kind is in scarce supply currently in the Third World. To base a notion of political development exclusively on the emergence of liberal democracy, or even of some less specified form of expanded participation, does not allow us sufficiently to discriminate between the array of existing and overwhelmingly authoritarian Third World regimes.

Liberation

More radical conceptions of political development derive from the failure of liberalism in the first development decade of the 1960s and coincide with the rise of dependency theory. They emphasise 'emancipation', 'liberation' and 'freedom from exploitation' rather than the 'participation' of the first approach. Thus Ocampo and Johnson: 'Development involves the liberation of man from the conditions of exploitation and oppression. Politics is the means of human liberation' (Ocampo and Johnson, 1972, p. 424).

Soon after Ocampo and Johnson we find Gavin Williams maintaining that political economy should be concerned with the 'emancipation of people' rather than with 'the management of society and the containment of conflict' (Williams, 1976, p. 4). Unfortunately neither Ocampo and Johnson nor Williams are prepared to go into detail as to what they mean by such terms as liberation and emancipation and as to how these conditions are to be realised. However, Julius Nyerere's essay 'Freedom and Development' is useful here as the President of Tanzania isolates the components of 'freedom' as follows: firstly there is 'national freedom' which is the ability of the citizens (of Tanzania) to determine their own future, and to govern themselves free from interference by non-Tanzanians. Secondly there is freedom from hunger, disease and poverty; and thirdly we have the personal freedom of the individual. That is to say the right of individuals to live in dignity and equality with others, freedom of speech, freedom to participate in decisions which affect their lives and freedom from arbitrary arrest (Nyerere, 1979).

It is important to note here that Nyerere is focusing on two separate but interrelated levels of analysis: first there is the ability of the Tanzanian state to exercise some acceptable degree of jurisdiction within its borders, an ability which will be significantly affected by Tanzania's resource base and its consequent position in the international economic and political system: its degree of dependence on a narrow range of exports, on foreign imports, aid and so on. The second level embodies the classical liberal pre-occupation with the position of the individual vis-à-vis the state. Before looking more closely at the interrelationships and possible conflicts between the two freedoms, of the state and of the individual, let us turn briefly to another writer, Dudley Seers, who has usefully elaborated on the notion of national independence. Writing in 1969 Seers itemises the components of national independence to include: the proportion of capital inflows (including capital goods and intermediaries); the proportion of assets including subsoil assets which are owned by foreigners; and the extent to which one trading partner dominates patterns of trade and aid. Interestingly Seers also refers to qualitative indicators such as the existence of foreign military bases and overflying rights, and the extent to which a given country follows the lead of one of the great powers at the United Nations. But Seers gives greater emphasis to the rights and needs of individuals: the need for sustenance, employment, ultimately for 'the realization of the potential of human personality' (Seers, 1979, p. 10). In fact for Seers development is basically about individual needs:

The questions to ask about a country's development are therefore: What has been happening to poverty? What has been happening to unemployment? What has been happening to inequality? If all three of these have become less severe, then beyond doubt this has been a period of development for the country concerned (Seers, 1979, p. 12).

Almost ten years later, however, a markedly pessimistic tone has crept into Seers' conception of development. The individualistic focus has almost dropped out of sight. The practicality of reconciling redistribution with growth is questioned. The attainment of fundamental human physical and social needs are now seen as contingent upon the achievement of 'true independence' or 'self-reliance'. Some of the economic aspects of self-reliance are: a reduction in dependence on imports especially of food, petroleum, capital equipment and expertise, as well as a reduction in cultural dependence in the sense of greater use of indigenous languages and home-produced programmes in the mass media. In many countries (which ones are not specified), self-reliance would also involve expanding the ownership of national assets, especially those below the soil. Ownership of leading economic sectors would be one of the chief targets for governments in pursuit of national independence. The Third Malaysian Plan of 1976 and Japanese development strategy as a whole are examples of what Seers sees as desirable approaches (Seers, 1979, pp. 27, 28).

Without embarking upon a detailed critique of Seers' position it will be fairly obvious that the self-reliance option, as he presents it, must produce tension between the needs of the economy and the needs, particularly the consumption needs, of the masses. It is difficult to see that curbs on imports, particularly oil and cereals, specifically mentioned by Seers, would not hit the living standards of the urban masses. Would such curbs be compatible with free collective bargaining? Would the inevitable demand for increased food production not lead to a squeezing of surplus out of the peasantry? Accordingly it is hard to avoid the conclusion that self-reliance, in so far as it is attainable, can only be at the expense of the masses.

Seers is to be congratulated for detecting the gaps in previous somewhat airy discussions of freedom and self-reliance, particularly the failure to examine the linkages and potential contradictions between national self-reliance and the freedom of the individual. Seers may be criticised for not coming clean and openly declaring his allegiance to the strong government school. The logic of Seers' argument is surely that self-reliance is incompatible with democratic participation along western lines as its attainment requires the state to hold down consumption in order to promote capital accumulation and overcome external dependence.

Its implicit authoritarianism apart, a number of writers have become increasingly sceptical as to whether the notion of self-reliance has much relevance to the reality of underdevelopment. The opening-up of the Chinese economies since the death of Mao has been taken to indicate that withdrawal or semi-with-drawal from the world economy can at best be a temporary phase, necessary perhaps for the building up of indigenous industries and markets. In today's world the idea of an hermetically-sealed economy, without any form of aid from outside, seems far fetched to say the least. Aidan Foster-Carter has suggested that in so far as such a situation is realisable, it is unlikely to be without some variant of the 'agro-barbarism' that was implemented in Kampuchea by the Khmer Rouge (Foster-Carter, *Guardian*, 10 September 1980).

Interestingly the self-reliance school, whose initial impetus was a radical one, has also come under attack from those who favour a Marxist perspective. We touched on this issue in the previous chapter, when discussing the changing meaning of 'socialism' under the influence first of Stalinism and then of dependency theory. Anne Phillips, for example, has charged dependency theory with advocating a 'national' solution to the problem of underdevelopment: 'National capital has been given the opportunity to put itself forward as representing the "national interest" and has ultimately been rejected, not because it is *capital*, but because it is unable to be sufficiently *national*' (Phillips, 1977, p. 19: italics in text). In other words the dependency-type approach, whilst appearing to reject capitalist development, sees the alternative largely in terms of the replacement of the metropolitan bourgeoisie by an indigenous class which in some unspecified way represents the interests of all the progressive classes and fractions in the society concerned. Although the *dependistas* talk about socialism and socialist revolution this socialism, maintains Phillips, is little more than a 'series of enlightened planning policies' introduced from above by the new 'progressive' government. Socialism cannot be merely 'chosen' for its superiority over capitalism, it can only be the outcome of the dynamic of the class struggle (Phillips, 1977, p. 20). At the end of her article Phillips implies that the way towards socialism (in Africa) is via the development of a proletariat. This presumably means that she would regard the penetration of capitalism and capitalist relations of production with approval.

We thus encounter in radical notions of political development two contrary strains: the first, an outgrowth of dependency theory, stresses the inability of capitalism to promote development and advocates some kind of withdrawal from the world capitalist system. The second, far from being anti-capitalist, follows orthodox Marxist-Leninist lines emphasising the desirability of capitalist development as this will eventually produce the contradictions needed for a revolutionary upheaval. This latter view entails a re-affirmation, albeit often tentative, of the working class as the bearer of revolution.

Political stability and economic growth

The third conception of political development which we identify is one which arises from the strong government school and emphasises institutional stability, the creation of a context favourable to long-term policy making and, by implication, one that is conducive to economic growth. This set of political arrangements usually entails the accumulation and concentration of power at the centre. The experience of South Korea may be seen as a typical example of this type of political development:

> Korean economic development has been in large part due to the consolidation and stabilization of political power and the determination with which policy has been implemented by political leadership and an increasing administrative capacity. With the exception of the brief interlude of the Chang government in the early 1960s constitutional reforms in Korea have tended to augment the authority of central, and particularly executive institutions and have moved away

from the pluralistic power systems conventional to parliamentary and limited presidential systems (Wade and Kim, 1978, p. 240).

We note here the close relationship between political change and economic growth. In fact the logic of this position is ultimately to equate political development with economic growth for if economic growth is desirable then its attainment must to a considerable extent depend upon an appropriate set of political arrangements, arrangements which will facilitate the optimal employment of such resources as are available. We note also the distinctly authoritarian character of these arrangements in the Korean example; the '*determination* with which policy has been implemented by political *leadership* and an *increasing administrative capacity*'. Such authoritarianism is familiar enough from our consideration of the writings of the strong government school in Chapter 3 and elsewhere. However, we would like to stress the point already touched upon that an authoritarian strain is implicit in the writings of a number who are not open advocates of strong government. Indeed many of them are ostensibly pre-occupied with liberation, freedom from exploitation, revolution and so forth. We saw above that under closer examination the self-reliance option reveals a pronounced authoritarian streak. Not only self-reliance but its Marxist-Leninist critique must implicitly condone strong governments in so far as they promote capitalist development. The logic of the Marxist position is surely that Korean development since the 1960s is progressive since it has created and consolidated a proletariat as well as a bourgeoisie, and so has established a context in which the appropriate contradictions may emerge.

Basically what we are saying is that this authoritarian strain pervades a good deal of the analyses of social and political change in the Third World and is by no means restricted to acknowledged proponents of strong government. An essential task for political scientists is to face up to the authoritarian implications of their own analysis as well as the prevalence of authoritarian regimes. That is to say, we must rid ourselves of the Eurocentric conviction that authoritarian regimes are deviant in the sense of diversions from the true path towards liberal democracy, or alternatively that they are a, perhaps necessary, stage *en route* to revolution. In addition to their Eurocentrism both positions are manifestly evolutionary and accordingly may be subjected to similar criticisms to those levelled against modernisation theory. Authoritarian state structures are not only typical throughout the Third World but have been typical throughout human history, or at least since the neolithic revolution made state formation possible. We cannot even assume that liberal democracies will remain the characteristic political form of the industrialised world.

To emphasise once more, the above arguments must not be taken to imply blanket approval of authoritarian regimes nor the abandonment of a commitment to the principles of human liberty. On the contrary we were at pains to point out in Chapter 3 that most of the proponents of strong government have chosen to ignore the grosser aspects of authoritarianism. We also criticised the strong government school for its assumption that authoritarian political structures are more likely to promote political stability and economic growth. We saw that ostensibly centralised authoritarian regimes in Chile, Brazil, Indonesia and Syria are by no means immune to personalism, factionalism, the widespread appropriation of office and economic stagnation.

What we would urge is that future political analysis of the Third World centres its inquiry around the bases and ramifications of authoritarianism. Is it possible for us to develop criteria which will enable us to differentiate between authoritarian regimes? Of key significance here is the ability to distinguish progressive authoritarian regimes: that is to say regimes which, whilst restricting political activity to a degree which would be unacceptable in the developed world, nonetheless make efforts to institutionalise genuine mass participation and in the process establish checks on the abuse of power. What constellation of social forces underpins the emergence of such regimes? Are they associated with certain levels of economic development? Are they more likely to appear in Tropical Africa (Ghana, Burkina Fasso?) than in the more developed states of Latin America? The successive approaches to Third World politics examined in this book have cumulatively helped us to identify these questions. We would finally urge that answers to them be strongly grounded in empirical research.

Bibliography

Ake, C. (1974) 'Modernization and Political Instability', *World Politics*, Vol. 26, pp. 557–91.

Alavi, H. (1965) 'Peasants and Revolution', in R. Miliband and J. Saville (eds.), *The Socialist Register 1965* (London: Merlin Press).

—— (1979) 'The State in Post–Colonial Societies', in H. Goulbourne (ed.), pp. 38–69.

(1982) 'State and Class Under Peripheral Capitalism' in H. Alavi and T. Shanin (eds.), *Introduction to the Sociology of 'Developing Societies'* (London: Macmillan).

Almond, G. (1970) *Political Development: Essays in Heuristic Theory* (Boston: Little, Brown).

—— and Coleman, J. (eds) (1960) *The Politics of the Developing Areas* (Princeton University Press).

—— and Powell, B. (1966) *Comparative Politics: A Developmental Approach* (Boston: Little, Brown).

Amnesty International (1973) *Report on Torture* (London: Duckworth).

Anber, P. (1967) 'Modernisation and Political Disintegration: Nigeria and the Ibos', *Journal of Modern African Studies*, vol. 5, pp. 163–79.

Anderson, P. (1979) *Lineages of the Absolutist State* (London: Verso).

Apter, D. (1965) *The Politics of Modernisation* (Chicago University Press).

Arrighi, G. and Saul, J. S. (1968) 'Socialism and Economic Development in Tropical Africa', *Journal of Modern African Studies*, vol. 6, no. 2, pp. 141–70.

Bailey, F. G. (1963) *Politics and Social Change: Orissa in 1959* (Oxford University Press).

—— (1971) 'The Peasant View of the Bad Life', in T. Shanin (ed.) pp. 299–321.

Baran, P. (1957) *The Political Economy of Growth* (New York: Monthly Review Press).

Bendix, R. (1967) 'Tradition and Modernity Reconsidered', *Studies in Comparative Society and History*, vol. 9, no. 3, pp. 292–346.

Bernstein, H. (1979) 'Sociology of Underdevelopment vs Sociology of development' in D. Lehmann (ed.) *Development Theory. Four Critical Studies* (London: Cass).

Bienen, H. (1970) *Tanzania: Party Transformation and Economic Development* (Princeton University Press).

Black, C. E. (1966) *The Dynamics of Modernization: A Study in Comparative History* (New York: Harper & Row).

Blair, H. W. (1972) 'Caste as a Differential Mobilizer in Bihar', *Comparative Politics*, vol. 5, no. 1, pp. 107–27.

Boissevain, J. (1977) 'When the Saints Go Marching Out: Reflections on the Decline of Patronage in Malta', in E. Gellner and J. Waterbury (eds), *Patrons and Clients in Mediterranean Societies* (London: Duckworth).

Booth, D. (1975) 'André Gunder Frank: An Introduction and Appreciation', in I. Oxaal, T. Barnett and D. Booth (eds), *Beyond the Sociology of Development* (London: Routledge & Kegan Paul).

Bretton, H. L. (1958) 'Current Political Thought and Practice in Ghana', *American Political Science Review*, vol. 52, March, pp. 46–63.

Cammack, P. (1982) 'Clientelism and Military Government in Brazil', in C. Clapham (ed.), *Private Patronage and Public Power* (London: Frances Pinter).

Cardoso, F. H. (1973) 'Associated Dependent Development: Theoretical and Practical Implications', in A. Stepan (ed.), *Authoritarian Brazil* (New Haven, Conn.: Yale University Press).

—— and Faletto, E. (1979) *Dependency and Development in Latin America* (translated by M. M. Urquidi) (Berkeley, Ca: University of California Press).

Clapham, C. (1982) 'Clientelism and the State' in C. Clapham (ed.), *Private Patronage and Public Power* (London: Frances Pinter).

Cliffe, L. (1972) 'Democracy in a One-Party State: the Tanzanian Experience', in L. Cliffe and J. Saul (eds), *Socialism in Tanzania*, vol. I (Nairobi: East African Publishing House).

—— (1982) 'Class Formation as an "Articulation" Process: East African Cases' in H. Alavi and T. Shanin (eds), *Introduction to the Sociology of 'Developing Societies'* (London: Macmillan).

Cohen, R. (1982) 'Workers in Developing Societies', in H. Alavi and T. Shanin (eds.), *Introduction to the Sociology of 'Developing Societies'* (London: Macmillan).

Cohen, R., Gutkind, P. C. W. and Brazier, P. (eds) (1979) *Peasants and Proletarians: The Struggles of Third World Workers* (London: Hutchinson).

Coleman, J. S. (1958) *Nigeria: Background to Nationalism* (Berkeley, Ca: University of California).

Collier, D. C. (1979) 'Overview of the Bureaucratic–Authoritarian Model' in D. C. Collier (ed.), *The New Authoritarianism in Latin America* (Princeton University Press).

Coquery-Vidrovitch, C. (1978) 'Research on an African Mode of Production', in David Seddon (ed.), *Marxist Approaches to Economic Anthropology* (London: Cass).

Crouch, H. (1979) 'Patrimonialism and Military Rule in Indonesia', *World Politics*, vol. 31, July, pp. 571–87.

Crumney, D. and Stewart, C. C. (eds) (1981) *Modes of Production in Africa* (London: Sage).

Cutright, P. (1963) 'National Political Development: Measurement and Analysis' *American Sociological Review*, vol. 28, no. 2, pp. 253–64.

Deutsch, K. (1961) 'Social Mobilisation and Political Development', *American Political Science Review*, vol. 55, September, pp. 493–514.

Dodd, C. H. (1972) *Political Development* (London: Macmillan).

Dowse, R. (1969) 'The Military and Political Development' in Leys, (ed.), *Politics and Change in Developing Countries* (Cambridge University Press).

Drake, P. (1978) 'Corporatism and Functionalism in Modern Chilean Politics', *Journal of Latin American Studies*, vol. 10, no. 1, pp. 83–116.

Easton, D. (1965) *A Systems Analysis of Political Life* (New York: Wiley).

Eisenstadt, S. (1966) *Modernisation: Protest and Change* (Englewood Cliffs, NJ: Prentice-Hall).

Emmanuel, A. (1974) 'Myths of Development Versus Myths of Under-development', *New Left Review*, no. 85, pp. 61–81.

Erickson, K. P. (1972) 'Corporatism and Labour in Development', in H. J. Rosenbaum and W. G. Tyler (eds), *Contemporary Brazil: Issues in Economic and Political Development* (New York: Praeger).

Evans, P. (1979a) *Dependent Development: The Alliance of Multinational, State and Local Capital* (Princeton University Press).

Evans, P. (1979b) 'Beyond Centre and Periphery: A Comment on the Contribution of the World System Approach to the Study of Development', *Sociological Inquiry*, vol. 49, no. 4, pp. 15–20.

Fanon, F. (1967) *The Wretched of the Earth* (Hammondsworth: Penguin).

Foster-Carter, A. (1978) 'The Modes of Production Controversy', *New Left Review*, no. 107, pp. 47–77.

—— (1980) 'The Dogma of Self-Reliance', *Guardian Third World Review*, 10 Sep.

Fox, R. G. (1970) 'Avatars of Indian Research', *Comparative Studies in Society and History*, vol. 12, pp. 59–72.

Frank, A. G. (1969) *Capitalism and Underdevelopment in Latin America: Historical Studies of Chile and Brazil* (New York: Monthly Review Press).

—— (1970) 'Destroy Capitalism, not Feudalism', in A. G. Frank *Latin America: Underdevelopment or Revolution* (New York: Monthly Review Press).

—— (1971) *The Sociology of Development and Underdevelopment of Sociology* (London: Pluto Press).

—— (1978) *World Accumulation 1492–1789* (London, Macmillan).

Gould, H. A. (1977) 'The Hindu Jajmani System: A Case of Economic Particularism', in S. Schmidt, J. C. Scott, C. Landé and L. Guasti (eds), *Friends, Followers and Factions: A Reader in Political Clientelism* (Berkeley, Ca: University of California).

Graham, B. D. (1975) 'Studies on Indian Elections', *Journal of Commonwealth and Comparative Political Studies*, July.

Grindle, M. (ed.) (1980) *Politics and Policy Implementation in the Third World* (Princeton University Press).

Gusfield, J. (1967) 'Tradition and Modernity: Misplaced Polarities in the Study of Social Change', *American Journal of Sociology*, vol. 72, January, pp. 351–62.

Halpern, M. (1962) 'Middle Eastern Armies and the New Middle Class', in J. Johnson (ed.), *The Role of the Military in Underdeveloped Countries* (Princeton University Press).

Heeger, G. (1974) *The Politics of Underdevelopment* (London: Macmillan).

Higgott, R. A. (1983) *Political Development Theory* (London and Canberra: Croom-Helm).

Hill, F. (1975) 'Ujamaa: African Socialist Productionism in Tanzania', in H. Desfosses and R. Levesque (eds), *Socialism in the Third World* (New York: Praeger).

Hobsbawm, E. (1975) *The Age of Capital* (London: Weidenfeld & Nicolson).
Hoogvelt, A. (1982) *The Third World in Global Development* (London: Macmillan).
Hoselitz, B. F. (1964) 'Social Stratification and Economic Development', *International Social Science Journal*, vol. 16, no. 2, pp. 237–51.
Huntington, S. (1965) 'Political Development and Political Decay', *World Politics* vol. 17, no. 3, pp. 386–430.
—— (1968) *Political Order in Changing Societies* (New Haven, Conn.: Yale University Press).
—— (1971) 'The Change to Change', *Comparative Politics*, vol. 3, no. 3, pp. 283–32.
Hyden, G. (1980) *Beyond Ujamaa in Tanzania: Underdevelopment and an Uncaptured Peasantry* (London: Heinemann).
Inkeles, A. and Smith, D. H. (1974) *Becoming Modern: Individual Change in Six Developing Countries* (London: Heinemann).
Ionescu, G. and Gellner, E. (eds) (1969) *Populism* (London: Weidenfeld & Nicolson).
Jessop, B. (1982) *The Capitalist State* (Oxford: Martin Robertson).
Johnson, J. J. (ed.) (1962) *The Role of the Military in Underdeveloped Countries* (Princeton University Press).
Johnson, M. (1977) 'Political Bosses and Their Gangs', in E. Gellner & J. Waterbury (eds).
Joshi, B. R. (1982) 'Whose Law, Whose Order – Untouchables, Social Violence and the State in India', *Asian Survey*, vol. 22, no. 7, pp. 676–87.
Kasfir, N. (1979) 'Explaining Ethnic Political Participation', *World Politics*, vol. 31, no. 3, pp. 365–88.
Kesselman, M. (1973) 'Order or Movement: the Literature of Political Development as Ideology', *World Politics*, vol. 26, no. 1, pp. 139–54.
Laclau, E. (1971) 'Feudalism and Capitalism in Latin America', *New Left Review*, no. 67, pp. 19–38.
—— (1977) *Politics and Ideology in Marxist Theory* (London: New Left Books).
Leeds, A. (1964) 'Brazilian Careers and Social Structure: an Evolutionary Model and Case History', *American Anthropologist*, vol. 66, pp. 1321–47.
Legg, K. and Lemarchand, P. (1972) 'Political Clientelism and Development', *Comparative Politics*, vol. 4, no. 2, pp. 149–78.
Lehmann, D. (ed.) (1979) *Development Theory: Four Critical Essays* (London: Cass).
Lenin, V. I. (1966) *Imperialism: the Highest Stage of Capitalism* (Moscow: Progress Publishers).
—— (1970) *The State and Revolution* (Moscow: Foreign Language Press).
Lewis, W. A. (1955) *Theory of Economic Growth* (London: Allen & Unwin).
Leys, C. (ed.) (1969) *Politics and Change in Developing Countries* (Cambridge University Press).
—— (1971) 'Politics in Kenya: the development of a peasant society', *British Journal of Political Science*, 1, pp. 307–37.
—— (1976) 'The "Overdeveloped" Post Colonial State: A Reevaluation', *Review of African Political Economy*, vol. 5, pp. 39–48.
—— (1978) 'Capital Accumulation, Class Formation and Dependency: the

Significance of the Kenyan Case', in R. Miliband and J. Saville (eds), *Socialist Register 1978* (London: Merlin Press).

Linz, J. J. (1970) 'An Authoritarian Regime: Spain', in E. Allardt and S. Rokkan (eds), *Mass Politics: Studies in Political Sociology* (New York: Free Press).

Lofchie, M. (ed.) (1971) *The State of the Nations: Constraints on Devleopment in Independent Africa* (Berkeley, Ca: University of California Press).

Macridis, R. C. (1955) *The Study of Comparative Government* (Garden City: Doubleday).

Malloy, J. (ed.) (1977) *Authoritarianism and Corporatism in Latin America* (University of Pittsburgh).

Marx, K. (1973) 'The Eighteenth Brumaire of Louis Bonaparte', in D. Fernbach (ed.), *Karl Marx: Surveys from Exile. Political Writings, Vol. 2* (Harmondsworth: Penguin).

Mazrui, A. (1976) 'Soldiers as Traditionalizers: Military Rule and the ReAfricanization of Africa', *World Politics*, vol. 28, pp. 246–72.

McClelland, D. (1961) *The Achieving Society* (Princeton: Van Nostrand).

Meillassoux, C. (1970) 'A Class Analysis of the Bureaucratic Process in Mali', *Journal of Development Studies*, vol. 16, pp. 97–108.

—— (1973) 'Are there Castes in India?', *Economy and Society*, vol. 2, no. 1, pp. 89–111.

Melotti, U. (1977) *Marx and the Third World* (London: Macmillan).

Meyerson, M. and Banfield, E. C. (1969) 'A Machine at Work', in Edward C. Banfield (ed.), *Urban Government, A Reader in Politics and Administration* (New York: Free Press).

Migdal, J. S. (1977) 'Policy and Power: a Framework for the Study of Comparative Policy Contexts in Third World Countries', *Public Policy*, vol. 25, no. 2, pp. 241–60.

Miliband, R. (1965) 'Marx and the State', in R. Miliband and J. Saville (eds), *The Socialist Register 1965* (London: Merlin Press).

—— (1969) *The State in Capitalist Society* (London: Weidenfeld & Nicoloson).

—— (1977) *Marxism and Politics* (Oxford University Press).

Morris-Jones, W. (1979) 'The West and the Third World', *Third World Quarterly*, 2, 1, pp. 31–42.

Murray, R. (1967) 'Second Thoughts on Ghana', *New Left Review*, no. 42, pp. 25–39.

Nehru, B. K. (1979) 'Western Democracy and the Third World', *Third World Quarterly*, vol. 1, no. 2, pp. 53–70.

Nordlinger, E. A. (1970) 'Soldiers in Mufti: The Impact of Military Rule upon Economic and Social Change in the Non-Western States', *American Political Science Review*, vol. 64, pp. 1131–48.

Nun, J. (1967) 'The Middle-Class Military Coup', in C. Veliz (ed.), *The Politics of Conformity in Latin America* (Oxford University Press).

Nyerere, J. (1979) 'The Process of Liberation', in H. Goulbourne (ed.), *Politics and the State in the Third World* (London: Macmillan).

O'Brien, D. C. (1972) 'Modernisation, Order and the Erosion of a Democratic Ideal: American Political Science 1960–1970', *Journal of Development Studies*, vol. 8, no. 2, pp. 351–78.

O'Brien, P. (1975) 'A Critique of Latin American Theories of Dependency', in I. Oxaal, T. Barnett and D. Booth (eds), *Beyond the Sociology of Development* (London: Routledge & Kegan Paul).

Ocampo, J. F. and Johnson, D. (1972) 'The Concept of Political Development', in D. Cockcroft and A. G. Frank (eds), *Dependence and Underdevelopment. Latin America's Political Economy* (New York: Anchor Books).

O'Donnell, G. (1973) *Modernization and Bureaucratic-Authoritarianism: Studies in South American Politics* (Berkeley, Ca: University of California).

Packenham, R. A. (1973) *Liberal America and the Third World: Political Development Ideas in Foreign Aid and Social Science* (Princeton University Press).

Palma, G. (1978) 'Dependency: A Formal Theory of Underdevelopment or a Methodology for the Analysis of Concrete Situations', *World Development*, vol. 6, pp. 881–924.

Parsons, T. (1960) *Structure and Process in Modern Societies* (Glencoe: The Free Press).

Peace, A. (1979) 'The Lagos Proletariat: Labour Aristocrats or Populist Militants?' in H. Goulbourne (ed.), *Politics and the State in the Third World* (London: Macmillan).

Perkin, H. (1969) *The Origins of English Society* (London: Routledge & Kegan Paul).

Peters, E. (1968) 'The Tied and the Free', in J. G. Peristiany (ed.), *Contributions to Mediterranean Sociology* (The Hague: Mouton).

Petras, J. (1975) 'New Perspectives on Social Imperialism: Social Classes in the Periphery'. *Journal of Contemporary Asia*, vol. 5, no. 3, pp. 291–308.

Philip, G. (1980). 'On Putting the Politics into Political Economy: Some Reflections on Latin America', unpublished paper presented to Political Change and Underdevelopment Group of the UK Political Studies Association.

Phillips, A. (1977) 'The Concept of Development', *Review of African Political Economy*, vol. 8, January–April, pp. 7–20.

Pitt-Rivers, J. (1954) *The People of the Sierra* (New York: Criterion Books).

Portes, A. (1976) 'On the Sociology of National Development: Theories and Issues', *American Journal of Sociology*, vol. 82, no. 1, pp. 55–85.

Post, K. (1972). '"Peasantization" and Rural Political Movements in Western Africa', *European Journal of Sociology*, vol. 13, no. 2, pp. 223–54.

Poulantzas, N. (1973). *Political Power and Social Classes* (London: New Left Books).

—— (1975) *Classes in Contemporary Capitalism* (London: New Left Books).

Powell, J. D. (1970) 'Peasant Society and Clientelist Politics', *American Political Science Review*, vol. 64, June, pp. 411–25.

Purcell, S. K. (1973) 'Decision-making in an Authoritarian Context. Theoretical Implications from a Mexican Case-Study', *World Politics*, vol. 26, no. 1, pp. 28–54.

Pye, L. W. (1966) *Aspects of Political Development* (Boston: Little, Brown).

Riggs, F. (1963) 'Bureaucrats and Political Development: A Paradoxical View', in J. LaPalombrara (ed.), *Bureaucracy and Political Development* (Princeton University Press).

—— (1964) *Administration in Developing Countries: The Theory of Prismatic Society* (Boston: Houghton Mifflin).

—— (1981) 'The Rise and Fall of "Political Development" ', in S. C. Long (ed.) *The Handbook of Political Behaviour*, vol. 4 (New York and London: Plenum Press).

Roett, R. (1972) *Brazil: Politics in a Patrimonial Society* (New York: Praeger).

Rostow, W. (1962) *The Stages of Economic Growth: A Non-Communist Manifesto* (Cambridge University Press).

Roth, G. (1968) 'Personal Rulership, Patrimonialism and Empire-Building in the New States', *World Politics*, vol. 20, pp. 194–206.

Rothchild, D. and Curry, R. L. (1978) *Scarcity, Choice and Public Policy in Middle Africa* (Berkeley, Ca: University of California).

Roxborough, I. (1979) *Theories of Underdevelopment* (London: Macmillan).

—— O'Brien, P. and Roddick, J. (1977) *Chile: The State and Revolution* (London: Macmillan).

Rudolph, L. and Rudolph, S. (1967) *The Modernity of Tradition: Political Development in India* (Chicago University Press).

Rustow, D. A. (1967) *A World of Nations: Problems of Political Modernization* (Washington, DC: The Brookings Institute).

Sandbrook, R. (1972) 'Patrons, Clients and Factions', *Canadian Journal of Political Science*, V, pp. 104–19.

—— (1982) *The Politics of Basic Needs* (London: Heinemann).

Sartori, G. (1970) 'Concept Misformation in Comparative Politics', *American Political Science Review*, vol. 64, no. 4, pp. 1033–53.

Saul, J. (1976) 'The Unsteady State: Uganda, Obote and General Amin', *Review of African Political Economy*, vol. 5.

—— (1979) *The State and Revolution in Eastern Africa* (London: Heinemann).

Schapiro, L. (1971) *The Communist Party of the Soviet Union* (New York: Vintage Books).

Schmitter, P. D. (1971) *Interest Conflict and Political Change in Brazil* (Stanford University Press).

—— (1973) 'The "Portugalization" of Brazil?', in A. Stepan (ed.), *Authoritarian Brazil* (New Haven, Conn.: Yale University Press).

—— (1974) 'Still the Century of Corporatism?', *Review of Politics*, vol. 36, January, pp. 85–121.

Scott, J. C. (1969) 'Corruption, Machine Politics and Political Change', *American Political Science Review*, vol. 63, pp. 1142–58.

Seers, D. (1979) 'The Meaning of Development', in D. Lehmann *Development Theory: Four Critical Essays* (London: Cass).

Shanin, T. (1971) 'Peasantry as a Political Factor', in T. Shanin (ed.) *Peasants and Peasant Societies* (Harmondsworth: Penguin).

—— (1973) 'Peasantry, Delineation of a Sociological Concept and a Field of Study', *Peasant Studies Newsletter*, pp. 1–8.

—— (1979) 'Defining Peasants: Conceptualizations and Deconceptualizations Old and New in a Marxist Debate', *Peasant Studies*, vol. 8, no. 4, pp. 38–60.

—— (1982) 'Class, State and Revolution', in H. Alavi and T. Shanin (eds), *Introduction to the Sociology of 'Developing Societies'* (London: Macmillan).

Shils, E. A. (1962) 'The Military in the Political Development of the New States', in J. J. Johnson (ed.), *The Role of the Military in Underdeveloped Countries* (Princeton University Press).

Shivji, I. G. (1976) *Class Struggles in Tanzania* (London: Heinemann).

Shor, E. (1960) 'The Thai Bureaucracy', *Administrative Science Quarterly*, vol. 5, June, pp. 66–86.

Silverman, S. F. (1977) 'Patronage and Community – Nation Relationships in Central Italy', in S. Schmidt, J. C. Scott, C. Landé and L. Guasti (eds), *Friends, Followers and Factions: A Reader in Political Clientelism* (Berkeley, Ca: University of California).

Singer, M. (1971) 'Beyond Tradition and Modernity in Madras', *Comparative Studies in Society and History*, vol. 13, no. 2, pp. 160–96.

Skidmore, T. E. (1967) *Politics in Brazil, 1930–64: An Experiment in Democracy* (New York: Oxford University Press).

—— (1973) 'Politics and Economic Policy-Making in Authoritarian Brazil, 1937–71', in A. Stepan (ed.), *Authoritarian Brazil* (New Haven, Conn.: Yale University Press).

Sklar, R. (1979) 'The Nature of Class Domination in Africa', *Journal of Modern African Studies*, vol. 17, no. 4, pp. 531–52.

Skocpol, T. (1979) *States and Social Revolution* (Cambridge University Press).

Smelzer, N. J. (1962) *Theory of Collective Behaviour* (London: Routledge & Kegan Paul).

Smith, T. (1979) 'The Underdevelopment of Development Literature: the Case of Dependency Theory', *World Politics*, vol. 31, no. 2, pp. 247–88.

Srinivas, M. (1966) *Social Change in Modern India* (Berkeley, Ca: University of California).

Stepan, A. (1978) *The State and Society: Peru in Comparative Perspective* (Princeton University Press).

Theobald, R. (1982) 'Patrimonialism', *World Politics*, vol. 34, no. 4, pp. 548–59.

—— (1983) 'The Decline of Patron-Client Relations in Developed Societies', *Archives Européennes de Sociologie*, XXIV, pp. 136–47.

Tipps, D. (1973) 'Modernization and the Comparative Study of Societies', *Comparative Studies in Society and History*, vol. 15, pp. 199–226.

Trimberger, E. K. (1978) *Revolution From Above* (New Brunswick: Transaction Books).

Turner, T. (1980) 'Nigeria: Imperialism, Oil Technology and the Comprador State', in P. Nore and T. Turner (eds), *Oil and the Class Struggle* (London: Zed Press).

Uphoff, N. T. and Illchman, W. (1972) *The Political Economy of Development* (Berkeley, Ca: University of California).

Van Dam, N. (1983) 'Minorities and Political Elites in Iraq and Syria', in T. Asad and R. Owen (eds), *The Middle East* (London: Macmillan).

Vincent, J. (1969) 'Anthropology and Political Development', in C. Leys (ed.) *Politics and Change in Developing Countries* (Cambridge University Press).

Wade, L. L. and Kim, B. S. (1978) *Economic Development of South Korea* (London: Praeger).

Waiguchu, J. (1974) 'The Politics of Nation-Building in Kenya: A Study of Bureaucratic Elitism', in E. Morgan (ed.), *The Administration of Change in Africa* (New York and London: Dunellan).

Wallerstein, I. (1971) 'Ethnicity and National Integration in West Africa', in

J. L. Finkle and R. W. Gable (eds), *Political Development and Social Change* (Chichester: Wiley).

—— (1974) *The Modern World System. Capitalist Agriculture and the Origins of the European World Economy in the Sixteenth Century* (London: Academic Press).

Warren, B. (1973) 'Imperialism and Capitalist Industrialisation', *New Left Review*, no. 81, pp. 3–44.

—— (1980) *Imperialism, Pioneer of Capitalism* (London: Verso Books).

Weber, M. (1930) *The Protestant Ethnic and the Spirit of Capitalism* (London: Unwin).

—— (1968) *Economy and Society*, vols. 1–3 (New York: Bedminster Press).

Weingrod, A. (1968) 'Patrons, Patronage and Political Parties', *Comparative Studies in Society and History*, vol. 10, July, pp. 377–400.

Williams, G. (ed.) (1976) *Nigeria: Economy and Society* (London: Rex Collings).

Wolf, E. (1969) *Peasant Wars of the Twentieth Century* (New York: Harper & Row).

Wolf-Phillips, L. (1979) 'Why Third World?', *Third World Quarterly*, vol. 1, no. 1, pp. 105–13.

Wood, G. (1977) 'Rural Development and the Post-Colonial State: Administration and the Peasantry in the Kosi Region of N. E. Bihar, India', *Development and Change*, vol. 8, no. 3, pp. 307–23.

World Bank Development Report (1980) (Oxford University Press).

Worsley, P. (1967) *The Third World* (London: Weidenfeld & Nicolson).

—— (1970) *The Trumpet Shall Sound* (London: Paladin).

—— (1979) 'How Many Worlds?', *Third World Quarterly*, vol. 1, no. 2, pp. 100–8.

Zagoria, D. S. (1974) 'Asian Tenancy Systems and Communist Mobilization of the Peasantry', in J. W. Lewis and K. J. Hartford (eds), *Peasant Rebellion and Communist Revolution in Asia* (Stanford University Press).

Zeldin, T. (1979) *France 1848–1945* (Oxford University Press).

Zolberg, A. (1966) *Creating Political Order: The Party States of West Africa* (Chicago University Press).

Index